P.

Voices of France

Also available from Pinter
Population and Social Policy in France
Edited by Máire Cross and Sheila Perry

VOICES OF FRANCE

Social, Political and Cultural Identity

edited by Sheila Perry and Máire Cross

PINTER

London and Washington

PINTER
A Cassell Imprint
Wellington House, 125 Strand, London WC2R 0BB, England
PO Box 605, Herndon, VA 20172, USA

First published 1997

British Library Cataloguing in Publication Data
A catalogue record for this book is available from the British Library.

ISBN 1–85567–394–0

Library of Congress Cataloging-in-Publication Data
Voices of France/edited by Sheila Perry and Máire Cross.
     p.   cm.
  Includes index.
   ISBN 1–85567–394–0 (hardcover)
   1. Political participation – France. 2. Mass media – France.
3. Civilization – France. 4. Popular culture – France. 5. National characteristics, French. I. Perry, Sheila, 1952– . II. Cross, Máire.
JN2916.V65 1997
306'.0944–dc20

96–38316
CIP

Typeset by York House Typographic Ltd, London
Printed and bound in Great Britain by
Biddles Ltd, Guildford and King's Lynn

Contents

Notes on contributors

Marc Abélès is Director of Research at the Centre National de la Recherche Scientifique and Lecturer at the Ecole des Hautes Etudes en Sciences Sociales in Paris. His research is in the field of political anthropology on the subject of France and more recently on European institutions. He is the author of a number of works, including: *En attente d'Europe* (Hachette, 1996), *Politique symbolique en Europe* (Duncker et Humblot, 1993), *Le Défi écologiste* (L'Harmattan, 1993), *La Vie quotidienne au Parlement européen* (Hachette, 1992) and *Quiet Days in Burgundy: A Study of Local Politics* (Cambridge Studies in Social and Cultural Anthropology, 1991).

Inès Brulard is Senior Lecturer at the University of Northumbria at Newcastle, where she teaches French language and area studies. She taught applied linguistics and socio-linguistics at the Université Catholique de Louvain, where she completed a PhD in the history of linguistic ideas. Her publications and research interests include contrastive French–English linguistics, French socio-linguistics and French civilization.

Patrick Champagne is Researcher in Sociology at the Institut national de la recherche agronomique and the Centre de sociologie de l'éducation et de la culture and Lecturer in Sociology at the Université de Paris I and the Ecole des Hautes Etudes en Sciences Sociales, in Paris. His research areas include the crisis of rural reproduction in France, politics and the media (mass demonstrations, opinion polls and their effects on political practice in France), and media treatment of the 'contaminated blood affair'. His works include: *Initiation à la pratique sociologique* (Dunod-Bordas, 1989), *Faire l'opinion. Le nouveau jeu politique*

(Editions de Minuit, 1990) and he has collaborated with Pierre Bourdieu in *La Misère du monde* (Le Seuil, 1992). He is currently working on changes in journalism and media treatment of environmental issues in France.

Máire Cross is Senior Lecturer in French at the University of Sheffield where she teaches aspects of contemporary French politics at postgraduate and undergraduate level. She has co-authored two books on French feminism, contributes items regularly to the journals *Modern and Contemporary France, European History Quarterly* and *French Studies* and is a member of the Editorial Board of *Modern and Contemporary France*.

Hanna Diamond is Lecturer in French History in the School of Modern Languages and International Studies at the University of Bath. She has published on women's experience of the Second World War in Toulouse for which she used oral history extensively. She is now preparing a book on women and the Second World War in France for Longman which will also draw on oral source material.

D.W.S. Gray is Principal Lecturer in Cultural History at the University of Northumbria at Newcastle. He has been course leader for the BA (Hons) History of the Visual Arts in the Modern Period, and his teaching and research are mainly in illustration and the graphic arts, with a focus on France in the long nineteenth century (1789–1914).

Sue Harris is Lecturer in French at the University of Stirling. She is currently carrying out research into the way in which performance styles in modern French cinema have been influenced by developments in French theatre. She has written articles on Samuel Beckett and on the films of Bertrand Blier.

Joanna Helcké is conducting doctoral research at Loughborough University on ethnic minorities and the media in France. Her work, which focuses on France's North African community, aims to analyse the influence of ethnicity on the ways in which audiences 'decode' television messages. She is also interested in the media representations of this minority group, and has published articles in *Hommes et Migration* and *Migrations Société*.

Simon Kitson lectures at the University of Paris XII. He is the author of a doctoral thesis entitled 'The Marseille police in their context, from Popular Front to Liberation' (Sussex University, 1995). His publications include 'The police in the liberation of Paris' in H.R. Kedwood and N. Wood (eds) *The Liberation of France: Image and Event* (Oxford, 1995); 'La Reconstitution de la police à Marseille (août 1944–février

1945)', *Provence Historique* 178 (October 1994) and a forthcoming article entitled 'Les Policiers marseillais et le Front Populaire' which will also appear in *Provence Historique.*

Philippe Marlière is Lecturer in Political Sociology and Social Theory at University College, London. He is currently writing a book on the work of Pierre Bourdieu. He has published articles on French and Italian politics, and recently a book on the French Socialist leader and thinker Jean Jaurès (1995). He has also been working on the collective memory of French Socialist activists, conducting numerous interviews with rank and file Socialists in northern and southern France.

Susan Milner is Senior Lecturer in European Studies at the University of Bath. She is the author of a book (*Dilemmas of Internationalism*, Berg, 1990) and several articles and book chapters on the French labour movement. She is currently involved in two comparative research projects, one dealing with socio-political change in France, Italy and Spain, the other looking at alternative unemployment policies in Western European countries.

Pamela Moores is Lecturer in French and Senior Tutor in the Department of Languages and European Studies, Aston University, Birmingham. After graduating in Modern and Mediaeval Languages from Girton College, Cambridge, she completed a PhD on journalist, writer and revolutionary Jules Vallès. Her main research interest is the French media, and she has written on regional and national newspapers in France, press agencies, media celebrities in politics, political communication and electoral coverage.

Sheila Perry is Principal Lecturer in French and the Modern Languages Departmental Research Coordinator at the University of Northumbria at Newcastle, where she teaches French language and politics at undergraduate and postgraduate level. She specializes in the study of politics and the media in France and has published articles and conference papers on French television and political communication. She is currently researching the development of political programmes on French television since the 1960s.

Brigitte Rollet is Lecturer at the University of Portsmouth where she teaches French Literature and Cinema. Her research interest lies in the field of French cinema and feminist and gender theories in film. She has published articles on contemporary French cinema. She is currently writing a book on the film director Coline Serreau for MUP.

Chris Warne is Lecturer in the Department of French Studies at Keele University. His research interests are broadly concerned with the nature of popular culture in twentieth-century France. He has published pieces on different areas of contemporary French youth culture and popular music, and is currently engaged in writing a book on youth and society in post-war France.

Steve Wharton is a Lecturer in French and Communication at the University of Bath. His current work, on perceptions and portrayals of (homo)sexuality and perceptions and portrayals of AIDS in Britain and France, draws on his work on persuasion, propaganda and political control. He is also working on gay activism, representation and identity, the 'pink economy' being part of this latter research.

TRANSLATORS

John J.A. Cullen has the Institute of Linguists Diploma in French with a Distinction in technical translation. He specializes in translation from French in engineering and has an interest in economics and politics.

D.W.S. Gray: please see above.

Grania Rogers is a free-lance translator and Associate of the Institute of Linguists. She has the Institute of Linguists Diploma in French and in German and specializes in translation from these two languages in the following areas: European Union, wind and other forms of renewable energy, mechanical and civil engineering.

Introduction

SHEILA PERRY

A nation speaks with many voices and is represented in various forms.
Whose voice is the legitimate one, and which form of representation is
most valid, are subjects of social, political and cultural debate. This
book explores the myriad forms of representation of the French public
as a whole and of specific socio-cultural groups in French society,
through self-expression or collectively shared myths and metaphors,
through visual, linguistic or textual media, through political participation and practice. It examines questions of belonging and marginality,
social struggle and social cohesion, and how the various forms of
identity are created and maintained.

Taken collectively, the chapters in this book provide a multifaceted
study of French socio-cultural identity and citizenship. Imposing any
kind of order on this rich tapestry is open to debate in much the same
way as the different identities and voices analysed here are themselves
the subject of controversy and socio-political struggle. Nevertheless, it is
part of our intellectual tradition to analyse, categorize and classify, and
so for the sake of cohesion the chapters have been grouped into three
parts, each with its internal unity which is explained below. It should,
however, be borne in mind that different combinations are possible
and that the boundaries between the three parts are also meant to be
fluid, as we hope to show in what follows.

Part One broaches a question which is central to any study of this
nature: who are the French and how does one ascertain what 'ordinary'
French citizens think and believe? How can they be given a voice, and
whose voice is it we hear when references are made to 'the French', 'the
public', 'public opinion', 'ordinary people', 'the people'? Are pre-
electoral opinion polls scientifically valid for this purpose, and if so,

what kind and in what conditions? Do televised debates provide an appropriate forum for self-expression – for whom, and in what circumstances and with what effect? Who does the French language belong to: the mass of ordinary people who speak it, or the legislators who sit on the ministerial terminology commissions and issue decrees regarding officially approved usage? How can researchers and students of French society ascertain what certain groups of French people think or wish to say: are they to adopt the interviewing techniques developed by the leading French sociologist Pierre Bourdieu, or should they establish methods of their own, and how? What constitutes a valid approach and what contribution can such testimonies make to French history or the study of contemporary France? Part One brings together a number of chapters which consider questions of methodology in the way in which people's voices are captured and recorded to be transmitted to others, be it through opinion polls, television programmes or sociological surveys, and examines the question of whose voice it is we hear in the various forms of expression and representation which are currently in use.

Part Two looks at cultural voices, and here the term is used in its broadest sense to mean any kind of expression, physical, visual and musical as well as through language. This part analyses nineteenth-century illustrations of *les Français* and their contribution to common conceptions of the French population and of French identity – conceptions which have outlived the techniques used initially to produce them. It illustrates the way in which three filmmakers, Serreau, Balasko and Blier, make use of earlier, popular, theatrical forms, giving them new meaning and fresh voice in film, and their treatment of notions of gender and family roles. The section considers the role of television as a means of aiding and encouraging integration of ethnic minorities, using interviews to examine the ways in which people from different social backgrounds interpret television messages. Integration is also approached through an analysis of new forms of immigrant and youth culture, such as hip-hop and ragga, and the ways in which they express different notions of what it is to be French. Looking at popular (as in working-class) culture, ethnic identity, youth culture, gender and notions of 'Frenchness', this section explores the transmission (or transformation) of self-image and expression from generation to generation, from one social group to another.

Part Three looks at what we have termed alternative voices, that is, often, voices from the margins of society, those voices which are often silent or silenced, or which are finding new forms of expression. For example, the homeless have a new outlet in the specialist press which champions their cause and provides a source of income: are these newspapers the instrument of social integration they claim, or aspire, to be? Similarly, how is one to assess the phenomenon of 'pink money' in France, and its role as a medium of identification – or ghettoization – of the homosexual community? How does a particular group in society, such as the police, go about improving its image among the public? What are the factors which shape reciprocal mistrust and how are relations improved through communication? And when urban policy has destroyed traditional collective identities, can they be created anew, how, and by whom? For example, can the Communist Party, which has traditionally spoken on behalf of working-class people, re-establish itself and speak in the name of the new urban 'underclass'? Why is it that the ecologists, whose voice has been increasingly heard and heeded, have not managed to translate this success into political power? This section raises the question of how and when and in what circumstances different voices are heard or go unheeded and charts the fluctuating fortunes of a number of different social groups in contemporary France.

The chapters in this book are based on a selection of papers delivered at the annual conference of the Association for the Study of Modern and Contemporary France at the University of Northumbria at Newcastle from 7 to 9 September 1995, on the theme of 'France: Population and People(s)'. They are written by specialists in the fields covered and are based on their most up-to-date research; explanations and translations have been provided to make them accessible to a wider readership.

Our thanks go to the following for financial assistance at the time of the conference: the French Embassy; North East Water; Tyne and Wear Passenger Transport Authority; and Newcastle Airport. Our thanks also to the Association for the Study of Modern and Contemporary France for assistance in the production of this book.

Part One

The People's Voice?

1.

Pre-election opinion polls and democracy

PATRICK CHAMPAGNE

TRANSLATED FROM THE FRENCH BY GRANIA ROGERS

With the onset of each election, the debate on opinion polls in politics re-emerges in the media with the same arguments being exchanged. On one side are the advocates of opinion polls: the political pundits, but also large numbers from political and media circles who claim to be 'modernists' and 'liberals'. They defend this technique which they consider 'democratic' and 'scientific' and which they claim plays a part in improving political debate insofar as these opinion polls provide citizens and politicians with reliable information enabling them to reach a decision with full knowledge of the facts. On the other side are the opponents, who are also to be found in political and journalistic circles, but particularly among the intellectual set. The arguments, equally scientific and political, put forward by the latter appear to be just as well founded. They question the reliability of these opinion polls, criticizing them for the fact that the samples are too small, the adjustments dubious, the questions badly worded, and the interpretation of responses improper or imposed (not to mention the self-interested political bias of certain leading members of polling agencies). And they explain that these opinion polls, sometimes rigged or irrevelant, disturb the tranquillity of the voter at the time of voting and play a part in changing the 'normal' election result. In short, for one side opinion polls are perfectly integrated into democratic political life, whereas for the other they pervert its natural course substantially.

A recurrent debate

The 1995 presidential election campaign in France, through the very excesses which it generated, above all revealed the tensions which prevail in the area of politics, and which the introduction of opinion poll technology into this very special sort of process has simply brought to a peak. Never before perhaps was the presence of the pollsters so strong at the time of an election, but nor were they ever subjected to such strong criticism. However, if some people were induced to question the political neutrality and scientific validity of opinion polls, it is on the basis of directly political interests and not for scientific reasons, as the propensity for politicians to doubt opinion polls or to believe in their validity depends largely on how favourable or unfavourable they are towards them. Thus, for example, a certain politician who early in the campaign used the position in the opinion polls of the candidate he supported to make a case for voting for him ('il faut voter pour lui parce qu'il a la préférence ... dans le cœur des Français'[1]), violently lost his temper with the polling agencies on the evening of the first round.

The same goes for journalists who, having played a significant role in placing opinion polls at the heart of the election campaign, were quick to criticize them on the evening of the first round, calling for customary caution regarding the presentation of results (margins of error, the instantaneous (i) nature of opinion polls (p) which would only be valid at the moment (m) when it was conducted, etc.), caution which they had scarcely ever respected beforehand, and which they would cease to respect within a matter of hours. It must be said that the results of the first round of the presidential election had hardly confirmed the forecasts which the specialists felt they were in a position to make on the basis of the pre-election opinion polls, since the latter pronounced Jacques Chirac (RPR candidate) at the top, followed by Edouard Balladur (Prime Minister) and Lionel Jospin (Socialist Party candidate). In fact, it was Lionel Jospin who came first easily, followed by Jacques Chirac.

An expanding market

This interest by politicians, journalists and political commentators in opinion polls undoubtedly has much to do with the fact that the polls are clearly devised and adapted to respond directly to their most immediate and most relevant concerns: even though poorly conceived and badly interpreted, these surveys provide them with data structured accordingly to the very logic of the field of politics and have a forecasting value which is in principle far superior to their own intuitive and unscientific evaluations.

Politicians are of course the choice clients of polling agencies. Public opinion polls in the true sense of the word, besides providing information on 'the state of opinion', can be used as a specific political resource by giving the impression that a majority of citizens approve of a particular opinion or action supported by a particular political leader (*legitimizing effect*). As for pre-election opinion polls, they make it possible to 'test' political leaders' chances in the elections and contribute towards the choice of candidates: they are an *instrument of forecast* or *simulation*.

Moreover, we know that the polling agencies are called upon more and more to direct government policy from day to day (at least as far as the media are concerned) as well as the election campaigns of the various parties. In particular they provide the opportunity to follow the popularity rating of the candidates according to their performance in the media, and to determine the themes which, because they appeal most to voters, can be given priority in political programmes. They can equally serve to give the parties' leadership a precise idea of predictable political power struggles and thus play a part in identifying strategies for mustering support or for regrouping. Although the introduction of the opinion poll has changed the traditional portrayal of political activity, the fact remains that this practice is inscribed in the logic of the most mundane political work which involves, in particular, converting options and choices devised and developed in the restricted milieu of the political professionals into proposals which can muster the greatest possible support among 'lay' people, or more precisely, among categories of population specially targeted by the campaign teams in view of their position in the field. The political opinion poll therefore fits into a very general process of rationalizing action ('helping towards the decision' as the pollsters say), which makes particular use of the resources offered by social science.

The success of the political opinion poll with radio and television can be explained by a whole variety of reasons, the first of which is a belief in the political validity of this type of survey which appears as natural as an election itself (isn't an opinion poll in fact similar to a referendum?) and secondly a belief in the scientific validity of these surveys, a belief which is in general all the stronger since the competence of journalists (in the area of the sociological survey) is weak, or forms an exception (social science training in schools of journalism remains almost non-existent today). At the same time, the complexity of the methodological problems to which every survey inevitably gives rise tends to escape them, and all the more so because journalistic logic inclines rather towards simplification.

Added to this is the fact that the opinion poll is a product particularly well adapted to the specifically technical and political constraints which, for most of the mass media, hamper the production of information today. In a situation characterized by increasing urgency and competition, opinion polls provide an opportunity to combine speed and apparent scientific validity, which is not the case for the traditional 'vox pop' in the streets. The presentation in figures in particular has the appearance of objectivity and precision: it seems to stand by itself and can, apparently at least, manage without long technical commentaries. An opinion poll can be presented in graphic form which provides a picture and lends itself to a more spacious layout. Insofar as opinion polls offer, besides, the possibility of inventing 'events' or 'scoops' practically at will ('An astonishing opinion poll reveals to us that . . . ', 'Exclusive: French people judge America!', etc.), they contain a flexibility which allows them to adapt to the demands of current events. In the area of politics they allow journalists to intervene in the debate with the apparent guarantees of science, the popularity ratings and the public opinion polls demanding a response from the politicians.

As regards surveys on voting intentions, they serve to heighten suspense and this plays a part day after day in maintaining the attention of readers and viewers, the majority of whom are not very interested in the political debate with its propensity to be complex, difficult and therefore boring for lay people. In particular they make it possible to present the political struggle modelled on the sporting event or the confrontation of personalities, more familiar to the 'public at large', and allow journalists from the main media to intervene in the political debate by focusing the discussion with the political leaders not so much on their programmes or political ideas, which requires a competence and legitimacy which the interviewers do not always have, as on the latest opinion polls, and the position they occupy in the election 'race'.

Political censure and scientific censure

The most radical censure of opinion polls in politics (which would also be the most efficient) would be for the press not to order or publish results any more – in short, to ignore them, as *Le Monde* newspaper did until the end of the 1970s. The least that can be said is that this sort of censure by action is hardly practised today in the media. On the other hand, a certain routine censure of opinion polls does exist, which has become integrated as it were, in the practice itself. It has the appearance of running counter to the publication of opinion polls, revealing a sort of persistent 'guilt' among political journalists who feel, themselves, that they might be going too far, perhaps because they sense instinctively the negative effects on the democratic debate. This sort of accompanying criticism, frequent in most of the main media, enables opinion polls in fact to be published while giving the impression of not believing in them too much nor of attaching too much importance to them: journalists give the statistical distribution but often with a note of irony or while remaining aloof ('it's only an opinion poll', 'if you can believe the latest opinion poll' ...) which seems intended to display a certain incredulity. When the newspapers decide, as they do periodically, to devote a special report to condemning 'the extensive manipulation of opinion polls', it is in most cases only another opportunity to give indirect publicity to the various polling agencies whose leading members are introduced favourably and invited to justify themselves at length.

Even the criticism which appears to be strictly scientifically founded, is in fact almost always politically based. Thus, for example, if, during the course of the 1995 presidential election campaign, the pollsters were criticized more vehemently than usual, it is just *because they were wrong* in that they failed to predict the candidates' results – an apt criticism which in all logic indicates that these same pollsters would conversely have drawn praise from the same people if, as is often the case, their predictions had been closer to the true results. Thus 'their amazing skill' would have been commended, and it is likely that we would find journalists or commentators wondering gravely in an editorial if 'the opinion poll did not extinguish the vote'. They would then have suggested, with the same assurance with which they condemned the pollsters this time round, organizing a debate, not on the validity of opinion polls but on the usefulness of the vote, since a simple pre-election opinion poll seemed to be capable of reliably pinpointing the people who would be elected. The opinion poll would be praised as a rational instrument of democracy, removing the need for traditional procedures which, like the vote or the referendum, would be pronounced archaic, too cumbersome and too costly in time and money.

The introduction of opinion poll technology into public debate has deeply affected the legitimate portrayal of political practice by shaking – especially amongst the political professionals – the basic structures of political perception and the election rules which were acceptable until then. No doubt it is not going too far to say that, for a significant proportion of political personnel, the activity of pollsters is viewed as a sort of illegitimate political exercise. Therein lies undoubtedly the main reason for the negative reaction which they provoke: by conducting these types of mini-referenda which claim to measure 'public opinion', in other words the 'will of the people', in a precise and unquestionable manner, and by continually encouraging these samples of population, supposedly representing the electorate, to vote, are the pollsters not in fact playing a part in weakening the real power of those elected by changing the philosophy which governed the old form of democratic regime?

A paradoxical criticism

Perhaps the most surprising element in this debate is the fact that the most virulent criticism is directed towards the opinion polls which are, in themselves, the least contestable. Under the generic term 'opinion polls', we actually know that very different surveys are normally grouped together which have virtually nothing in common, except that they all (or almost all) involve samples (supposedly) representative of the French population of voting age, that they involve asking questions, they are carried out by polling agencies, are published by the press and are quite often intended to produce more or less direct political effects. From a scientific point of view, each type of opinion poll should be viewed on the basis of its individual characteristics. The type of criticism which applies to some is not necessarily valid for others. Now, we generally confuse very different types of opinion poll. For example, asking respondents which newspaper they read, or whether they have taken part in a demonstration or strike, comes under *capture of behaviour*. These questions are not in the same league and do not pose the same epistemological and technical problems as those which involve asking respondents if they are, for example, 'in favour of French intervention in Bosnia', 'in favour of a five-year presidential mandate' or 'in favour of limiting the right to strike'. These are *opinion surveys* in the true sense of the word, and it is these which cause very complex problems of capture and interpretation.

During the 1995 presidential election campaign the debate was not about opinion polls but about that very specific type of poll, the *pre-election opinion poll*, whose purpose is to capture intentions of political behaviour. Now, this is precisely where polling agencies and political pundits seem to escape the criticism normally directed at opinion polls: are they not beyond reproach since they are capable of identifying, shortly before an election, the probable distribution of ballot papers between the candidates? And is the election not the best guarantee of the seriousness of the pollsters in that it enables declarations made in the opinion polls leading up to an election to be compared with the votes actually recorded? In fact, French pollsters have acquired an indisputable *savoir-faire* in this field, on which they have established their reputation with the media. It is true that the pre-election opinion poll hardly poses any scientific problems since it simply involves getting voters to vote a little before the legally determined date. Criticism denouncing the imposition of a problematical framework which is valid for every question put to a socially and culturally very heterogeneous population is unfounded here, since this type of survey simply involves getting a representative sample of the population of voting age to vote in the very format established by the democratic political process. If a problematical framework is imposed (particularly through the choice of possible candidates and the programme themes suggested to respondents, in other words the voters), it is the fault not of polling agencies but of the political process itself.

The specificity of pre-election opinion polls

The pre-election opinion polls which were the most severely criticized at the time of the presidential election campaign were the least questionable in their essence provided that they were carried out in the days preceding the election. In this case, and only in this case, they record *a true political situation* since they capture the voting intentions of a population urged to choose *on a given date* between clearly and finally designated candidates, at the end of a mobilization campaign which was planned in accordance with this date and which is precisely intended to allow, in principle, each voter to take up his or her position in the political arena and to make his/her choice. The question put to respondents in this type of opinion poll, which is generally of the type 'If you had to vote tomorrow, which candidate would you choose?' records, since it is asked *at a good moment politically,* that is to say on the eve of an election, a declaration of behaviour which is more or less called for through the operation of the democratic political process itself.

From a technical point of view, the discrepancies to be found between the last opinion polls carried out (within 15 days or so of the election) and the results recorded at the time of the count are generally acceptable in view of the method of composition and the size of the samples, but also because of the specific problems arising from this type of survey (in particular the varying degree of sincerity of respondents' statements and the increased or decreased percentage of 'don't knows'). Another factor has more recently been added to these traditional sources of inaccuracy, increasing a margin of error which is both inevitable and irreducible. This has emerged because a number of voters, still probably small in number but not insignificant, are taking account, when making their decision, of the results of the latest opinion polls and numerous commentaries on them published by the press, and this is a factor which could well increase in the future. The publication of pre-election opinion polls can only create among certain voters a new type of vote which is well known and usually practised by the professionals in politics. This is the *strategic vote* which involves not voting directly and naively for your candidate but for the one expected to produce a political effect which is not necessarily or always achieved by the direct vote for 'your' candidate (you can vote for the opponent in order to 'teach a lesson' to your own party which you hope however will win but not by too big a margin; or vote 'usefully' by focusing on a candidate of second choice to prevent his or her elimination in the second round; etc.). If this strategic vote – which can be decided at the last minute, sometimes even in the polling booth, when all elements of essential information are available, and particularly the last opinion polls which are supposed to indicate the probable shape of the election – only affects a rather small and politically aware proportion of the electorate today, and if undoubtedly some of these ultimate decision changes often end up cancelling each other out, the outcome in certain political circumstances may be the production of vote transfers of two or three points, which may be enough to change the expected results.

It is not going too far to uphold the view that it is normal to have a discrepancy between the last pre-election opinion polls published and the actual election result. The existence of such a discrepancy even provides proof that the publication of such opinion polls is necessary since it has an effect on citizens' decision-making. It is not very logical to blame the polling agencies for not identifying the distribution of votes to within one point, and in other respects to regard the publication of pre-election opinion polls as essential. If this publication in no way changed voters' decisions, it would be hard to understand that it is regarded so essential to democracy and freedom. A *published* pre-election opinion poll can no longer be a forecast: it becomes information which intervenes in the electoral process. We can even speculate that, at the time of the 1995 presidential election campaign, the unexpected reversal of the first and second place was due precisely to the accuracy of the pre-election opinion polls and to the effects that their publication managed to produce in the electorate.

A debatable presentation

Nevertheless, these remarks do not mean that the pollsters, and in particular the political pundits in the media, have not themselves had a hand in encouraging scientifically unorthodox use of pre-election opinion polls in politics and the media: in fact they should probably be criticized less for the technical quality of their surveys than for the quality of presentation and interpretation which they give of the results or leave to be expanded in the press. From a scientific point of view, the margins of error in these surveys are acceptable and, besides, scarcely hamper the cross-sorting which can be done between variables, or even the calculation of correlation coefficients which can be carried out in the framework of some or other research on the social determining factors of the vote. This accuracy is, on the other hand, inadequate if, maintaining the confusion, the pollsters claim to say who should be elected; in other words, they claim to stand on political ground, ground on which each vote counts since one single vote can determine the election and therefore completely change the final result. In spite of their denials, the pollsters try to respond to the demands of their clients and often go well beyond what their skill can reasonably guarantee, forgetting in particular the basic caution required for this type of survey.

The harsh reactions of politicians to the opinion polls carried out and published *at the end of the campaign*, which were supposed (wrongly) to give the results of the vote, tend to mask the fact that the opinion polls which were the most fanciful, the most artificial and above all the most formative politically were not these ones, but were those opinion polls also termed 'pre-election' (we will keep the inverted commas in order to distinguish them), which were carried out *at the beginning and throughout the election campaign*. Numerous and repetitive, these premature 'pre-election' opinion polls weighed heavily upon politicians but also upon the press and, in particular, on the main national media (radio and television) which invite politicians, organize debates and comment on the election campaign in relation to the results delivered daily by these surveys. It would be interesting to evaluate the influence of these opinion polls on the structure of the public debate, measuring the proportion of commentaries and questions which in the course of the campaign in radio and television could be traced back directly or indirectly to an opinion poll.

Now these opinion polls, which are such a determining factor in the formation of the media campaign, are the least reliable (the issue is what they implicitly claim to be assessing, namely, the probable result of the approaching election) because they do not capture mobilized opinion but simple statements mainly created by the survey itself. These are voting intentions which are often fictitious, potential and not yet crystallized. To ask a question about voting intentions on the eve of an election is not the same thing as asking the same question three months (or indeed one year or even more) before an election, in other words at a time when not all the candidates are yet known, and when the election campaign has not yet started, or at least the candidates do not all have the same degree of involvement. In this case it is a *hypothetical and largely unreal question* because it is asked more or less outside the context which creates it and gives it meaning for the simple voter. For this reason it can only drive a large portion of the electorate, prematurely consulted in this way, to give provisional replies, often short-lived and of no importance. It is true, it is not easy to understand that the same question (for whom do you think you will vote?) can produce answers which do not have the same technical meaning, nor the same epistemological status, depending on the moment when it is asked. And this applies all the more because it is obviously impossible to determine the moment, which varies according to the dynamics peculiar to the mobilizing ability of each election, when individual voting intentions are crystallized in a sufficient proportion that the pre-election opinion poll tends to become more reliable and enables sensible predictions to be made, or, if you like, near-forecasts.

In the 'pre-election' opinion polls the rate of 'don't knows' and non-returns, which is normally very high at the beginning of an election campaign (more than 60 per cent at the time of the 1995 presidential campaign), is in fact the most important information, more important in any case than the distribution of votes of those who have apparently already made their final choice of party or candidate. If, as leading members of polling agencies reiterate, these surveys do not provide forecasts but are only 'snapshots' of the state of voting intentions, the least that can be said is that they are not drawing all the consequences of this when they give the results of these surveys as if they were actual votes, that is to say when they give the distribution *excluding non-returns and 'don't knows'*. Now this rate of 'don't knows' and non-returns, at a particular moment in a campaign, forms the decisive feature. Without a doubt the political journalists following the pollsters generally mention this rate in their commentaries, but it is more so that they can get it out of the way immediately and present the distribution of voting intentions excluding 'don't knows'.

The effects of opinion polls on the political process

The problem of the effects of opinion polls on the political process was raised as soon as the press started publishing these surveys. Attention was then focused above all on pre-election opinion polls because for politicians and journalists they were the most 'interesting' but also the most disturbing and the most spectacular. Because of ethnocentrism they were interested mainly in the effects which these surveys could have *on the voters* without seeing that by far the most important effects were those created on politicians and the media. The political pundits in the media only brought scientific backing to those spontaneous and directly self-interested concerns of the political players, transforming naive questions – Do opinion polls influence the vote? Do opinion polls affect the choice of candidates? Does television determine the election? etc. – into research subjects. Above all preoccupied with 'justifying' this new practice of which they were the instigators and specialists, and to which they owe the distinguished position (between expert and guru) which they now occupy in the political field, the political pundits in the media hastened to conclude, using the illustration of a particular opinion poll or a particular counter-example, that opinion polls do not affect the vote, without seeing the much more powerful effects which they themselves were producing, either directly by henceforth occupying the space for political commentary in the main media, or indirectly by profoundly changing the 'media coverage' of political campaigns through their surveys, and in this way producing a certain presentation and portrayal of the political struggle.

It is in this way, amongst others, that pollsters (and journalists) have played a large part in shifting public attention in politics to 'behind the scenes' political work with its inevitable manipulations, its conflicts of personal ambitions or its leadership struggles, weakening at the same time the public vision of politics which politicians form (and/or suggest to their voters), which is also a clash of programmes and ideologies, and opposing visions of the world – in short, a struggle to impose a certain definition of the common good. The political pundits, with their pre-election opinion polls which are supposed to identify the position of candidates in the election 'race', push the media to focus the debate not so much on ideas to be discussed (it is true, this is not very easy in radio and television which are obsessed with audience numbers) as on votes to be won or to be taken from the opponent, not so much on sincere convictions as on more or less cynical election strategies directed towards one or other category of voters to be targeted, categories created by the pollsters for the purpose of political marketing surveys ('women', 'young people', 'the working classes', etc.), not so much on social projects as on themes to be developed in order to seduce – or deceive? – the voters, not so much on the leaders' political qualities as on 'media coups' on which they have to embark in order to improve their 'public image' when it is judged, again through pollsters' surveys, to be insufficiently 'nice' and they are deemed incapable of 'getting their teeth into' a particular layer of society which needs to be conquered.

The presentation of 'pre-election' polls, already guilty of putting the electoral struggle into figures, tends, furthermore, to give a largely fictitious portrayal in the media of the progression of the election and the respective results of the various candidates, with falls and rises as spectacular as they are artificial. It encourages those endless commentaries about false graphs and those questions repeatedly put to candidates by journalists on their assumed position in the race, on the reasons for their apparent 'breakaway' or their potential 'fall' in the ratings, as if, supposing that these developments were true, the political leaders were in a position to understand the reasons, and above all as if, supposing that they understood them, they would be naive enough to announce them in front of the television cameras.

Reinventing the polling booth

Sociological analysis enables us to observe that the persistence of the debate on the problem of political opinion polls stems from the fact that it is badly presented and therefore badly thought out. All the regulations made and all the proposals which are regularly formulated, more often than not in haste and indignation, remain ineffectual or are unrealistic because they stem from the old methods of political thinking and are linked in a way which has not been analysed to the ambiguities inherent in democratic regimes. The combination of interests as established by the old form of political struggle, and strictly economic interests which have been grafted onto this practice, have even led to quite *the reverse* of thinking about the steps which should have been taken to preserve the logic of the vote, which is the principle behind the invention of the polling booth.

In fact, enforcing, as did the July 1977 law on the regulation of opinion polls, the publication of the technical details for each opinion poll, indicating the date on which the survey is carried out, as well as the size and structure of the population sample questioned, is an indispensable device which prevents undesirable political manipulation through the production of fictitious opinion polls. But such a regulation does not broach the main issue in that the major effects created today by the use of opinion polls in politics are, we know, more subtle and in part more subconscious (they lie particularly in the formulation of questions asked and, above all, in the interpretation of responses). As for the second device which consists of banning the publication of pre-election opinion polls in the week before an election, it is completely inadequate: a product of the hysteresis of structures of political perception, it is based on an old portrayal, fetishist and sacred, of the election ritual symbolized by the polling booth. This device (quite falsely) reassures politicians by in fact installing a sacred barrier, mainly mythical, a 'cordon sanitaire' or a 'decompression chamber' between opinion polls and the vote; furthermore, it has the advantage of scarcely hampering the main commercial activity of polling agencies which have all the time necessary outside of this short period to conduct their business and receive publicity; it suits journalists perfectly as they can retrieve material amongst the data figures published throughout the campaign for use in articles, more subtle forms of political manipulation and easy methods of entertainment (in particular the build-up of election suspense), enabling the public at large to take an interest in 'politics'.

Now, what needs to be preserved is not the polling booth but the logic behind its invention. Historically, the polling booth was imposed, after considerable debate, to protect voters from the pressures, seen as unwarranted, exerted on the act of voting. The secrecy of the vote was aimed at putting an end to threats or attempts at corruption, to which the members of the rural working classes were subjected by the *notables* and local élite who tried to maintain their power by forcing the people, who were often 'their people', to 'vote well'. If this type of pressure has not completely disappeared, it has become very marginal. Without a doubt, the polling booth no longer has the practical importance it had at the time it was established. Its function has progressively changed. A relic of an ancient form of political system which sought to set the minimum rules for the efficient operation of (male) universal suffrage, it has become the symbol of the philosophy which is the basis for the political creation of the 'citizen-voter': if the citizen has to be in isolation before voting, it is not so much to resist external pressures but more because the logic of democracy ensures that s/he votes as an individual and according to his/her conscience.

The unwarranted pressures which influence voting today have changed. They still need to be identified clearly since they have become more subtle. The steps which, only recently, were envisaged, often in anger, by certain political representatives after the first round of the last presidential election, in fact only serve to compound the initial errors caused by an inadequate appreciation of the problem, and at the same time increase the unwanted effects which opinion polls have on the vote through their impact on public debate. In fact, extending the period of the publication ban on pre-election opinion polls from one week to 15 days or even a month before the election date amounts to keeping a ban on the most technically authentic opinion polls (those preceding the election) and allowing the most fictitious opinion polls (those which are very remote) to be published and commented on; it is these polls which conversely weigh very heavily on the structuring of political campaigns in the media and play a part in virtually transforming the essential public debate into a discussion between specialists in political marketing. The solution recommended by the political pundits in the media, which involves lifting all publication bans, is not any more satisfactory inasmuch as this arrangement has no effect either on the 'pre-election' opinion polls carried out well before the election and throughout the campaign, and yet we know how misleading these can be. Now, the genuine pressures on voting, which are considered unwarranted today even by the people working in the fields of politics and the media – the numerous articles in the press which denounce 'opinion poll mania' bear witness to that – stem precisely from this type of 'pre-election' opinion poll.

If we wish, therefore, to remain faithful to the logic of the polling booth and to the idea of democracy which it implies, *we must do the exact opposite to what we are doing at present* and put back on its feet legislation which is turned on its head. We must allow the publication of pre-election opinion polls, but on two express conditions. The first is that the results are presented in a way which is scientifically beyond reproach, that is to say without excluding the 'don't knows' and the 'non-returns' and clearly showing the margin of error. The second condition is that this publication should *only* be authorized *during the week just preceding the election*. The opinion polls are then at their most reliable and, above all, they are presented at the right time, when the voters must reach a decision. Apart from this short period, a ban on publishing 'pre-election' opinion polls can only be desirable, both from a scientific point of view (they have little meaning) and from a political point of view (they give too much encouragement to the media who create a 'horse-race' out of the political struggle).

Note

1. 'You must vote for him because he is the favourite ... in French people's hearts' (Nicolas Sarkozy speaking in favour of the Prime Minister, Edouard Balladur).

2.

Public participation in French television debates

SHEILA PERRY

Technological progress (in particular the introduction of fibre optic cable) means that the television of the future will be interactive. Spurred by the need to compete, the terrestrial channels are introducing interactive television today: *Sans aucun doute, J'y crois, j'y crois pas, 90' pour agir,* are just some of the discussion programmes recently introduced by TF1 in the interactive mode, while France 2 has imported a Brazilian concept, a mixture of interactive fiction and reality, with *A vous de décider.* Designed to '[faire] sortir le public de sa passivité'[1] (Cauhaupé, 1995), such programmes claim to be constructing a different social rapport between television and the viewer, one in which television ceases to be an object to be viewed or consumed passively, and becomes an integral part of the viewer's social space. The television set is no longer simply a screen through which one can view the world, but an instrument through which one can act upon and influence that world. Having brought the outside world into people's sitting-rooms, it is now the channel through which people can make their mark upon that world without leaving their own homes.

A parallel, and related, development is the increase in public debate programmes, conducted on a large scale and with audience participation, on a wide range of social and moral issues. Examples of this are *Ça se discute, Chéla ouate* (France 2). So-called 'reality shows' (*Bas les masques, Perdu de vue, et al.*) feature members of the public who recount real-life experiences as their contribution to the theme of the debate. The proliferation of such programmes creates the impression, fostered by the channels themselves in the interests of self-promotion, that the viewing public are being offered opportunities never before available, and that this is a measure of the progress made by television in giving the appropriate respect and importance due to viewers.

In fact, as this chapter will aim to show, these opportunities are by no means as new as they seem. What is new, perhaps, is the amount of time they occupy in the television schedule (corresponding to the overall increase in television programmes on offer), which of course is of social significance, and which in turn can affect the way in which they are constructed. In televisual terms, that is in programme design and presentation, public participation has been a constant feature of French television debates on social, political or literary subjects. As a result, there are many variations on the theme, and we shall seek to explore and categorize those variations.

Historical overview

Table 2.1 shows the list of programmes on which this study is based.[2] There are few programmes (only seven out of 46),[3] which do not have any form of *representation* (as opposed to participation) of the public whatsoever, and three of those seven are from the 1995 presidential election campaign and so are among the most recent. Of the remaining 39, 22 take place in the presence of a studio audience ('en public et en direct'). It is the fact that the programmes are 'en public', before a studio audience, which represents and substantiates their being 'en direct' (live): the English expression, a 'live' broadcast, underlines this, as a programme seems more authentically 'live' for those at home watching because it is live for those in the studio, for whom it is a real-life experience. Those at home can rest assured that the programme is authentic, free from editorial distortion, because there are people *really there*. The studio audience presents a microcosmic mirror to the wider target audience; because the television viewers can watch other people watching, they can trust in the transparency of the medium; transparency is equated to truthfulness, and so legitimates the programme concerned.

Legitimation is the major motivating factor governing access to programmes by members of the general public, of course. The term 'media' implies an intermediary between two communicators, but in fact television has frequently attempted to be more than a channel between, say, the politician and the electorate; rather it has sought to stand as proxy, to represent the electorate. This is evident in the role adopted by journalists interviewing politicians, when they purport to speak on behalf of the viewing public or when they ask for, or provide, clarification on complex issues to help 'the ordinary person' understand.[4] Such positioning substantiates the claim that television is an element in the democratic process, in that it questions and calls to

Table 2.1 *Televised debates 1960–95*

Programmes are listed in chronological order of the start date. A blank in the 'End' column indicates that on 7 September 1995 the programme was still running. Dates marked with an * asterisk are uncertain (due to insufficient information available at the time of writing).

Start	End	Title	Channel
10 June 60	09 Feb. 62	Faire face	1
24 Jan. 66	12 Sept. 66	Face à face	1
03 Oct. 66	08 Apr. 68	En direct avec	1
06 Apr. 67	03 Sept. 91	Les Dossiers de l'écran	2
07 Feb. 69	08 Dec. 69	Face à face (suite)	1
17 Feb. 70	28 Mar. 73	A armes égales	1
22 Feb. 70	27 Sept. 70	L'Avocat du diable	2
20 Jan. 71	07 Sept. 72	L'Actualité en question	1
07 Jan. 72	19 Dec. 72	L'Heure de vérité	1/2
15 Sept. 72	18 Nov. 74	Actuel 2	2
18 Apr. 73	19 Sept. 73	Feux croisés	1
27 June 73	24 July 74	Les Trois vérités	1
10 Jan. 75	22 June 90	Apostrophes	2
20 Sept. 76	11 July 77	L'Huile sur le feu	2
10 Oct. 76	17 Sept. 78	L'Homme en question	3
18 May 77	30 Mar. 81	Cartes sur table	2
09 Sept. 80	16 Dec. 81	Le Grand Débat	1
08 Sept. 81		Sept sur sept	1
12 Dec. 81	19 Sept. 87	Droit de réponse	1
20 May 82	25 June 95	L'Heure de vérité	2
28 Feb. 84	22 May 84	Politiques	1
11 Jan. 85	25 Apr. 86	Face à la Trois	3
28 Mar. 85	28 Mar. 89	Questions à domicile	1
28 Apr. 85	02 Mar. 86	Ça nous intéresse, Monsieur le Président	1
17 Sept. 87	17 Mar. 88	Le Monde en face	1
30 Sept. 87		La Marche du siècle	2/3
10 Jan. 88*	11 Feb. 90*	Forum RMC-FR3	3
26 Sept. 88	29 Apr. 92	Médiations	1
29 Sept. 90		Bas les masques	2
04 Oct. 90	27 Jan. 93	Le Point sur la table	1
09 Nov. 90	06 Apr. 94	Le Droit de savoir	1
11 Sept. 91	10 June 92	Direct	2
23 Sept. 91	13 Jan. 92	Les Absents ont toujours tort	5
07 Sept. 92	29 June 93	Durand la nuit	1
10 Oct. 92	12 Dec. 93	Repères	3
12 Jan. 93	13 Nov. 93	Jury d'honneur	1
11 Feb. 93	25 Feb. 93	Audition publique	2
07 Mar. 93		Zone interdite	6
23 Feb. 94	22 June 94*	Les Coulisses du destin	1
26 Sept. 94		Ça se discute	2
18 Oct. 94		Je suis venu vous dire	1
22 Oct. 94		Chéla ouate	2
19 Jan. 95	06 Apr. 95	Face à la Une	1
21 Jan. 95	18 Mar. 95	La Revue de campagne de Michèle Cotta	2
26 Jan. 95	31 Mar. 95	Carnet de campagne	2
30 Jan. 95	06 Apr. 95	La France en direct	2

account those in power on behalf of those who put them there. From speaking on behalf of the citizen, it is a relatively small step to inviting the citizen to speak in his – and occasionally, but not too often! – her own name.[5]

French television has been inventive in the variety of forms of public participation which have been introduced: studio panels, phone-ins, straw polls and, of course, the ubiquitous opinion poll, instantaneous or otherwise. *L'Heure de vérité* (1982–95) is probably the most famous for having combined several of these, and using state of the art technology to provide them, but none of the forms of participation were new even in 1985 when *L'Heure de vérité* introduced them. SVP (the telephone) had been used in the 1960s by *Faire face* and became famous with *Les Dossiers de l'écran*, when the phrase 'SVP – Guy Darbois' became 'une phrase toute faite' (a catch-phrase) (Arthur in *Les Enfants de la télé*, France 2, 1 October 1994). Opinion polls had already been widely used, albeit with less advanced technology: *A armes égales*, for example, used cartoon drawings to illustrate the polls conducted specifically for the programme. There was even a kind of interactive television in the 1970s: *Feux croisés* allowed the public to choose the surprise guest. In other words, virtually all main types of public participation had been tried in the 1960s and 1970s when television was still in its infancy. However, this very fact is what has given rise to the great ingenuity of variations on the theme of public participation, as directors and producers have sought to differentiate their programme from the others: those variations have been multifarious and as a result almost defy classification. It is important to attempt such a classification, however, as, for example, the presence of a large, vociferous audience in a huge brightly lit auditorium does not have the same impact or significance as a small intimate audience sitting in the dark: one of the ways in which *L'Huile sur le feu* lived up to its promise in the title was with a highly responsive (though strictly speaking non-participatory) audience.[6]

Classification of public participation

A word should be said here about the notion of public participation. The expression has meaning in common parlance, but in scientific discourse is problematic, as the term 'the public' is used mythically for political ends (especially, for example, in reports on opinion polls) and the referent is a fluid one. It is my contention that the programme defines what is meant by the public, and so a preliminary definition is not possible: it is precisely this – the way in which programmes construct the meaning to be attributed to the notion of public opinion – which is the subject of this chapter.

Consider a political interview, for example. In this context, a member of the public is someone who is not a politician and not a journalist, although journalists (and indeed, politicians) are also citizens and in other contexts are members of the general public. It is their participation in the programme which requires journalists to leave behind their personal preferences and – theoretically at least – become neutral and objective. Is a celebrity a member of the public? In opposition to the politician, yes, but in relation to the audience, no. There is not a single definition of the public, the public is a spectrum of many hues. In fact, it is not one spectrum but three.

A survey of French programmes from the past 30 years invites classification of forms of public participation along three axes. Any individual or group of participants is situated at a particular point along each of these axes and their combination indicates the significance constructed by their participation in the programme. The three axes are CSP (*Catégorie socio-professionnelle*), Number and Positioning (see Figure 2.1).

The first axis: CSP (Catégorie socio-professionnelle)

When introduced during a programme, all participants are almost invariably defined by their socio-professional category. In this sense, as Figure 2.1 shows, they may belong to one of a number of subsets, positioned from one end of the axis to the other: the experts, the representatives, the witnesses or the 'anonymes' (those without any social designation).

The 'experts': these may be subject specialists, such as doctors, psychologists, historians, etc., called upon for their scientific knowledge of the area in question. Examples of programmes having recourse to experts are: *Les Dossiers de l'écran, La Marche du siècle, Médiations, Le Point sur la table, Le Droit de savoir, Durand la nuit, Zone interdite* and *La France en direct*. In their analysis of British television debates, Sonia Livingstone and Peter Lunt (1994: 123) comment that 'In audience discussion programmes, experts are very much alone in an alien environment'. Two elements make the television environment alien: the fact that rational discursive argument, which is the usual discourse of the expert, has to be reduced to the media sound bite; and the criticism experts receive from the more numerous 'ordinary' people, who value lived experience more highly than scientific knowledge, accusing experts of being 'out of touch'. French experts face similar problems, but they do have some advantages over their British counterparts. The usual programme slot in France is one and a half hours, considerably longer than the British equivalent (half, three-quarters or one hour), and the timetable is less rigorously respected, allowing programmes to run over. Also, as Patrick Champagne (1990) has pointed out, there is a new group of experts, generally designated 'politologues' (political pundits), whose role and function is to comment on an event or a debate 'à chaud' (on the spot): the term 'politologue' designates the combination of expert scientific knowledge (sociologists, political scientists, etc.) and the degree of media exposure as a result of their readiness to act as opinion leaders on the television stage, and their ability to be at ease with the medium. What is particularly interesting, and specifically French (at least in comparison with Britain), is the way in which academics (*universitaires*)

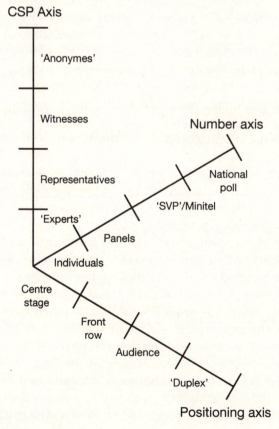

Figure 2.1 *The three axes*

sit alongside those representing economic interests (representatives of polling agencies for example). Indeed, the importance of CSP springs precisely from the involvement of such agencies in the composition of panels and audiences in order to make them 'representative' of the population at large. It may also be true that the reverence with which intellectuals are traditionally regarded in France means that their expert knowledge is treated with greater respect than may be the case in British programmes. However, more importantly, the construction of the programmes presents a different form of social interaction between expert and lay person, which means that it is rare for the 'expert' to feel out of his or her depth; this will be dealt with more fully in the section on positioning.

The second subset on the CSP axis is that of *representative of a particular social group or organization*, such as a trades union representative or the head of a company. The representative function may be official (as in the former) or implied and assumed: the juxtaposition, for example, of a managing director of a large company with that of a small one would constitute an unofficial form of representation, whereas the head of the CNPF (Conseil national du patronat français) – roughly the equivalent of the British CBI – would be official. In this category, there is almost always an unemployed person (preferably young) as a sign that producers recognize the importance of unemployment as a theme of 'public concern'. Increasingly, there are members of Associations set up to help the unemployed and fight against other forms of 'exclusion'.

People in this category share with the expert the fact that they owe their presence on the programme to expert knowledge, but here it is knowledge of lived experience, rather than scientific knowledge, though the two are not mutually exclusive of course. The difference is that where the expert is expected to be neutral and objective, the representative can, indeed is meant to, be partisan, to speak on behalf of a particular group and from their perspective. To do this, they may use their personal, individual experience as typical of what happens to others in their social group. They are thus situated midway between the expert and the next subset, the *témoins* or witnesses.

The *witnesses* are interested parties related in some way to the theme of debate: for example they may be victims or their relatives in a debate about crime. The difference between witnesses and the previous subset, representatives, is that the witnesses gain their link with the theme uniquely through experience, rather than through their profession (e.g. police officers or magistrates would be representatives). One group is concerned primarily with the public sphere and their public role, the other with the private (though the lines of demarcation may not be quite so clear). If the witnesses represent others, it is simply through shared experience, and not in any official capacity. Many programmes have recourse to both representatives and witnesses: in addition to those using experts, listed above, are: *L'Heure de vérité*, *L'Homme en question, Droit de réponse, Bas les masques* and *Les Coulisses du destin*.

Finally, there are the *anonymes*, those without any social designation. It is rare on French television for people to go unnamed, and even rarer for them to have no socio-professional label. This rarity is a measure of the importance of CSP for the legitimacy of participation. Television is not giving access to just anybody, but to those with a legitimate right to an opinion on a particular subject. As the television presenter Michel Field rightly said (on the radio programme *Mon œil*, Europe 1, 6 June 1995): 'La télévision ne donne pas la parole aux gens, elle la leur confie'[7] and, equally, conserves the right (contested by some) to withdraw access, as in the case of *Audition publique* (16 February 1981), which was simply taken off the air when the presenters lost control of the debate.[8] The CSP is provided as an implicit guarantee of a participant's right to be present.

The exception to this is the *télé-trottoir* or vox pop, where it is precisely the anonymity which legitimates the participation: it is, quite literally, the opinion of 'the man or woman in the street'.[9] Yet the pressure to provide a socio-professional label is strong: *Sept sur sept*, for example, introduced a *télé-trottoir* in September 1994 but frequently labelled the interventions with subtitles. The labelling can be verbal or visual; that is, subtitles may appear on screen to designate the speaker, but the setting used and the dress of the person interviewed also act as markers. The first edition of *Le Monde en face* (17 September 1987), for example, had a vox pop in which, among others, a farmer, a labourer and a bartender figured, identifiable by their dress and setting. Interestingly enough, some of the others were recognizable celebrities: the writer Jean d'Ormesson, the Archbishop Monseigneur Lustiger, the singer Michel Jarre, although unnamed. So even when overt labelling is absent, recognition can take place. This is frequently true of the so-called 'public' which constitutes the audience and which is composed of well-known faces (e.g. *Le Point sur la table*). And just in case the viewers were not sufficiently *au fait* with the latest stars, *L'Heure de vérité* began to label some of the more 'relevant' but lesser-known members of its otherwise passive audience.

There are few examples of genuine anonymity: in spite of reference to 'the public', 'public opinion', 'the French' in their broadest terms, participants are situated nearer to the expert/celebrity end of the CSP axis than to the anonymous end. This seems to signify that France has yet to open its television studios to the 'ordinary masses': it favours representativity over access, and frequently has recourse to celebrities. There is still a tendency to label, and hence to categorize and separate, even to hierarchize.

There is one further form of designation which is sometimes made in addition to any of the above categories, and that is age. In the early stages, the panels which participated in *A armes égales* were seated at three separate tables according to generation: 'les jeunes', 'les gens d'entre les deux guerres' and 'les gens de 40'[10] (*Télérama*, 17 February 1970); nowadays, *Chéla ouate* is geared exclusively towards young people and the studio audience is composed mainly of young people. The contrast is interesting and shows a shift in the way in which age is on the public agenda, the problems of youth having displaced the conflict of generations as a topic considered to be 'of public concern'. Also interesting in this context is the fact that gender or ethnic origin is never a factor in its own right but only when it makes the participant a witness: e.g. a programme may invite a 'Beur président de groupe industriel' when the subject for debate is the integration of immigrants (*Le Point sur la table*, 18 September 1991), but would be unlikely to do so when the debate centres on the economy.[11] This is not blatant racism or sexism: it is the fear that the face and voice would be too 'marked' and insufficiently representative of the social group concerned: too individual and insufficiently typical. There is a rejection in France of tokenism or positive discrimination for any social groups, especially where this concerns women: programmes frequently feature only men. Where politicians are concerned, the argument used for the small number of women participants is their scarcity in public office (see Perry, 1995); in the case of the public, no such excuse can be possible, but *La France en direct*, for example, had a clear majority of male participants (almost two men for every woman) and in three out of ten programmes (the first two and the seventh) featured only male members of the public.[12]

The second axis: number

If, as I have suggested, French television is concerned less with access, and more with representation, this poses a serious problem: How can a small number of participants in a debate represent the public at large?

The CSP makes it possible for individuals to represent particular social groups, but not necessarily therefore 'the public'. The advantage of a witness is that s/he may move or inspire, but the disadvantage is that the experience may be too individual to be shared, too specific for the public at large to identify with it, too personal for general conclusions to be drawn. On the other hand, logistically only a limited number of people can actively participate in any given programme: *A armes égales* began with panels of 30, and reduced them to 15 to make the programme more manageable. Aided and abetted by polling agencies, French programmes have constantly sought to claim representativity with even the smallest of panels: *Jury d'honneur* and *Le Point sur la table*, for example, had panels of seven and four respectively, each claiming scientific credibility. By comparison, *L'Heure de vérité*'s much maligned 'instantaneous poll' through Minitel, with its access to 250, then 500, households, seems positively generous, though in fact, of course, it had no scientific validity whatsoever, since statisticians argue that 1000 respondents are essential to get an accurate picture – and that is without entering into the debate about what is meant by an accurate picture.[13] One programme, *Face à la Trois*, tried an even more spurious, technology-led measure of 'public opinion' which included the element of time in its recordings: as the politician was interviewed, a superimposed moving graph showed a dynamic, second by second, positive or negative response by a panel of 15 people with their fingers on the button: fortunately this experiment was quickly dropped. The point here is simply that producers have sought not only to give flesh and voice to particular points of view by inviting members of the public to participate, but also to represent public opinion at large through contact with the greatest number technologically and logistically possible.

However, this aspiration to quantitative validity leads to loss of the qualitative (no face, voice, or setting, the loss of the personalization of opinion and its potential identification), and to criticism of selection and control by the media. An alternative method for increasing the number of voices, therefore, is to multiply the nature and type of participation in a single programme. A prime example is *Audition publique*, introduced for the legislative elections of 1993, using Minitel on a vast scale, the telephone, personal intervention from members of the audience, letters and national polls. The representation of the public at large springs therefore from the interraction between these different 'voices', which if they echo each other become mutually reinforcing as representative of a wider public, and if they contradict each other create the impression of a mosaic of voices, equally indica-

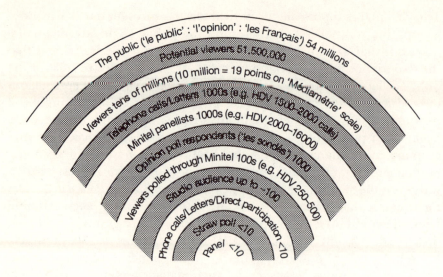

The smaller numbers towards the centre constantly
reflect and represent the larger groups in the outer circles

Figure 2.2 *The public in concentric circles*

tive of a wider number. Participation is like a pool of outwardly moving
concentric circles when a stone has been thrown into the water, the
smaller ones in the middle moving (symbolically) towards the larger
outer ones (see Figure 2.2). The programmes using several types of
participation are too numerous to cite; the most varied have been *A
armes égales, L'Heure de vérité* (1982–95), *Le Monde en face, Durand la nuit,
Audition publique* and *Les Coulisses du destin*.

The third axis: positioning

This is the most important axis of all in the construction of meaning, for
it provides the contextualization of the other two and so influences the
way in which they are to be interpreted. There are two types of
positioning: spatial and temporal.

Spatial positioning consists of the various types of physical space which
are constructed to host studio debates: there is the theatrical-style stage
set (e.g. *A armes égales* in the 1970s and *Ça se discute* in the 1990s), the
circle (which the development in camera technology has made the
most common) and the variation on the circle which is the large
rectangle, with an audience on all sides, particularly used by Guillaume
Durand (e.g. *Les Absents ont toujours tort*, based on the British House of

Commons, *Durand la nuit* in the Salle Wagram) and which figured also in *Audition publique* for the 1993 legislative elections. Whatever the configuration, all have a focal point, which is the centre of activity and where the main guests sit. Where one sits (or stands) in relation to this focal point defines one's role, to a certain extent. For example, a politician may be the central figure, the subject of the debate (whatever the subject of the exchanges which take place during the course of the programme), by being in the centre of this stage (e.g. *L'Heure de vérité*, *La France en direct*), or one voice among many, as other guests join the central platform (thematic debates such as *Le Droit de savoir* or *La Marche du siècle* – except in electoral periods when the former style takes over). Similarly members of the public adopt a different stance by being centre stage (and so subjects, equal voices with other guests, which separates them from the public at large, usually still present on the periphery) or in the audience (where they are *alternative* voices to those on stage and keep their association with the non-participating public), or even further still from the centre, in the outside world, with a television link to the studio (*en duplex*): see Figure 2.1. As their titles suggest, both *Le Monde en face* and *La France en direct* staged the outside world, but, curiously enough, the first of these sometimes attempted to mask the outside link with the use of a 'life-sized' screen, making it appear in certain shots as though the participant was in the studio with the guest! *La France en direct* had multiple voices in terms of positioning: there were question and answer sessions with celebrities seated in a semi-circle round the main guest, questions put by members of the public in a television link-up with different French regions, a pre-recorded portrait drawn by two acquaintances of the main guest (pre-sented in alternative sequence), a documentary film, a one-to-one debate in centre stage, questions from journalists, also seated with the celebrities. Through the use of spatial positioning, an impression of multiplicity was created, symbolizing **La France** *en direct* and partially masking the very small numbers of the general public (between three and six for each programme) who took part in the live debate, and their minor role as posers of one-line questions. In fact, by and large, putting questions (rather than putting forward points of view) seems to be the primary function of members of the public (unless they are centre stage – and even then not always – the further 'out' they are on the spatial positioning axis, the more likely they are to play this role).

One common feature in political programmes is the panel. This positions members of the public as *contradicteurs* (opponents) to the politician, a jury (one programme at least uses this terminology) with the right to judge, those to whom the politician is accountable. It is interesting to note that in this they are supplanting (or at least supplementing) the journalists: it is the traditional pattern of *Face the Press*, imported from the USA. Members of the public are granted access to speak for themselves, the journalist is no longer speaking on their behalf. However, with the clear preparation of the questions, often read from a piece of paper, one wonders whether in fact it is not the public who are speaking on behalf of the journalists: they ask the same questions, in almost the same language. They simply add variety of face and voice, but do not substantially alter the direction of the debate. In *Sept sur sept*, for example, Yolande Rambaldi, a model maker, asked Philippe Séguin: 'Pour qui roulez-vous?'[14] The question was more brutally expressed than is usually the case when put by journalists, but otherwise it is a typical media preoccupation: the alignment of personalities with each other, warring factions within party groupings, in short *la politique politicienne*. The question carries more weight from a member of the public, who adds variety but also legitimacy for the themes of the discussion: but are members of the public just proxy journalists, since it is they, and – Patrick Champagne (1990) would argue – the polling agencies, who set the agenda?

This is an interesting question as the journalists themselves claim the opposite. They frequently claim to be obeying the imperatives of public demand: the public are supposedly setting the agenda. To illustrate this, the public are often used as a launch pad, either at the start of the programme, or at spaced intervals, to introduce another theme (e.g. *Politiques*). This brings us on to the second type of positioning, *temporal positioning*. In effect, because the public is supposedly setting the agenda, they serve as a useful tool in the construction of a programme, to give it rhythm and to sustain interest. Bruno Masure repeatedly stated in his introduction to *La France en direct* that '[L'émission] sera *rythmée* par des interventions de citoyens ordinaires' (my emphasis),[15] and indeed the structure of the programme substantiates this (see Table 2.2). The programme was cut into segments which hopefully did not outlast viewers' attention spans and was made visually more appealing. It also enabled greater clarity, since questions on similar themes were juxtaposed. This was possible because of tight editorial control.

Conclusion

The point regarding both types of positioning is that a television programme is a construct, aesthetic as well as political, which the

Table 2.2 La France en direct; *programme structure*

1. Sarkozy	2. Hue	3. Barre	4. Juppé	5. Aubry	6. Le Pen	7. de Villiers	8. Balladur	9. Jospin	10. Chirac
Introduction	Introduction	Introduction	Introduction	Introduction	Introduction	Introduction	Introduction	Introduction	Introduction
Celebrity 1	Portrait	Portrait	Portrait	Portrait	Portrait	Portrait	Portrait	Portrait	Portrait
Celebrity 2	Celebrity 1	Celebrity 1	Celebrity 1	Celebrity 1	Celebrity 1	Celebrity 1	Celebrity 1	Public 1	Celebrity 1
Public 1	Public 1	Public 1	Public 1	Public 1	Public 1	Public 1	Public 1	Public 2	Public 1
Public 2	Public 2	Public 2	Public 2*	Public 2	Public 2	Public 2	Public 2	Celebrity 1	Public 2
Celebrity 3	Celebrity 2	Celebrity 2	Celebrity 2	Celebrity 2	Celebrity 2	Celebrity 2	Doc. Film	Public 3	Celebrity 2
Celebrity 4	Celebrity 3	Celebrity 3	Celebrity 3	Celebrity 3	Celebrity 3	Public 3	Celebrity 2	Celebrity 2	Celebrity 3
Journalist	Celebrity 4	Public 3	Public 3	Public 3	Public 3	Public 4	Celebrity 3	Public 4	Public 4
Journalist	Public 3	Public 4	Public 4	Public 4	Public 4	Celebrity 3	Public 3	Celebrity 3	Celebrity 4
Celebrity 5	Celebrity 5	Celebrity 4	Celebrity 4	Doc. Film	Doc. Film	Public 5	Public 4	Public 5	Doc. Film
Public 3	Doc. Film	Doc. Film	Doc. Film	Celebrity 4	Celebrity 4	Debate	Celebrity 4	Doc. Film	Public 5
Debate	Debate	Debate	Debate	Debate	Debate	Journalists	Debate	Debate	Debate
Doc. Film	Public 4	Public 5	Journalists	Public 5	Journalists	Close	Public 5	Journalists	Public 6
Journalists	Journalists	Public 6	Close	Public 6	Close		Public 6	Close	Journalists
Close	Close	Poll		Journalists			Journalists		Close
		Journalists		Close			Close		
		Close							

Note: *plus an unforeseen intervention by 1 woman

journalists and producers create according to criteria of entertainment and attractiveness. The lobby for freer access to television will always come up against the fact that a television programme *is* a constructed social space; it is not just a chance encounter with free access to anyone who happens to come along. Let it be said that in this respect television is no different from any other form of unspontaneous social inter-action, such as (an example chosen at random) an academic con-ference – though even academic conferences cater for elements of spontaneous interaction within the structured programme. To date (1995), this has been rare in French television. Little use has been made of the 'roving microphone' in the manner of *The Oprah Winfrey Show* or *Friday Live*, and this is a major factor in the lack of anonymous people in French debates. The forum, in the sense of a general free-for-all, rarely involves those people generally regarded as ordinary citizens. These people are kept to a subsidiary role, in spite of titles such as *Le Monde en face* or *La France en direct*. The audience participation programme on the American model does not exist as such; it is not the ordinary people who determine the style of the debate. It is they, rather than the experts, who are entering a social sphere which may not resemble their normal milieux and to which they therefore have to adapt. For example, a number of participants in *La France en direct* were clearly overawed by the medium and momentarily went blank when it was their turn to speak. There is a process of acculturation which takes place as people enter and leave the studio, or the café which is no longer a normal café but has been transformed into a temporary studio. Just as with oral interviews conducted for the purposes of sociological or historical research, one has to take into account the effects of the interview situation, and this raises the question as to whose voice it is we are hearing.[16]

The process of acculturation can even hit at the heart of the pre-sumed legitimacy of the public as the fountain of political wisdom. Normally, the public, like the customer, is always right: so much so, that one politician, Jean Foyer, even thanked a student for raising a certain question when he had already openly admitted that he had not under-stood what the question was! (*A armes égales*, 17 November 1970). But there are exceptions, such as people who ask unforeseen questions that are a little too awkward to answer, as in one edition of *La France en direct*. *La France en direct* was a carefully constructed programme, totally lacking in any spontaneity, in which Bruno Masure knew in advance which question was coming next – with one notable exception, when a woman insisted on putting a question to Alain Juppé and was given

rather short shrift by the latter, for her pains. M. Juppé's response
sought to discredit the woman's question:

> On dit souvent que les hommes politiques sont sectaires, polémiques: les
> Français sont comme ça. Je regrette un peu que cette dame ait un tel
> regard – j'allais utiliser des mots peut-être un petit peu forts – chargé de
> sentiments qui ne sont pas amicaux. Je ne vais pas polémiquer avec elle
> sur le fond. ... Je voudrais revenir à une question qui, elle, n'est pas
> polémique et qui n'est pas du niveau un peu du café du commerce pour
> répondre au premier intervenant parce que lui a posé une vraie ques-
> tion.[17]

(Alain Juppé, *La France en direct*, 25 February 1995)

Interestingly enough, Bruno Masure made no attempt to follow the
unexpected question through (as he had with other questions).

Because television programmes are designed and produced according to pre-set patterns, they create a carefully constructed social space
which exists in its own right, and which people engage in between
entering and leaving. Television is not just a window on the world, it is
a part of it, and effects a transformation of the world it portrays. In that
sense it is truly interactive. This can never be otherwise, except if one
takes the fly-on-the-wall approach, with a hidden camera. One programme at least simulated this idea: *Le Monde en face* asked Mitterrand
to comment on a recording showing a family and friends at dinner in
which racist comments abounded. But this was no longer interactive,
live television, but a pre-recorded document, and placed Mitterrand in
the false position of having to comment on what had been said without
the possibility of exchange.

This overview of French television debates shows that producers have
been inventive in creating new forms of public participation, but that
representation and mediation dominate over access to the ordinary
masses or particular social groups, and issues of entertainment and
visual attractiveness dominate in the construction of programmes. This
is not to say, however, that the question of access is an easy one to solve.
Television can never fully reflect the world through the medium of a
studio debate, it is constantly reconstructing it. So although it may be
true that French producers still have some way to go towards opening
up television studios to more 'ordinary' people, this ultimate limit on its
effects and achievements should not be forgotten.

Notes

1. 'to stir the public out of their passivity.'
2. This list is by no means exhaustive but covers the main programmes shown over the past 30 years. I am grateful to the Institut National de l'Audiovisuel (INA) for access to their television archives.
3. Strictly speaking, 45 or even 44, as *Face à face* and *Face à face (suite)* were really the same programme, listed separately here because of the intercalation of *En direct avec* – which in fact followed exactly the same formula but under a different title! On the other hand, *L'Heure de vérité* legitimately occurs twice, as they were two quite distinct programmes.
4. This representation is a long-standing tradition, as testified in the opening words of Pierre Sabbagh in his historic interview with Guy Mollet in 1956: 'M. le Président du Conseil, tout d'abord je tiens à vous remercier de bien avoir voulu recevoir le spectateur français que je suis, car je représente ici l'ensemble des spectateurs français ... ' ('Prime Minister, first of all I would like to thank you for kindly agreeing to receive the French viewer that I am, since here I am representing all French viewers ... '). See Neveu (1989) for a discussion of this representation in relation to *L'Heure de vérité*.
5. See note 12 for details of women's participation in *La France en direct*.
6. The programme title means '[to add] fuel to the flames'. Its presenter, Philippe Bouvard, is better known as a variety show host. He denies that the audience was 'warmed up' prior to the programme, and claims that their responsiveness was due to the fact that they were supporters of the guests (interview with the author, 14 February 1994), but many programmes have selected their guests in this way, without the same results.
7. 'Television does not give people the opportunity to speak, it entrusts it to them temporarily.'
8. *Audition publique* is a title which has frequently been used for one-off debates on a major current theme, as well as for the short series prior to the 1993 Legislative elections which is listed in Table 2.1. The programme referred to here was interrupted when militants from the Communist Party and the affiliated trade union, the CGT, protested vociferously against the failure to invite representatives of these two organizations to participate.
9. See below for the significance of positioning.
10. 'The young, the 1940s generation and the generation from the inter-war years.'
11. The young man in question (a *Beur* – that is the son of immigrants but born in France – chairman of an industrial group) was Jean-Pierre Bianco's 'suppléant' (supporter) for the programme. The panel included 'une Malienne devenue Française' (a naturalized Malian woman) and 'un sportif d'origine maghrébine' (a sportsman of North African origin), each 'representing' different forms of integration.
12. The total numbers of women for all ten programmes were as follows: in the television link-up with various French regions, 17 women out of 46 participants (37 per cent); in the studio, eleven out of 40 celebrities (27.5 per cent) and one in ten of those who took part in the one-to-one debate with the main guest.
13. For details of the margins of error related to the size of the survey sample, see Meynaud and Duclos (1985: 60–3). For a critique of opinion surveys as constructing (rather than reflecting) social reality, see Champagne (1990). See also

Chapter 1 in this book.
14. Meaning 'Whose side are you on?' but with a slightly cynical tone in the use of the verb *rouler* (untranslatable in this context).
15. '[The programme] will be *punctuated* by interventions from ordinary citizens.'
16. See Chapters 4 and 5.
17. 'People often say that politicians are sectarian and argumentative: the French are like that. I'm slightly sorry that this lady sees things in such a – I was going to use words which are a bit strong, perhaps – in a way which is suffused with unfriendly sentiments. I'm not going to argue with her over what she says. . . . I would like to come back to another, uncontroversial question, which isn't on the level of bar talk, in order to answer the first person who intervened because *he* asked a genuine question.'

References

Cauhaupé, V. (1995) 'Quand les téléspectateurs ont le mot de la fin', *Le Monde Radio-Télévision*, 9–10 July.

Champagne, P. (1990) *Faire l'opinion. Le nouveau jeu politique.* Paris: Editions de Minuit.

Livingstone, S. and Lunt, P. (1994) *Talk on Television: Audience Participation and Public Debate.* London: Routledge.

Meynaud, H. and Duclos, D. (1985) *Les Sondages d'opinion.* Paris: Editions La Découverte.

Neveu, E. (1989) '*L'Heure de vérité* ou le triangle de la représentation', *Mots* 20 (Sept.): 57–73.

Perry, S. (1995) 'French television and women politicians' in J. Still and D. Knight (eds) *Representations of Women.* Nottingham: Nottingham University Press.

3.

The loi Toubon: *linguistic interventionism and Human Rights*

INÈS BRULARD

The *loi Toubon* is a linguistic law which was promulgated on 4 August 1994 on the basis of a bill introduced in 1993 by the Minister of Culture and Francophone Affairs, Jacques Toubon. The controversies surrounding the Toubon bill reached their highest point when on 1 July 1994, 60 deputies called for it to be amended on the grounds that, as the bill then stood, it was unconstitutional. The Conseil Constitutionnel divested the law of two of its most contentious clauses: firstly, the obligation on private individuals and the media to use the official terminology,[1] and secondly, making the allocation of public funding for research subject to an explicit undertaking to publish the work in French.

In this chapter, the *loi Toubon*, as it was amended by the Conseil Constitutionnel, will be presented as an instance of what I call a *tensorial relationship* between two types of linguistic interventionism. By 'tensorial relationship' is meant a relationship in which two terms or concepts are considered as tensors, that is as terms which are *both* opposed to each other *and* complementary. It is distinct from the classical structuralist concept of opposition, which presupposes strict disjunction, an either/or relationship. Therefore the terms in a tensorial relationship are not just conceived of as mere dichotomies; they complement each other as well.

Two kinds of interventionism

The debates concerning the *loi Toubon* seem to revolve around the dual nature (and function) of linguistic interventionism: a *pragmatic* and an

ideological sort of interventionism. Broadly speaking, linguistic interventionism consists either in improving communication between members of a particular society or in spreading a particular ideology.
Underlying these two types of interventionism are two different views of
language: in the case of pragmatic interventionism, language is considered as a mere instrument of communication; linguistic interventionism will therefore consist in developing new lexical sources, diction-
aries, spelling reforms, etc. The idea is that these modifications in the
language will improve communication between the individuals of a
particular linguistic community. In the case of ideological interventionism, language is the symbol of values external to the language itself: it is
no longer viewed as a mere instrument of communication but as
symbolic of a particular ideology. This could be represented as shown in
Figure 3.1.

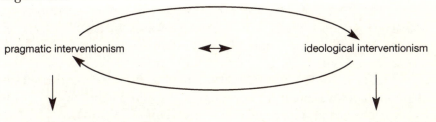

Figure 3.1 *Tensors*

Clearly, these two approaches can occur simultaneously (this is often
the case in France) but interestingly, they are often polarized during
debates relative to linguistic measures. For instance, for Mr Toubon (*Le
Monde*, 14 April 1994), language is 'une affaire d'Etat' (the business of
the state); the use of French must be promoted because all consumers,
employees, the public at large have the right to be informed in a
language that they understand. Conversely, some people do not accept
that the state should legislate on language matters, on the grounds that
language belongs to the 'masse parlante' (the people who use it) and
that no legislation whatsoever should alter the right of individuals to
express themselves as they see fit. Jacques Toubon's reply to the *laissez-
faire* argument is evidence of the conflictual nature of these opposi-
tions: 'Je suis étonné de voir ceux qui prétendent ''défendre le peuple''
m'expliquer que rien n'est plus beau que d'employer des mots qui sont
incompris de 95% des gens'[2] (in *Le Monde*, 23 March 1994).

This chapter, however, will not attempt to assess the necessity or the
validity of the *loi Toubon*. Rather, I am interested in highlighting the

interplay between these recurrent positions in French linguistic policy, and in the *loi Toubon* in particular. Like the 1975 law (*loi Bas-Lauriol*), the *loi Toubon* offers a sort of defence of the consumer,[3] and, to that extent, it can be seen as an instance of pragmatic (or instrumental) interventionism; however, as the debates and, more importantly, the amendments of the Conseil Constitutionnel clearly showed, the *loi Toubon* represented a lot more than that. Two types of tensorial relationships will emerge from this discussion: one concerning the relationship between pragmatic and ideological interventionism, the other concerning the relationship between the French state and the citizen.

References to previous instances of linguistic interventionism kept being made during the controversies surrounding the Toubon bill. Two of these will serve to illustrate the dual aspect of linguistic interventionism: the Villers-Cotterêts Ordinances (a series of edicts) and the decree of 20 July 1794. The Villers-Cotterêts Ordinances, promulgated in 1539 by François I, marked the first step towards the establishment of French as the official language. The text ostensibly outlawed Latin from legal procedures in order to ensure better understanding between the various parties, but it was in fact also aimed at superseding the vernaculars other than French. In contrast to the 1490 Ordinance of Moulins, which imposed the use of 'the French language *or* the vernacular' for all court interrogations and verbatim reports, the Villers-Cotterêts edict specified that only the French vernacular could be used. This edict must be interpreted in the context of the codification of the law but also in the broader ideological context of an attempt, on the part of the French state, to establish stronger administrative and political centralization, with the French language as the symbol of a new national identity (on the connection between language and national identity, see Lodge, 1993: 130–1 and Brulard, 1997).

A second attempt towards the establishment of French was made during the Revolution. At its beginning (1790), Abbé Grégoire had been asked to study the linguistic situation of France: however, his detailed survey, 'On the necessity and the means of annihilating the use of *patois* and of universalizing the use of the French language', was only submitted to the Convention in 1794. It emerged from the survey that a vast proportion of French people could not read or communicate in French. At first, the measures which were taken in view of that fact were of an essentially instrumental nature: it was decided that revolutionary texts and the decisions of the Constituent Assembly would be translated or transmitted orally in the various languages used in the country. So at first the French language was just seen as a vehicle for communication.

Later, however, it appeared that the objective was no longer communication but acknowledgement of a new authoritative discourse, connected with new interests (Bourdieu, 1982: 31): in a climate of fear of counter-revolution, the translation policy was abandoned in favour of policies to spread the French language and stamp out the others. The decree of *thermidor an II* (20 July 1794) stated that all public notices should be published in French. The law condemned all those who infringed it to destitution and six months' imprisonment (in Hagège, 1987: 196).[4]

This change in language policy was connected to a change in the way the French language was thought of: French had become the symbol of an ideology, a symbol of republican unity and identity. As Abbé Grégoire himself put it, 'L'unité de l'idiome est une partie intégrante de la Révolution ... Il faut identité de langage'[5] (quoted in *Le Monde*, 4 May 1994). The French language became the 'language of liberty' and, following Condillac's theory, a link was created between revolutionary *language* and revolutionary *thought.* As Bourdieu (1982: 31) rightly puts it, 'L'imposition de la langue légitime ... fait partie des stratégies politiques destinées à assurer l'éternisation des acquis de la Révolution par la production et la reproduction de l'homme nouveau'; what is at stake is 'la formation ou la réformation des structures mentales'.[6] The following equation thus appeared: national unity, stability and identity are based on linguistic unification. At the same time as the Revolution announced the triumph of reason and democratic principles, it set out to erase all the particularisms which were seen as a danger to the nation. Language issues were thus cast as public safety issues, as insurrection and treason were associated with different languages. Barrère, in a speech to the Comité de salut public (Committee of Public Safety) conveyed this idea very clearly:

> le fédéralisme et la superstition parlent bas-breton; l'émigration et la haine de la République parlent allemand [alsacien]; la contre-révolution parle italien [corse] et le fanatisme parle basque. Cassons ces instruments de dommage et d'erreur. ... Citoyens, la langue d'un peuple libre doit être une et la même pour tous.[7]
>
> (in Lodge, 1991: 107–8)

A territorial approach to language

Let us now turn to Toubon's linguistic bill and see how it is characterized both by an instrumental and by an ideological approach. Mr

Toubon stated in *Le Monde* (23 March 1994) that his intention was to devise 'une loi de service' (a service law). The bill was presented as the affirmation of a 'droit au français pour les consommateurs, les salariés, le public'[8] (in *Le Monde*, 25 February 1994). This instrumental conception of language is reflected in the law itself: the measures which impose translations from a foreign language into French and/or regional languages go in that direction (see for example Articles 3 and 4 concerning public notices, and Article 6 concerning any documents distributed to conference participants in France, in *Journal officiel*, 5 August 1994).

However, in addition to this pragmatic approach, Mr Toubon also took an ideological stance: he declared in *Le Monde* (5 May 1994) for instance, that his bill opposes the idea of 'l'anglo-marchand' (or 'commercial English'). Mr Toubon opposes the world-wide creation of uniform structures, the advent of 'un seul modèle culturel, politique, économique, inspiré de l'économie de marché, avec ses bienfaits, mais, aussi, avec ses tares'. He also stresses that 'Préserver le français, langue de la liberté, de l'égalité et de la démocratie, est un enjeu pour tous les peuples épris de nos valeurs'[9] (in *Le Monde*, 5 May 1994). This passage represents language as the symbol of abstract values such as liberty, equality, democratic principles. Interestingly, a few lines further, this interpretation is shifting to an *instrumental* view of language, which entails a different view of the concept of liberty as well: Mr Toubon makes it clear that his bill will not lead to a reduction but, on the contrary, to an increase in the individual's freedom, as his only wish is to 'interdire qu'on interdise l'usage du français' ('to prohibit the prohibition of French'; in *Le Monde*, 5 May 1994). Clearly here, the reference is not to the abstract concept of freedom but to the *free usage* of a language, thus to a pragmatic sort of interventionism.

The tensorial relationship between pragmatic and ideological interventionism became evident on 29 July 1994, when the Conseil Constitutionnel partly censured the law. The Conseil's amendments relate to what was ideologically perceived as unacceptable: the Conseil ruled that certain elements in the law were going against fundamental liberties proclaimed in the 1789 *Déclaration des droits de l'Homme*: freedom of thought, freedom of speech and freedom of opinion. However, this ideologically oriented intervention related to a point in the law which was based on the instrumental character of language. Indeed, one of the central points of the law was to encourage the use of neologisms, i.e. the terms elaborated by ministerial commissions and published in *Le Dictionnaire des termes officiels* (see note 1). Such a measure is not surprising, since it is generally acknowledged that the problem for the French language is to express a rapidly changing technical reality; from that point of view, creating neologisms and 'naturalizing' borrowings from foreign languages is justified. If a strict pragmatic approach is to be followed, then one has to accept that modernizing the French language goes together with a widespread diffusion of neologisms, supported by the media, whose help to promote particular usages is invaluable.

However, by referring to the universal concept of Human Rights, the Conseil Constitutionnel sought to balance the purely instrumental logic in the law; it was decided that official neologisms would only be imposed on corporate bodies and on individuals in public office. The Conseil Constitutionnel judged that, according to the principle of free communication of thoughts and opinions enshrined in the Declaration of Human Rights, any individual (except those acting in the name of the Republic), including the media (whether public or private), should be allowed total freedom in language usage and therefore could not be forced to use the official neologisms.[10] As some commentators have pointed out, the Conseil Constitutionnel's censorship would have gone further if the 1992 constitutional amendment had not included that 'la langue de la République est le français'.[11] The Conseil Constitutionnel's intervention has established the following tensorial relationship: Mr Toubon has obtained a major victory since his instrumental vision has, to a large extent, been accepted by the Conseil Constitutionnel. The use of French will be reinforced on television and radio (Articles 12 and 13), publicity (Articles 12 and 14), in all the contractual relationships between employers and employees (Articles 8, 9, 10), in the description and directions for use of products, on bills and receipts (Article 2), etc. (in *Journal Officiel*, 5 August 1994). However, the Conseil decided that this instrumentalist policy could only be exercised within the limits imposed by the concept of freedom of speech.

In contrast to this tensorial approach, some reactions following the decision taken by the Conseil Constitutionnel kept highlighting the conflictual nature of the two types of linguistic interventionism, together with the ambiguities inherent in universal concepts such as that of freedom. Jacques Toubon's interpretation of the concept of freedom was in fact underpinned by his essentially instrumental view of language. In the letter published in *Le Monde* (4 August 1994), he denounces 'une interprétation abusive de la liberté d'expression' which has the consequence that 'on distinguerait de nouveau, après cinq siècles de progrès, une langue de l'administration et une langue des citoyens'.[12] Let us first note that this comparison is somewhat incongruous since in contemporary, as opposed to fifteenth-century, France, most people speak French.[13] Moreover, if his comment is to be interpreted in linguistic terms, Mr Toubon seems to regret that language is no longer uniform. However it is a mistake to believe that it ever was: this uniform view of language is, as many sociolinguistic studies have shown, pure fiction. Rather, this 'langue de l'administration' can be seen as *one* of the varieties of French amongst all those used by Toubon's 'French citizens'.

As suggested in the following passage, Mr Toubon's concern is with language as an instrument of social and cultural integration: 'les socialistes ont pris le risque d'aggraver les ségrégations, l'échec scolaire et les entraves à l'intégration et à la promotion sociale'[14] (in *Le Monde*, 4 August 1994). It is true that access to French language and culture is crucial for any individual wishing to integrate and progress in a society which, as Bourdieu (1982: 30ff.) has shown, is characterized by a close link between language and social advancement and therefore power; and this is precisely the role, amongst other institutions, of the *école de la République*. However, it is exaggerated, to say the least, to claim that imposing official neologisms (this is after all what Jacques Toubon was left to advocate) on every French individual is a solution to the social problems in question!

Another example of sterile dichotomies is found in the reaction of Jack Lang, who criticized what he called 'la philosophie ultralibérale' of the Conseil Constitutionnel on the grounds that the revolutionaries who contributed to formulating the principles of the Declaration of Human Rights 'concevaient une politique volontariste pour la langue française'[15] (in *Le Monde*, 2 August 1994).

Conclusion

According to Jack Lang, Toubon's interventionist policy was defeated by an 'ultra-liberal' *laissez-faire* attitude. As was shown previously, the position adopted by the Conseil is far less clear-cut and goes beyond these dichotomies, precisely in that it has established a tensorial relationship between the two types of linguistic interventionism and between the state and the individual. The position taken with regard to the media (Articles 12 and 13 in *Journal officiel*, 5 August 1994) seems to be another case in point: apart from some exceptional cases, the use of French will be compulsory in all radio and television broadcasting and advertising; however, the Conseil has suppressed the interdiction on using a foreign term if a French equivalent exists. Whether public or private, it was important that the media should be recognized as an essential place of freedom in a democratic society (see Jacques Rigaud's letter, published in *Le Monde*, 9 August 1994). On the other hand, the Conseil Constitutionnel has increased the powers of the broadcasting regulatory body, the Conseil supérieur de l'audiovisuel, so that it can see to the 'respect de la langue française et [au] rayonnement de la francophonie'[16] (Article 13). It is up to the professionals to decide whether or not they should use the neologisms which are imposed on civil servants.[17]

As mentioned earlier, the role of the media to promote a certain usage is important. In the seventeenth century it made sense to say, like Malherbes, that the people are 'sovereign lords of their own language'; since the advent of the twentieth century (and even more so in the second half of the century), the impact of the media is such that one can wonder to what extent this is true of 'ordinary people'. However, it is still true to say that, at the end of the day, it is always up to the individual to accept or reject new usages (like the neologisms imposed in some walks of life). The law, as it has been amended, thus reflects both poles of the opposition: it preserves the necessary freedom of the media and, at the same time, highlights their pivotal role in the diffusion of new French usages.

Notes

1. Each Ministry has its own Commission ministérielle de terminologie, whose task is to create new French equivalents of foreign words. The work done by the various terminological commissions and approved by ministerial decree is then published in the *Dictionnaire des termes officiels*. These terms 'must be used in all official documents and in all documents produced by those contracting with the state' (Ager, 1990: 242).

2. 'I am surprised that those who claim to "stand up for the people" tell me that it is wonderful to use words which are not understood by 95 per cent of the population.'

3. The 1975 law established the compulsory use of French in three areas: 'in commercial and advertising contexts, to protect the consumer; in work contracts, to protect the employee; and in the context of information given to consumers either by private firms or public bodies, usually in the form of leaflets' (Judge, 1993: 21). The problems with that law lay first in its actual implementation and secondly in its limitations by Common Market laws (it appeared to clash for instance with Article 30 in the Treaty of Rome, which outlaws measures which would restrict, or have the effect of restricting, imports amongst the European member countries). As a result, few cases actually led to convictions, and when they did, the fines incurred were too small to act as a deterrent.

4. Political ideology was to be reinforced by the education system: the effective extension of standard French throughout France and the consequent decline in the use of dialects and regional languages only came about in the nineteenth century, with the greater availability of, and access to, education (especially with the establishment by Jules Ferry of a free, universal and secular education system).

5. 'Unity of language is an integral part of the Revolution ... There should only be one language in this country.'

6. 'Imposing a single legitimate language ... was but one of the political strategies which were to ensure the permanence of the revolutionary changes by producing and reproducing "the new man".' At stake is 'the shaping or re-shaping of mental processes'.

7. 'Federalism and superstition speak Breton; emigration and hatred of the Republic speak German (Alsatian); the counter-revolution speaks Italian (Corsican) and fanaticism speaks Basque. Let us smash these faulty and harmful instruments. ... Citizens, the language of a free country must be one and the same for all.' The term 'federalism' was used pejoratively in the French Revolution because it was thought that it was linguistic differences which had divided the nation. Now it was crucial for the nation to be united.

8. The 'right of the consumer, the worker, the public to use French'.

9. He opposes 'a single cultural, political, economic model inspired by a beneficial but also flawed market economy' and stresses that 'Preserving French, the language of liberty, equality and democracy, is a challenge for all the peoples who cherish our values'.

10. Interestingly, this shift from an instrumental to an ideological position is reflected in the language that is used: no mention is made any more of neologisms, a neutral term used in linguistics; instead, one speaks of *français officiel* (official French) or of *français codifié* (codified French). Also the issue is no longer so much the modernization of the French language as the *imposition d'une langue d'Etat* (imposing a state language on the citizen, and thus violating the principle of freedom of speech).

11. 'The language of the Republic is French.' The addition of this article to the Constitution in 1992 has to be read in the context of the ratification of the Maastricht Treaty. Lynne Wilcox (1994) has underlined the contradiction between France's desire to ensure a place for the French language on the international scene, and the apparent disregard for minority languages within French territory.

12. He denounces 'an excessive interpretation of the notion of the freedom of speech' which has the consequence that 'after five centuries of progress, one would re-establish a distinction between the language of the administration and the language of the people'.

13. Although this chapter is not directly concerned with the assessment of the influence of English on the French language, it has to be borne in mind that French syntax, morphology, pronunciation and even lexicon have not been affected by English to such an extent that one can speak of the imminent death of French (see Hagège, 1987: 24–74).

14. 'The socialists have taken the risk of increasing segregation, academic failure and the obstacles to integration and social advancement.'

15. Jack Lang criticized this position as 'ultra-liberal' on the grounds that the revolutionaries 'devised an interventionist approach to the development of the French language'.
16. 'Respect for the French language and [to] the promotion of French abroad.'
17. Note, in this connection that Balladur's *Circulaire relative à l'emploi de la langue française par les agents publics* (Circular on the use of the French language by public servants; published in the *Journal officiel* of 20 April 1994) has passed relatively unnoticed. It states, however, that the appraisal of public servants will take into account the willingness and enthusiasm ('l'intérêt et le zèle') they show in respecting the French language (in *Le Monde*, 4 July 1994).

References

Ager, D. (1990) *Sociolinguistics and Contemporary French.* Cambridge: CUP.

Bourdieu, P. (1982) *Ce que parler veut dire.* Paris: Fayard.

Brulard, I. (1997) 'Linguistic policies' in S. Perry (ed.) *Aspects of Contemporary France.* London: Routledge.

Hagège, C. (1987) *Le français et les siècles.* Paris: Odile Jacob.

Journal officiel de la République française, 20 Apr. 1994.

Journal officiel de la République française, 5 Aug. 1995.

Judge, A. (1993) 'French: a planned language?' in Sanders, *French Today*, 7–26.

Lodge, R.A. (1991) 'Authority, prescriptivism and the French standard language', *Journal of French Language Studies* 1(1): 93–111.

Lodge, R.A. (1993) *French: From Dialect to Standard.* London: Routledge.

Sanders, C. (1993) (ed.) *French Today.* Cambridge: CUP.

Wilcox, L. (1994) 'The amendment to Article 2 of the Constitution: an equivocal interpretation of linguistic pluralism?', *Modern and Contemporary France* NS 2, 3: 270–8.

4.

Social suffering 'in their own words': Pierre Bourdieu's sociology of poverty

PHILIPPE MARLIÈRE

Pierre Bourdieu has long been a dominant figure in French social theory, and over the last 15 years, his research has aroused increasing international interest and comments.[1] Bourdieu's latest main empirical investigation into social poverty in France (Bourdieu, 1993) is, in many respects, intellectually and politically challenging for all those – academics, politicians, but also, more generally, any citizens – who feel concerned with the constant rise of diverse forms of misery and exclusion[2] in our societies today.

The most striking feature of the book is certainly the audience it wishes to target: deliberately 'non-intellectual' – or perhaps one should say, 'non-jargonizing' – Bourdieu intends his research to be read by a large circle of people, going far beyond the academic specialists on the topic. This constitutes a rather unusual aspect of this particular work, especially if one compares it with the highly theoretical style of his previous publications. Not surprisingly, *La misère du monde* has been for the last two years one of the best sellers in sociology in France.

The method and the object of his vast research are unique: more than 150 interviews were conducted by 24 researchers (including Bourdieu) between 1989 and 1993 in different regions of France and among very diverse segments of the French population. Fifty-eight interviews have been published *in extenso*, and the book contains nearly a thousand pages (Bourdieu, 1993: 7).

Bourdieu's survey of social poverty concretely shows why some people, in certain conditions of social suffering, behave as they behave, or think what they think. It is above all an attempt to understand how a social situation, understood or seen as a personal destiny by the social agent him/herself, stems in fact from social constraints which are themselves rooted within the very structures of the social market, of the educational system, etc.

In the Hippocratic tradition, real medicine begins with the treatment of invisible illnesses, i.e. with the knowledge of facts about which the ill person does not say anything, because s/he is not aware of them, or because s/he forgets to mention them. Using this Hippocratic method to tackle the question of poverty in French society, Bourdieu above all makes an effort to circumscribe poverty where it is – in bodies and minds – and to make it understandable and visible for potential political therapy.

Three main issues can be picked up and discussed from the book. The first one poses a direct social challenge: to what extent does Bourdieu's comprehensive sociology help us to grasp the nature and the content of suffering and malaise in French society? The second one involves an epistemological consideration about Bourdieu's use of interviews and oral testimonies: in other terms, what heuristic credit can be given to a survey which builds its observations from oral sources and the unusual social situation of interview? The third issue is on Bourdieu's critique of the 'state's withdrawal' (in the education system, in the police, in health services, or in housing) and has a more obvious political implication.

Limited and profound misery

The assumption which underlies Bourdieu's research is that today people carry conflicts which are 'politically inexpressible'. This is the reason why he and his team have decided to go and meet ordinary citizens and listen to them. The major preoccupation is to find out, far from the official discourses of the political class or of the media, what these people's concerns are from their own perspectives. This social suffering is difficult to perceive, even physically and morally painful to express, because often it has been repressed for a very long time. Bourdieu says that it is necessary to 'briser l'écran de projections, parfois absurdes, parfois odieuses, derrière lequel la souffrance se cache'[3] (Bourdieu, 1992: 173), referring here to racism or xenophobia, as current manifestations of social hatred. The survey tackles and shows the ordinary world of 'possessed people', captured by a 'réalité extérieure qui, à la façon du monstre d'*Alien*, les habite et les hante'[4] (Bourdieu, 1992: 174).

Tackling the social poverty issue, Bourdieu offers new perspectives, introducing the concept of *relative misery* (what he literally calls *positional misery – misère de position –* i.e. misery one experiences in relation to one's relative position in society). This notion involves the understanding of a plurality of social situations which are very rarely evoked, or known as such in academic surveys on poverty. It shows that relative misery is to be found primarily in the context of material misery, but that it en compasses another type of misery, relative and not quantifiable, which is to be met in every social field, and in every social class. Bourdieu summarizes his approach in a short introductory chapter where he states that merely taking into consideration manifestations of material misery prevents us from being aware of and understanding the patterns of social suffering, characteristic of a social order which might have softened the most blatant social disparities, but has also given rise to new forms of miseries, both relative and subjective, depending on the point of view of the social agent who suffers (Bourdieu, 1993: 11).

The departure from traditional research on poverty from a macro level is patent here. Scrutinizing people's misery as it is expressed throughout the interviews, he is bound to pay attention to what he calls *limited misery* ('petite misère') (Bourdieu, 1993: 11), which he opposes to *profound misery* ('grande misère'). Limited misery is what people suffer from because of their position in society. Profound misery is what society objectively recognizes as such: long-term unemployment, poor housing conditions, serious illness or accidents, manifestations of racism, etc. Social suffering is in this respect plural and exists across classes. Bourdieu and his team show that in any social class, some people suffer because they think they occupy a depreciated position within their social group. The paradigmatic use of Patrick Süskind's play *The Double Bass* illustrates this first important point. In this play, the main character plays the double bass in a socially prestigious group, a symphony orchestra. His love for one of the orchestra's soloists cannot be declared, in any situation, because he plays an instrument normally considered less prestigious in the orchestra. He therefore feels that he occupies a rather obscure position in this privileged world. Thus, his relationship with one of the stars of the group becomes very problematic in his own eyes.

Two principal forms of miseries are exposed in this survey. The first are those 'seen from below', i.e. miseries linked to social experiences of decline. Others, according to our example of the double bass player, have their roots in privileged social situations. In the first category, a series of interviews draws a quite alarming and sad panorama of shattered micro-universes which are about to disappear. There is the story of an old worker who has spent 30 years assembling Peugeot cars on an assembly line. He has been a trade union representative for a long time, with marked communist sympathies. He keeps insisting on three main points throughout the interview: the ever more difficult working conditions in his factory imposed to increase the total production of cars, the loss of the 'feeling of comradeship' among workers, and the individualization of social life in general: he sees the young workers as terribly individualistic, with absolutely no class consciousness or political belief. He simply comments, in his own words, on the drastic cultural changes which have occurred in the working class over the last three decades, aware that he is one of the last survivors of a bygone age. This is also the situation of the farmer who has just invested a lot of money to buy some very expensive equipment to cultivate his land (Bourdieu, 1993: 519–31). He is poor and burdened with debts. At the time of the interview, he has just learnt that his only son has decided to go and live in the town, and refused to become a farmer in his turn. This decision is for the father a betrayal, undermining, in his view, the work and efforts of an entire life. With no heir, he sees his life and his work totally ruined. Or again, there is, among the numerous cases exposed in this survey, the example of the independent wine seller who cannot compete with the discounts on alcohol offered at the nearby supermarkets, and who slowly loses his clients (Bourdieu, 1993: 551–68). Three representative examples from important sectors of industrial and rural France which are on the verge of vanishing, taking their associated populations down with them.

Other landscapes of social decline, but representing increasing populations this time, and especially affecting young people, include: the broken social dream of a young northerner who left his region because he had been promised a temporary job in a car factory in Central France. He is now unemployed again, and rootless, looking for an elusive temporary job (Bourdieu, 1993: 349–65). Also the case of the young *Beur* – the son of an Algerian, but born in France – who sees school just as a nice way to spend time and speaks of the 'useless degree' for which he has been preparing himself (Bourdieu, 1993: 605–20).

A third of the book is devoted to the second type of suffering Bourdieu puts forward: the kind of malaise which arises after experiencing a particular social success. In this case, success is apprehended as a failure, or as the transgression of the 'family project'. A young man, son of a primary school teacher, after going to the Ecole Normale Supérieure has now become a physics researcher in a laboratory. He nonetheless cannot help considering what his career could have been, if he had not resigned from the Polytechnique, the most prestigious military French *Grande*

Ecole. Bourdieu explains the young man's decision to leave the Polytechnique to which he had been admitted, by the initial contradiction
contained in his father's project: i.e. the more the son is successful (i.e.
accomplishes his father's will), the more he fails, because he then feels he
is betraying his father (who is a left-wing, anti-militarist teacher, whereas
the Polytechnique is known as a far right-wing military milieu).

This new case-study shows what Bourdieu's main point is: even the
most personal forms of social suffering or frustration, even the most
silent and interiorized ones, are to be explained by the objective
contradictions of the social market. In other words, the suffering is to
be found in the antinomic social constraints which one given individual
has to endure. The situation of malaise stems from the fact that the
double constraints do not offer an alternative. It is not possible for the
social agent to choose just one of the two positions, instead s/he has to
try to cope with these antinomic tensions. In this respect, Bourdieu
speaks of 'victimes structurelles' (structural victims) (Bourdieu, 1991:
3–6). He widely discusses the notion of *double bind* to try to explain the
suffering which arises from the social position that an individual occupies. As currently used in the social sciences, the notion of double bind
determines a situation in which a first injunction is addressed to an
individual by a relative, a friend, or a colleague. This first injunction is
contradicted by a second main injunction. The person who has to deal
with these two contradictory orders is incapable of deciding which one
of the two injunctions s/he is going to opt for. From this ensues a
situation of total uncertainty, or even profound self-doubt.

In this book, many striking examples of double binding are to be
found in the educational system. A lot of working-class children are
unconsciously encouraged by their parents to continue their education, beyond the *baccalauréat.* These young people from lower classes
are urged to invest in school while the social conditions of their
eventual success are far from being present. They find themselves in a
situation where going to school becomes the end as such. They keep
deferring the time when they will have to leave school, the moment of
truth when they will realize for good that time spent in the institution
has only been 'un temps mort, un temps perdu' (dead time, lost time)
(Bourdieu, 1991: 600). Until the end of the 1950s, the situation was
based on the early and brutal exclusion of the working class from the
education system. A certain 'democratization' of the system took place
from the 1960s onwards: conditions of selection were relaxed, in order
to let more pupils enter college or university. For Bourdieu, this new
situation has provoked a 'social dream', particularly in working-class

families for whom the belief in a sure and definite social progression for their children through education has been aroused. But due to the lack of real democratization of the social conditions of access to education, working-class children tend to be the first victims of this false openness. It is no great surprise to hear from Bourdieu that educational institutions remain as exclusive as they were in the past. Besides the transmission of a cultural capital (what Bourdieu calls 'reproduction'), the whole system itself, under the appearances of 'democratization', continues to be fiercely selective. It turns out that today, the education system keeps in its realm children who are in fact already rejected. They are, in Bourdieu's words, 'les exclus de l'intérieur' (excluded on the inside) (Bourdieu, 1993: 597–603). These pupils study degrees which are very poorly valued in the job market. They rapidly get the feeling that all their efforts are bound to fail. They are forced to lie: to lie to their parents who equate education with social progression, to lie in order to satisfy the 'family project'. On the other hand, they come to terms with the fact that education will not provide them with better chances later. The effect of double binding is particularly obvious here. Incapable of filling the gap between family desires and the demands of the education system, some of these working-class pupils affect a certain distance *vis-à-vis* the institution and education. This explains the violent, or casual, behaviour of some of them in class. They do not attempt to hide a kind of 'résignation désenchantée' (disenchanted resignation) (Bourdieu, 1993: 603) which shows that, for them, 'real life' is not at school but in an indefinite 'somewhere'.

To summarize the main aspects of this first point, it would no doubt be a mistake to see in the voluminous presentation of the diverse forms of misery a kind of litany of complaints. Bourdieu's comprehensive sociology makes an effort to take seriously the diversity and complexity of manifestations of poverty in French society today. In particular, Bourdieu's interviews concretely show the terribly human aspects of social poverty. The survey deals with individuals who suffer, differently and for different reasons, dismissing aseptic and incomprehensible macro-research on poverty, which provides the reader with a lot of figures, tables and diagrams, but very little explanation of the reasons and the nature of the social malaise. It is definitively a political book, a contribution to a debate which has been at the top of the agenda for many years in France, and even more in the run-up to the 1995 presidential election. With this research, the coherence of Bourdieu's 'objectivation participante' (participating objectification) appears here with even more acuity. It is a kind of attempt to act politically, not within political parties or within the state, but via social agents themselves. Moreover, it is a project aiming to 'convertir le malaise social en symptômes lisibles, susceptibles d'être traités politiquement'[5] (Bourdieu, 1992: 173).

Social maieutic and symbolic violence

Pierre Bourdieu has widely used the interview technique since he started his sociological research. In this respect, this survey is not innovative. What is more original however is that this survey relies purely on oral testimonies. Each interview is preceded by a short text written by the interviewer, allowing indications which do not appear in the interview text (description of the interviewee, of the place where the interview was conducted, summaries of bits of conversations off the record, etc.). But more importantly, the introductory text helps to draw the reader's attention to the 'traits pertinents que la perception distraite et désarmée laisserait échapper'[6] (Bourdieu, 1993: 8). It aims to give more data on the social conditioning of such a discourse (social trajectory, body language, class or regional accent, silences, slips of the tongue; all kind of details which cannot be read in the interview text). The written information about all the interviewees which is provided suggests the extent of Bourdieu's fear of seeing the content of some interviews misunderstood or stigmatized.

The systematic use of the interview in this survey leads us to an epistemological point: to what extent can the content of the interviews be taken for granted? In other words, do the interviewees tell who they are and what they really feel, or, inversely, do they tend to construct an artificial discourse inferred by the exceptional situation in which they find themselves when they are interviewed? This is an old debate. The widespread use of life stories in the social sciences today leaves open the question of the reality of the material collected. How is it possible to assess the authenticity of the interviewee's words? How can one be sure that what is being said corresponds to the reality of somebody's life? The American sociologist Howard Becker – himself a great adept of the interview method – acknowledges that when he reads a biography, he is always aware that authors (interviewees) tell only a small part of their story, that they select facts in order to present the image of themselves that they would like us to have of them, and that they neglect some secondary or unpleasant elements, which may be of great interest to the sociologist (Becker, 1986: 105). Bourdieu himself, in an article

published in the mid-1980s, denounced 'l'artefact socialement irré-
prochable' (the socially irreproachable artefact) (Bourdieu, 1986: 71)
that seems to constitute the life story. He finds that beyond the sociologist's so-called democratic attempt to let the people tell their prosaic
and genuine truth, the interview situation can be totally artificial if
some precautions are not taken by the researcher. For Bourdieu, most
interview practitioners tend to forget that their object (the interviewee)
is above all a social agent involved in a multitude of overlapping social
relationships. The researcher will only have a chance to grasp the reality
of the interviewee's life if s/he is aware of the mobile social frames in
which the agent is involved. Otherwise, the sociologist will unconsciously encourage the production of a discourse centred on the
individual, leaving aside the social determinisms which have shaped
her/his personality.

Bourdieu, wishing to avoid this pitfall, justifies his interview method
accordingly:

> Je fais des entretiens avec des gens très différents – des employés, des
> beurs, des cadres au chômage, etc. – et j'essaye, par un type de ques-
> tionnement assez compliqué, de mettre en œuvre une forme de maïeu-
> tique socratique, ou, si l'on veut, une socioanalyse, visant à faire dire aux
> gens des choses qu'ils ne savent pas complètement eux-mêmes.
>
> (in Biasi, 1992: 108)[7]

What is socio-analysis about? Bourdieu says that it is like a *directed self-
analysis* ('auto-analyse assistée') (Bourdieu, 1991: 3). The interviewee,
in many cases, seems to take advantage of the interview to question
him/herself, and to start the task of explanation, which in turn makes
him/her enunciate experiences and reflections which had been forgotten or repressed. The interviewer, in Bourdieu's socio-analysis, has
an active role to play. The sociologist must act as an 'obstetrician'
(Bourdieu, 1991: 3). Through a kind of empathic approach, s/he tends
to adopt the interviewee's language (for instance, interviews with
Algerian immigrants are conducted in Arabic; Bourdieu, 1993: 33–48;
823–44). The interviewees are very often old acquaintances of the
researcher, or at least are introduced to the interviewer by a common
acquaintance. A lot of guarantees seem to be taken to avoid the
construction of an artefact. What seems to underlie this is the desire to
know as much as possible about the interviewee's social conditioning so
as to be able to fill the gaps in her/his social trajectory.

However, Bourdieu says very little on the question of the symbolic
violence contained in an interview relationship. These 'possessed

people' are *par excellence* in a cultural or economic situation of distress. Therefore – and it is very evident in the case of drastic social poverty – the question of the violent imposition implied by the interview situation is not really taken into consideration. The choice of the accurate language is of course determinant. Some interviews conducted by Pierre Bourdieu himself with young *Beurs* or working-class youngsters in big urban areas (Bourdieu, 1993: 81–9; 605–20) show how artificial and acculturating the interview position can be. When he addresses these young men, Bourdieu himself sometimes hesitates between the generally legitimate use of the *vous* form, and the illegitimate use of the *tu* form which, in this context, seems more appropriate. How can we assess to what extent the effects of symbolic violence have an impact on the discourse of the interviewees? It is very difficult to answer this question, since each interviewer remains rather silent about the method used for each interview. No information is provided on the strategies of questioning used by each researcher in order to make visible the coding applied to every social relation. Besides, this socio-analytic method involves a question of professional ethics: what are going to be the effects of the interview on the interviewee? How are these people going to react when they know that their experience has been published in a book entitled *La misère du monde*? The role of the sociologist is not to defend or to condemn people's words or behaviour. Therefore, the scientist does not have to worry about the psychological consequences of the interview. However, to some extent, her/his moral responsibility could be engaged, considering that this social maieutic could, as a result, and in many cases, make people feel even more guilty or demoralized about their own situation.[8]

The left hand and the right hand of the state

The increase of contradictory constraints (double binds) becomes more and more painful for people because of the rapid disinvestment of the state. One chapter of *La misère du monde* is entitled 'La démission de l'Etat'[9] (Bourdieu, 1993: 219–28). Bourdieu clearly differentiates between *state bureaucracy* (i.e. governing political élites, and technocratic power) and *street level bureaucrats* (the postman, the school teacher, the policeman, the public GP). He says that the former has espoused the rules of the market and today fails to provide ordinary citizens with the quantity and the quality of welfare provisions that they need. The latter feel abandoned or even disavowed (Bourdieu, 1993: 222) by state bureaucracy, and left alone to try to solve increasing problems. Most of this street level bureaucracy has the task of treating profound poverty. Its agents feel the double constraint which stems from their public service mission: on the one hand, they have to take on immense responsibilities (in education, housing or employment matters), while on the other, they are not provided with the means of doing their jobs correctly.

According to Bourdieu, the state's withdrawal and its adhesion to neo-liberalism started in the 1970s, and was achieved in the mid-1980s when the Socialists were in office (Bourdieu, 1993: 220–1). Running public services according to the profit standards of private economy (productivity, profit, efficiency) has slowly undermined the capacity of the public sector to face the urgent problems in education, housing, health or urban security. It especially undermined the 'civil servant spirit', made out of 'disinterested self-commitment' to public service (Bourdieu, 1993: 222). In accordance with the liberal vision, state provisions are often now merely a *state charity* given to the *deserving poor* as at times of religious philanthropy. The state does not try to act upon the structures of distribution, but only to correct the unequal distribution of cultural and economic goods. Bourdieu speaks of the 'right hand and left hand of the state'. The right hand is the state bureaucracy, and the left hand is the street level bureaucrat. According to Bourdieu's sketch, the right hand no longer knows – or does not want to know – what the left hand is doing.

Bourdieu's critique of the state's withdrawal is neither a political nor a philosophical critique as such. For instance, he never advocates social or economic solutions to solve the state crisis. Bourdieu's concern is strictly sociological: his objective on the question of poverty is to show, and only to show, the nature and the manifestations of misery in French society. He is not concerned with the making of a counter-project to improve the functioning of bureaucracy, as the politician or the philosopher would be.

However, Bourdieu does slightly more than merely observing. At this point in his work, there is a noticeable ambiguity. When he says that the 'right hand of the state does not know what the left hand is doing' (Bourdieu, 1993: 222), two different readings of this statement can be proposed. On the one hand, it can mean that the state apparatus and the political élites have betrayed their public service mission, in progressively adopting the logic and the mode of operation of the private sector. In so doing, they have failed to provide the public with the necessary social help. Consequently, to tackle the different forms of poverty in society, the state should be more active and present. This could be a kind of traditional social-democratic reading of Bourdieu's critique of the withdrawal of the state. On the other hand, it can also be read as proposing that the welfare state is totally useless and even has nefarious effects. A neo-liberal supporter could certainly refer to Bourdieu's research to justify the claim that 50 years of welfare state economy have, despite enormous financial and human efforts, finally worsened the social situation! This double reading is made possible by the 'epistemological tension' in Bourdieu's work. Bourdieu does not only show, listen to and observe the different forms of misery in society. In fact, he does much more than that: in Bourdieu's approach, there is a strong assumption that the state – and above all the political class – is basically responsible for this misery. On many occasions, he denounces political élites, assisted by 'young technocrats' who do not have the slightest idea of what is going on in the life of ordinary citizens (Bourdieu, 1993: 941). His words are extremely aggressive in their stigmatization of the vacuity of political organizations, or their 'arrogance technocratique' (technocratic arrogance) (Bourdieu, 1993: 942).

Conclusion

The 'epistemological ambiguity' perceived in Bourdieu is under no circumstances serious enough to portray him as standing on the side of the neo-liberal camp. A civil servant himself – belonging to the top élite in the educational system, as professor in the Collège de France – Bourdieu seems structurally influenced by public service. The problem is that his sociology condemns state bureaucracy in a very Manichaean way, insisting at length on the 'courage of the street level bureaucrats', while describing too promptly the political élites and the state bureaucratic apparatus as a whole as corrupt and useless social agents and structures.

Moreover, in refusing any clear normative statement on the role of the state, his sociology of poverty does not really do justice to the political issues raised in most interviews (i.e. what should be the mission of the state?; what should be the human and financial means involved in a real welfare policy?; what should this 'civil servant spirit' be about?; etc.). In the French tradition of sociology, the normative approach of social facts has very often been criticized and considered as the intrusion of subjectivity in the objectivity of research. In so doing, sociology appears to have been a useful discipline to X-ray and classify social events and behaviour. But no more than this. In this respect, Pierre

Bourdieu is a typical product of the French school. His sociology could be even more stimulating if it combined the rigour of the sociological approach with the taking of clearer positions in the realm of politics. In this case, Pierre Bourdieu would certainly have to use tools of comparison taken from other disciplines (economics, law and especially political philosophy). This would be likely to suppress the ambiguity of his approach: i.e. a claim of pure objectivism, where, *de facto*, political and normative statements are indirectly expressed or hinted throughout his observations, but never clearly argued.

However, it remains that Bourdieu's claim to adopt a Hippocratic posture (Bourdieu, 1993: 942–3) is genuine in the sense that there is a deliberate attempt – through the systematic use of interviews and the 'liberating force' of socioanalysis – to make 'people' (i.e. the economically and culturally dominated), whose voices are usually heard through the 'opinion makers'[10] rather than independently, be more aware of the structural reasons for their subordinate position. For this alone, Bourdieu's survey, despite some rather undefined aspects of its methodology, was worthy of being conducted.

Notes

1. Here is a sample of the most important contributions recently published in English on Bourdieu's theory: Robbins (1991 and 1995); Calhoun, LiPuma and Postone (1993); Jenkins (1992); Forbes and Kelly (1993).
2. The notion of 'exclusion' should be used with great circumspection, since it appears to have acquired over the last few years an ambiguous meaning in the fields of politics and the social sciences. Once a term which clearly designated the *act* of exclusion, it seems to refer more today to the situation, to the *fact* of being 'excluded'. In a recent article, Danielle Sallenave (1995: 35) sees in this new emphasis on the passive form of exclusion, a significant shift from the consideration of the causes of exclusion to the mere consideration of its effects. This, in turn, involves a shift from political concern to moral concern, or from responsibility to guilt. This outlines a society from which the actors and the profiteers of a system which allows, encourages or provokes exclusion, are evacuated, and in which they are replaced by spectators, witnesses of exclusion, who are asked to feel pity and compassion (two terms with intense Christian connotation) for the 'excluded'.
3. It is necessary to 'smash the screen of the sometimes absurd, sometimes hateful projections, behind which suffering hides'.
4. Captured by 'external reality which, like the monster in *Alien*, is within them and haunts them'.
5. A project to 'convert social malaise into visible symptoms, so they can be treated politically'.
6. The 'pertinent features [of the interview] that an absent-minded and unprepared reading might miss'.

7. 'I conduct interviews with very different people ... and I try, through a very complicated type of questioning, to apply a kind of Socratic maieutic, or in other terms, a socio-analysis, which aims to make people say things they do not really know about themselves.'
8. For a further discussion of the interview method, see Chapter 5.
9. Translated as 'the state's withdrawal' or 'the state's disinvestment', the term *démission* implies shirking one's responsibilities.
10. i.e. journalists, politicians; who are also called the 'doxosophes' by Bourdieu.

References

Becker, H.S. (1986) 'Biographie et mosaïque scientifique', *Actes de la Recherche en Sciences Sociales* 62–6: 105.

Biasi, P.-M. (de) (1992) 'Pierre Bourdieu: Tout est social!' *Le Magazine littéraire* 303: 104–11.

Bourdieu, P. (1986) 'L'Illusion biographique', *Actes de la Recherche en Sciences Sociales* 62–3: 71.

Bourdieu, P. (1991) 'Introduction à la socioanalyse', *Actes de la Recherche en Sciences Sociales* 90: 3–6.

Bourdieu, P. (1992) *Réponses*. Paris: Editions du Seuil.

Bourdieu, P. (1993) *La misère du monde*. Paris: Editions du Seuil.

Calhoun, C., LiPuma, E. and Postone, M. (eds) (1993) *Bourdieu: Critical Perspectives*. Oxford: Polity Press.

Forbes, J. and Kelly, M. (eds) (1993) 'Pierre Bourdieu', *French Cultural Studies* 4(3), no. 12: whole issue.

Jenkins, R. (1992) *Pierre Bourdieu*. London and New York: Routledge.

Robbins, D. (1991) *The Work of Pierre Bourdieu: Recognising Society*. Milton Keynes: Open University Press.

Robbins, D. (1995) *Bourdieu and the Analysis of Culture*. Oxford: Polity Press.

Sallenave, D. (1995) 'Guerres, catastrophes, exclusion: l'alibi de la compassion', *Le Monde diplomatique* 496: 35.

5.

Oral history: an assessment

HANNA DIAMOND

People, when talking about their lives, lie sometimes, forget a lot, exaggerate, become confused and get things wrong. But they are revealing truths. These truths don't reveal a past as it actually was, aspiring to a standard of objectivity. They give us instead the truths of our experiences.

(The Personal Narratives Group, 1989: 261)

Carrying out a series of interviews can be an ideal way of uncovering information for use in any number of kinds of historical studies concerned with the contemporary period. This kind of source material is generally referred to as oral history and there now exists quite a significant body of literature relating to it. The vocabulary reflects the fact that those who use oral history have drawn on a wide range of different disciplines ranging from literary criticism, anthropology, sociology and ethnography. Authors refer to life histories, life stories, in-depth interviews, testimonies, autobiographies, oral narratives and personal narratives which are collected through the process of recollection, reminiscence and memory from informants, interviewees, witnesses and narrators by interviewers and interpreters. This chapter will first show how oral history has developed in Britain and France, and will then examine some of the methodological and theoretical problems associated with it.

Although early British historians such as Macaulay used oral testimony in their work, oral history as a discipline did not come to the fore until the late 1950s, as a result of the meeting of two different currents both concerned with popular culture. The first was situated outside academia and came from village history, as exemplified by George Ewart Evans's *Ask the Fellows Who Cut the Hay*, published in 1956. The second centred on university-based historians, anthropologists and sociologists who, inspired by the work of Richard Hoggart (1958) and E.P. Thompson (1963), wanted to move towards a new kind of social 'history from below' or 'people's history'. The History Workshops that resulted from this saw in oral history an ideal way to have access to the history of those unrepresented in the documentary evidence. Community projects emerged which set about recording and writing the history of women, workers and migrant groups. This movement saw itself as moving towards 'democratizing' history (Samuel, 1981: 67–79).

The initial concerns of these British theorists were to legitimize oral history as source material as compared with documentary or written historical evidence. They had to respond to accusations that oral history was unreliable, arbitrary and lacking in methodology. As A.J.P. Taylor put it, 'In this matter I am almost a total sceptic . . . Old men drooling about their youth – No' (Thompson, 1978: 70). In 1978, Paul Thompson, originally a sociologist, published *The Voice of the Past*, which he put together as a defence for oral history:

> the opposition to oral evidence is as much founded on feeling as on principle. The older generation of historians who hold the Chairs and the purse-strings are instinctively apprehensive about the advent of a new method. It implies that they no longer command all the techniques of their profession. Hence the disparaging comments about young men tramping the streets with tape-recorders.
>
> (Thompson, 1978: 63)

Here and as editor of the journal *Oral History*, which emerged in 1973, Thompson tried to give scholarly respectability to the subject. He argued the case for oral history as compared with documentary sources, reminding traditional historians that the latter were no less selective and biased, and underlined the additional advantages that oral history has to offer. For him, oral history has three particular strengths. First, it can 'provide significant and sometimes unique information from the past'. Secondly, it can 'convey the individual and collective consciousness which is part and parcel of that very past'. And thirdly, 'the living humanity of oral sources gives them a particularly unique strength'. The early handbooks of oral history were concerned with assessing the reliability of oral memory and tried to offer some methodology (Lummis, 1987). They borrowed approaches from social psychology and anthropology to determine bias in the formulation of memory and the effects of the interviewer on remembering. From sociology came interviewing technique and representative sampling, and from documentary history came rules for checking the consistency of sources.

Oral history is generally considered to have become popular in France much later than in Britain or America (Thompson in Samuel, 1981).[1] However, French scholars have had a long-standing interest in autobiography and biography in terms of *témoignages* (personal testimonies) and *documents vécus* (documents which relate lived experiences). The work of Philippe Lejeune (1975 and 1980) is very much in this tradition. But a particular interest in oral history came more from French anthropologists and ethnographers than historians. Jan Vasina's *De la Tradition Orale* published in 1961 on oral tradition in Africa offered the first steps towards writing the histories of the 'illiterate' continents with no documentary evidence.[2] This kind of approach also became popular inside France in the context of regional and local history which examined oral tradition and cultural identity (Bouvier, 1980). As far as established French historians were concerned however, although the *Annales* school of history became interested in themes of *mentalités* (attitudes) and *vie quotidienne* (daily life) in the 1970s, they never really saw interviewing as being a relevant way of collecting this kind of information.

Parisian professional history was isolated from the kind of political motivations that drove the History Workshop movement in Britain. French labour history was quite separate from the labour movement at this time. It was therefore left to sociologists like Daniel Bertaux and Isabelle Bertaux-Wiame, who became frustrated with using quantitative methods in their research, to turn to what became known as the 'life history approach' (Bertaux-Wiame, 1981; Bertaux and Kohli, 1984). For Bertaux, the origins of this approach were in structuralism, life stories were collected in a single milieu with a focus on 'practices', not on perceptions or feelings. The task was to infer from recurrent practices the pattern of socio-structural relationships that were generating or constraining them. This kind of 'ethnosociological' approach is rather different from the work of another French scholar, Maurice Catani. He also used life stories but was more interested in values, and especially the values of migrants. His method of analysis consisted of looking for meanings hidden in the narratives – not only in their content, but also in their form (Catani and Maze, 1982).

Despite these differences of approach and attitude, by the mid-1980s oral historians on both sides of the Channel found common cause and united to defend themselves against Louise Tilly's attack on oral history for its lack of a scientific approach. Tilly claimed that oral history fell short of being a social science and called for a more coherent methodology and theory within the discipline.[3] Out of these debates came two main approaches to oral history. One was the more 'ethnographic' approach referred to above, which was concerned to locate testimony in society, to study it for what it tells about people and their relationship to other people and the world of production. This more sociological approach was applauded by Tilly. The other, known as the 'hermeneutic' approach, was concerned to use the latest techniques of literary criticism and communication theory on the life history. This approach aimed to discover the interpretative power of the text – levels of discourse, hidden meanings and its ability to transport a message. Through this analysis it was hoped to be able to show how people manipulate the truth, make history, tell stories and carry on collective memory. Such an approach ties in with the work of the British Popular Memory group and international oral historians like Luisa Passerini who rejected the work of those oral historians who sought respectability by trying to correct memory, since their main interest was to explore how individuals construct their memories in particular ways (Popular Memory Group, 1982; Passerini, 1986). Their focus was more on the investigation of the construction of public history and the interaction between public and private senses of the past.

The debate continues and to date no serious or standard methodology has as yet been established amongst oral historians, who have tended to congratulate themselves on the plurality of their approaches. The result has been that the vast majority of mainstream historians remain sceptical of oral history and though they look on with interest, steer clear of discussing it. Proof of the failure of oral history to penetrate into the main historical debates, in Britain at least, can be found in the fact that publications about oral history appear to be limited to two or three specialist journals.[4] Yet it would be erroneous to assume that this is a realistic reflection of the true state of oral history. As Chantal Bonazzi, until recently Director of the Contemporary Section of the Archives Nationales de France, observed in 1990: 'rares sont à l'heure actuelle les contemporanéistes qui n'ont pas recours aux témoignages et ce, quelque soit le thème traité ... [Le contemporanéiste] se sert des témoignages, mais il n'en parle que rarement'[5] (Bonazzi, 1990: 14–15). Researchers recognize the enormous potential that oral history has to offer, but in the absence of an established methodology they have tended to improvise their approaches, declaring themselves as oral historians to a greater or lesser extent, sometimes failing to give a proper account of their sources. In this context it seems of value to turn to some of the main methodological issues associated with oral history and to examine them more closely in an attempt to move towards a more coherent and acceptable methodology.

Valerie Raleigh Yow's recently published handbook *Recording Oral History* offers detailed practical advice and is, as such, extremely helpful (Yow, 1994; see also Diamond, 1996). But, surprisingly, despite their late arrival on the oral history scene, it is the recent French debates around the practical use and validity of oral history that most help us to move forward. Their anxieties force us to focus on what exactly we are looking for from oral history and how we intend to obtain it.

One question that needs clarification is that of terminology. As Danièle Voldman recently pointed out, we need to distinguish between 'l'histoire orale, les archives orales, les sources orales et les témoignages oraux'[6] (Voldman, 1992: 33). We can sympathize with Pierre Nora's worries that oral archives are being collected in an arbitrary way by people with their own particular agendas:

> De quelle volonté de mémoires portent-elles ... celles des enquêtés, ou celle des enquêteurs? L'archive change de sens et de statut par son simple poids. Elle n'est plus le reliquat plus ou moins intentionnel d'une mémoire vécue, mais la sécrétion volontaire et organisée d'une mémoire perdue.[7]
>
> (Nora, 1984: xxviii)

But this should not preclude the collection of oral archives under controlled circumstances. Still, we must bear in mind that the approach of the archivist is rather different from that of the historian. As the Directeur Général des Archives de France explains:

> pour l'historien, la création d'archives sonores est en général liée à un projet particulier, il 'fabrique' sa source, dont l'existence ne précède pas la recherche mais en compose la première étape; pour l'archiviste, la collecte est le plus souvent systématique et a pour but le rassemblement de matériaux qui seront mis à la disposition de chercheurs futurs.[8]
>
> (Favier, 1990: 9)

Our concern is that of the historian who wishes to use memories as source material. Another point to be wary of is that the term 'oral history' could be misleading since it might suggest that a historical study should be entirely based on oral sources. What is at issue here is the use of oral sources as a source amongst others and this is how oral history should be understood. What then are the main methodological problems that are under debate? The first issue to consider is to establish what represents a reasonable sample.

The sample

Who should be interviewed and how many informants should there be? The opinions of the experts vary on this. Some suggest interviewing up to a hundred people (Bonazzi, 1990: 100), others offer the experiences of just one individual. We would tend to agree with the historian Jean-Pierre Rioux that 'la taille du corpus est un signe distinctif d'une recherche probante ... trois, quatre ou cinq récits, si riches soient-ils, ne suffisent pas ... à donner un sens'[9] (Rioux, 1983: 27). It seems reasonable to assume that the most successful oral studies are likely to be those which focus on a particular community or group of people and are well anchored within a locality or region. In this context, oral sources can be an invaluable contribution to other existing sources by providing information that cannot be found in any other way. This kind of sample is much more likely to be 'representative'. It remains hard to see how an oral study could be conducted on a national scale and see itself as representative of the population as a whole. Quite apart from anything else, this would create dramatic logistical problems as the sample would have to be enormous and oral history interviewing is extremely time-consuming.

A reasonable sample will therefore largely depend on the context and the objectives of a research project, the way the testimonies are going to be used and the claims that will be made for the study. It does, however, seem essential that the sample should be described very clearly somewhere, perhaps in the introduction or the appendix. It is common practice to include a short life history of each informant. The sample of interviewees should be clearly introduced giving as much material about them as possible, but also indicating where there are omissions. The reader needs to be aware of the limits of a sample in order to interpret its findings.

Structuring, conducting and transcribing the interviews

The second main methodological issue centres around the structuring, conducting and transcribing of the interviews. Most commentators favour a non-directive interview procedure which allows the informants to improvise their account. A very loosely structured interview enables informants to talk about what they feel to be important about their own experiences. Part of what interests us as historians is to discover what marks people in particular and what they choose to recount. It is helpful to prepare a list of open questions[10] in advance of the interview to help to structure the interview and act as a guide. However, it is advisable to be as flexible as possible about these questions. There is no point in writing a questionnaire and then sticking to it religiously; better to use it as a kind of check-list of questions that you know you want to cover. It can be very frustrating to come away after a couple of hours and find that there is one vital question that you forgot to ask.

The interview ideally should be taped, but this does raise some issues. Before starting the interview the witness must be made to understand that the tape recorder is a tool to facilitate note-taking. Some people may be really intimidated by it, but using a tape recorder prevents the interviewer from having to scribble down notes during the interview and means that s/he can really concentrate on what the informant has to say and guide the discussion into areas of interest. The researcher is much more likely to give an accurate representation of the narrator's account if a recorded version exists. This has the added advantage that it can be made available to provide proof of what was said and can also be used by other researchers with different questions in mind.

The relationship between interviewer and interviewee has also been a subject of much debate. Commentators fear that the interviewer can unduly influence the interviewee, leading to what Jacques Ozouf has dismissed as *archives provoquées* (prompted archives) (quoted by Denis Peschanski in Voldman, 1992: 49). Denis Peschanski puts it thus: 'l'historien a souvent tendance à oublier qu'il est partie prenante de l'entretien, qu'il intervient dans la construction du témoignage qu'il enregistre'[11] (in Voldman, 1992: 48). Feminist oral historians are particularly concerned to address the 'problem of the distinct imbalances in power and privilege which characterize most women's oral history projects' (Berger Gluck and Patai, 1991: 3). The interpreter is seen as an active participant involved in the shaping of the narratives and both the narrator and the interpreter approach the process of creating a personal narrative with their own agenda. These affect the focus and form of the text (Personal Narratives Group, 1989: 201–3).

They therefore suggest that we should be sensitive to our own motives. Although these are valid concerns, it is also important not to underestimate the power of the informant who creates the life story as s/he organizes and tells it, and after all, the informant always has the choice of erasing or correcting his/her narrative (Dominique Veillon in Voldman, 1992: 49).

Ownership of material is another area of concern. Yow's proposal that the informant should sign a document she calls a *release form* seems helpful, as the copyright laws are not very clear on this subject (Yow,

1994: 85). Informants should have access to interview transcripts and copies of anything written or published as a result of meeting them. They should have the opportunity to decide whether their names will appear or whether they wish to remain anonymous.

Another important ethical or moral factor which is rarely addressed in the literature is the fact that the interview situation is such that informants sometimes impart intimate and traumatic experiences to a virtual stranger. This is problematic for both the interviewer and the witness. Interviewees tend to feel that by sharing their most intense experiences, experiences they find distressing to discuss, they have created a bond. This is all very well, but you cannot sustain a friendship with all the people you interview. The problem is compounded by the fact that the elderly can often be quite lonely. Witnesses are essentially giving away a large part of their lives and not really getting much in return for it. In this context it is encouraging to discover that therapists who use reminiscence therapy, something close to oral history interviewing, have found that it can be invaluable for the elderly to undergo an oral process of remembering. Furthermore, a key element in the success of the treatment is that there should be a product, an exhibition, a book or a sound tape, at the end of this process. According to Joanna Bornat, sharing the product with younger people, family members and the wider community does much to enhance the individual's sense of worth (Bornat, 1994: 3).

Transcribing is the most time-consuming and perhaps the dullest part of the process. Before any use can be made of the interviews they need to be written/typed up in full. How do we best represent in written form the oral versions that we are given?[12] Some feminists see transcription as being the point at which the witness, or narrator, loses control over the whole process:

> Rendering the oral narrative into an accessible form for public consumption requires considerable intervention on the part of the researcher/ editor. Punctuation is added, repetitions are deleted, words and passages are discarded, highlighted, and/or taken out of sequence. . . . Typically, the speaker is consulted, if at all, only once the editing process is complete.
>
> (Berger Gluck and Patai, 1991: 5)

This problem is further exacerbated in cases where translation is necessary, or even by the use of a third person as interpreter. Translation into another language carries its own set of problems and forces the presentation of the informant's narrative to change from the exact words used in the interview. In my experience witnesses tend to be extremely concerned that the way they express themselves should be improved if their words are to be used directly. When transcribing their words, the aim should be to keep the spontaneity of the witness's expression without making it impossible for the reader to understand.

Using the material

Interpretation of the material and how to present it is, for most oral historians, the most important issue to resolve and brings us back to the theoretical debates of the 1980s. For Luisa Passerini, who works on Italian Fascism, it is impossible to make direct use of oral memories as immediately revealing facts and events. But she offers the guiding principle that 'all autobiographical memory is true; it is up to the interpreter to discover in which sense, where, for which purpose' (Passerini in Personal Narratives Group, 1989: 189–99). Similarly, Anne-Marie Tröger, who has carried out research on German memories of the Second World War, explains how for her, memories are constantly being recreated and that there is no original and therefore accurate memory (Tröger, 1987: 286–98). She suggests that memories of the war have three levels of meaning. The first is on an existential level where the individual attempts to describe feeling and emotions for which there are no words. The second is a psychological level which represents the complex formation of the collective and individual memory. The third is a historical-political level which is a deliberate, generalized description conveyed by metaphors such as 'war as natural catastrophe'. Alastair Thomson's work on the First World War in Australia also offers new frameworks of analysis where he attempts to put the popular memory approach into effect, and explores the relationship between the Anzac[13] legend and the lives and the remembering of the Anzacs and shows how the two are very different (Thomson, 1994: 13).

Oral sources have proved particularly valuable to feminist and women's historians in both Britain and France where they have given us access to women's everyday lives in the past:

> Pour l'histoire des femmes, leur usage s'impose d'autant plus que les femmes ont bien moins manié l'écrit que les hommes: elles ont eu plus de façons de dire que de façons d'écrire. ... Ensuite appartenant – de tradition, de droit ou de nature – à la sphère de l'intime ou du privé leur histoire est davantage fait de traces orales qu'écrites.[14]
> (Van de Casteele-Schweizer and Voldman, 1984: 60–1)

Research has brought out interesting gender differences in the ways men and women tell their life stories, and what they emphasize about their past experiences. Isabelle Bertaux-Wiame noticed (1981: 256–7) that men's life stories revolve around a sequence of occupations whereas women talk more about their relationships. Luisa Passerini (1986) and Anne-Marie Tröger (1987) both found that their research interviews do not throw up the same things for women and for men. It would seem that oral historians have much potential to explore.

The variety of interpretations and uses of oral history described here serve to demonstrate that the way you process your material depends on what you are looking for from it. It is now well established that we are not really looking for 'fact' or 'truth'. We accept that what we hear may only be a representation of what really happened. We agree with feminists who have suggested that 'the typical product of an interview is a text, not a reproduction of reality, and that models of textual analysis are therefore needed' (Bertaux-Wiame, 1981: 256–7). The way you present the material also very much depends on the kind of study you carry out. Traditionally, life histories are presented and then commented upon. This can sometimes appear a bit laboured and it is also feasible to present the results of an oral study as one would any other historical study based on documentary evidence.[15] An oral study can often help to put together a historical interpretation and quotations from oral sources can serve to illustrate a point as from any other source. Such quotations can bring the historical accounts provided by written sources held in the archives – police reports, administrative documents and the newspapers – to life and make it possible for the voices of the actors themselves to be heard.

Conclusion

There is no doubt that oral history no longer deserves to be dismissed by traditional historians who cannot afford to ignore its potential. Researchers at the prestigious Institut d'Histoire du Temps Présent, the main CNRS laboratory responsible for research into twentieth-century France, now grudgingly accept the use of oral testimony. Their reluctance seems a shame, particularly if we consider the extremely interesting work of someone like Henri Rousso (1987 and 1994). His work concerns the Vichy past in France, and the extent to which this past is still present. He gives a penetrating analysis of the popular memory of the war and the influences which continue to act to help revise this memory without actually using oral history or asking people about it. Dominique Veillon, another member of the Institut, does refer to oral material in her recent book *Vivre et survivre en France, 1939–1947* (1995) but fails to list her oral sources or describe the oral study upon which it is based.

Oral history has an important role to play in our interpretation of the past and it brings history to life with incredible force and spontaneity. It would be unscholarly to use oral history in isolation, to let it stand in its own right as offering some kind of ultimate truth. But recording the experiences of what is necessarily a relatively small number of people can provide us with considerable insight into parts of the puzzle as we try to piece together a better understanding of our society.

Notes

1. This is refuted by Michel Trebitsch (in Voldman, 1992: 25) who both denies that oral history came to France late and offers reasons for its lateness.
2. Such oral tradition is also of great interest to British historians of the Third World and anthropologists: see Henige (1982) and Tonkin (1992).
3. This debate makes quite entertaining reading. See the *International Journal of Oral History* 6(1) (Feb. 1985).
4. *Oral History, Journal of the Oral History Society, The International Journal of Oral History* and *History Workshop Journal.*
5. 'Nowadays it is rare to find contemporary specialists who do not have recourse to testimony whatever the theme they are dealing with. They use testimony, but they only rarely talk about it.'
6. 'Oral history, oral archives, oral sources and oral testimonies.'
7. 'Whose memory do they represent ... that of the interviewees, or that of the interviewer? The archive can have a different meaning and status according to the emphasis. It is no longer the more or less intentional collection of what remains of people's experiences, but the voluntary and organized secretion of a memory.'
8. 'for the historian, the creation of sound archives is generally linked to a particular project, s/he "manufactures" her/his source, the existence of which does not precede the research but represents the first step; for the archivist, the often systematic collection has the aim of bringing together material that will be made available to future researchers.'
9. 'the size of the corpus is a significant indication of convincing research ... three, four or five accounts, however rich they may be, are not enough ... to give any meaning.'
10. Open questions are questions that require more than just Yes/No answers, and for which no pre-set selection of responses is suggested.
11. 'The historian often tends to forget that s/he is actively involved in the interview, that s/he intervenes in the construction of the account s/he is recording.'
12. Many archivists prefer to keep their oral sources in interview form on cassette.
13. Australia and New Zealand Army Corps.
14. 'For women's history, their use is essential, particularly since women used the written word less than men: they had more ways of saying things than of writing

them ... Subsequently, belonging – by tradition, by right or by nature – to the intimate or private sphere, their history consists more of oral than written evidence.'

15. A recent article by Martyn Cornick (1994) is exemplary in its use of oral history to examine a particular issue and an edited version of the interview is supplied as well as historical context.

References

Berger Gluck, S. and Patai, P. (eds) (1991) *Women's Words: The Feminist Practice of Oral History.* London: Routledge.

Bertaux, D. and Kohli, M. (1984) 'The life story approach: a continental view', *Annual Review of Sociology* 10: 215–37.

Bertaux-Wiame, I. (1981) 'The life history approach to the study of internal migration' in D. Bertaux (ed.) *Biography and Society.* London: Sage.

Bonazzi, C. (1990) 'Un nouveau territoire pour l'archiviste' in *Le Témoignage Oral aux Archives. De la collecte à la communication.* Paris: Archives Nationales: 11–20.

Bornat, J. (ed.) (1994) *Reminiscence Reviewed: Perspectives, Evaluations, Achievements.* London: Open University Press.

Bouvier, J.-C. (ed.) (1980) *Tradition Orale et Identité Culturelle, problèmes et méthodes.* Paris: Editions du CNRS.

Catani, M. and Maze, S. (1982) *Tante Suzanne, une histoire de vie sociale.* Paris: Librairie de Méridiens.

Cornick, M. (1994) 'Oral history, the BBC and the propaganda war against occupied France: the work of Emile Delavenay and the European Intelligence Department', *French History* 8(3): 316–54.

Diamond, H. (1996) 'Carrying out interviews for research' in S. Sellars (ed.) *Instead of Full Stops.* London: The Women's Press.

Evans, G.E. (1956) *Ask the Fellows Who Cut the Hay.* London: Faber and Faber.

Favier, J. (1990) 'Avant-Propos' in *Le Témoignage oral aux archives. De la collecte à la communication.* Paris: Archives Nationales: 7–8.

Henige, D. (1982) *Oral Historiography.* Harlow: Longman.

Hoggart, R. (1958) *The Uses of Literacy.* London: Penguin.

Lejeune, P. (1975) *Le Pacte Autobiographique.* Paris: Seuil.

Lejeune, P. (1980) *Je est un autre. L'autobiographie, de la littérature aux médias.* Paris: Seuil.

Lummis, T. (1987) *Listening to History.* London: Hutchinson.

Nora, P. (1984) 'Entre mémoire et histoire', *Les Lieux de Mémoire*, I: *La République.* Paris: Gallimard.

Passerini, L. (1986) *Fascism in Popular Memory.* Cambridge: CUP.

The Personal Narratives Group (eds) (1989) *Truths: Interpreting Women's Lives, Feminist Theory and Personal Narratives.* Bloomington and Indianapolis: Indiana University Press.

The Popular Memory Group (1982) 'Popular memory: theory, politics, method' in *Making Histories: Studies in History Writing and Politics.* London: Hutchinson.

Rioux, J.-P. (1983) 'L'historien et les récits de la vie', *Récits de Vie, Revue des Sciences Humaines* 191: 27–35.

Rousso, H. (1987) *Le syndrome de Vichy de 1944 à nos jours.* Paris: Seuil.

Rousso, H. and Conan, E. (1994) *Vichy, un passé qui ne passe pas.* Paris: Fayard.

Samuel, R. (ed.) (1981) *People's History and Socialist Theory.* London and Boston: Routledge (History Workshop Series).

Thompson, E.P. (1963) *The Making of the English Working Classes.* London: Gollancz.

Thompson, P. (1978) *The Voice of the Past.* Oxford: Oxford University Press.

Thomson, A. (1994) *Anzac Memories.* Sydney, Australia: Oxford University Press.

Tonkin, E. (1992) *Narrating Our Pasts: The Social Construction of Oral History.* Cambridge: CUP.

Tröger, A.M. (1987) 'German women's memories of World War Two' in M.R. Higonnet, J. Jenson, S. Michel and M.C. Weitz (eds) *Behind the Lines: Gender and Two World Wars.* New Haven: Yale University Press.

Van de Casteele-Schweizer, S. and Voldman, D. (1984) 'Les sources orales pour l'histoire des femmes' in M. Perrot (ed.) *Une histoire des femmes est-elle possible?* Paris: Rivages.

Vasina, J. (1961) *De la Tradition Orale. Essai de Méthode historique.* Annales du Musée Royal de l'Afrique Centrale, Sciences Humaines, 36. Translated and reissued (1984) as *Oral Tradition and History.* London: Routledge.

Veillon, D. (1995) *Vivre et survivre en France, 1939–1947.* Paris: Editions Payot.

Voldman, D. (ed.) (1992) *Les Bouches de la vérité? La Recherche historique et les Sources orales.* Les Cahiers de l'IHTP no. 21: whole issue.

Yow, V.R. (1994) *Recording Oral History: A Practical Guide for Social Scientists.* London: Sage.

Part Two

Cultural Voices

6.

Pictures of the French

D.W.S. GRAY

When in 1993 *L'Express* wanted to celebrate its fortieth anniversary it published a special supplement of 212 pages entitled *Les Français* (see Figure 6.1) (*L'Express*, 1993).[1] It was an unusual kind of survey of the present population of France – not a statistical study, nor an analysis, but a miniature encyclopaedia of characters perceived as typical of contemporary France, 124 items in all. Each was represented by a colour photograph and a piece of written text. All the pictures were by the photographer Yann Artus-Bertrand and his two assistants, and all the pieces of text were by named journalists and authors too many to name here, though all get proper credit in the special supplement. The items are assembled into six groups: *La République, La Famille, L'Esprit, La Rue, L'Entreprise, Le Pays.*[2] Each group has about 20 characters in it, all identified by a generic name establishing their position in the French cosmos. *L'Officier de carrière, le maire du village, le chercheur du CNRS* jostle with *le président de la République*[3] in the category of the Republic. There are some challenging newcomers, as one might expect, in the Family: not only *la mère célibataire,* but *le couple homosexuel,* and indeed *le doltomaniaque*[4] (who turns out to be a parent in thrall to his children). The curious reader might get curiouser when coming across some of the denizens of that most excoriating of French environments, the Mind. Where one might have expected to find that same CNRS researcher, one stumbles over *le dépanneur,* who here is the television repairman, and *l'amateur de foot,* though there may be less difficulty in swallowing *le chef cuisinier.*[5] No difficulties at all with the Street, with its *tagueurs, ados, prostituées,*[6] in the sense that they fulfil expectations; nor with the Business World, with *femme d'affaires* getting ready to elbow *le cadre dynamique.*[7] Some of us might experience a *frisson* of comfort when the Countryside gives us the golden oldies of *joueur de*

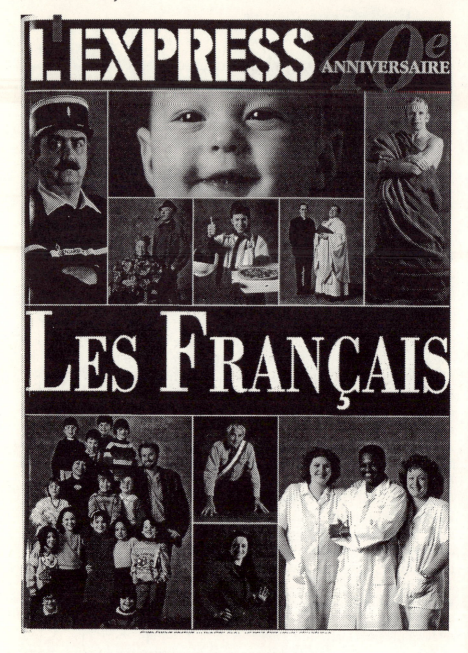

Figure 6.1 *Cover of special supplement* Les Français (L'Express, *no. 2184, 1993*)

pétanque, curé de campagne, gendarme, etc., so that sneaking in *l'écologiste*[8] right at the end has nowhere near the terrorizing effect it might have had.

The special supplement has a two-page introduction acknowledging its most immediate debt to journalistic innovations of the 1830s and 1840s in Paris, during the July Monarchy of Louis-Philippe: to the vogue for 'Physiologies' and especially the series of weekly fascicles republished in bound volumes as *Les Français peints par eux-mêmes* (Français, 1841–42). Quoting the *Dictionnaire Robert*, the editors of the supplement refer to 'works objectively describing a human reality'. They see these kinds of 'portrait' as a literary genre and as a publishing phenomenon, and in this they are undoubtedly right. It is clear that the editors are addressing their current audience and have no need to show any cultural, ideological or perhaps theoretical resonance in their idea for celebrating the 40-year achievement of their paper. The purpose of this chapter is to explore some of the resonances of this publishing phenomenon in order to show how fundamental the innovations were, not just as techniques, but as ideas which have entered our language and may now be taken for granted as unquestioned features of social reality.

I shall assume as requiring no argument here that the great ideological transformation of the revolutionary era, from a world of fixed social orders to a society of mobile classes, was the background against which new forms of expression emerged, reflecting new views of human nature. The new forms gave currency to new meanings in old ideas. The old image of 'the people' as a kind of picturesque cattle gives way to the modern, all-inclusive notion where 'people' and 'nation' can be treated as synonyms. The ideas ultimately relate to human nature. Notions of human character, individuality, identity and personality can be shown to have shifted in content as human society adjusted itself to new economic patterns, new knowledge, new lifestyles. In particular, the concept of the social or human type, so crucial to our contemporary media criticism and analysis, owes a significant conceptual debt to *Les Français peints par eux-mêmes*.[9] This chapter will offer an alternative perspective on the fascination for codifying human nature evident in this and several other sources of representation. The phenomenon has in fact been well studied by modern scholarship, though with an emphasis on the influence of Lavater's physiognomic theories which may have distracted us from other meaningful perspectives.[10] The explication of this publishing phenomenon should facilitate an approach to ideological contents, especially those involved in the construction of a new national identity for the French people.

Techniques of illustration

It is scarcely a coincidence, though no reference was made to it, that two months before *L'Express* published its supplement the Musée d'Orsay had opened one of its series of special exhibitions under the rubric of 'Les Dossiers du Musée d'Orsay' with the title of *Les Français peints par eux-mêmes* (Le Men and Abélès, 1993). It was an exhibition of the original publications, with related materials, giving an intense and concentrated experience of this product of a periodical press newly empowered with pictures. The first half of the nineteenth century had seen the development of several new techniques of picture reproduction. Photography came last, in the late 1830s, but only much later came into its own as a popular medium. Nevertheless, it deserves a moment's special attention here, both with reference to the special supplement of *L'Express* and because the comparison between photography and other means of image-making is helpful and instructive.[11]

An attempt to view the non-photographic traditions of reproduction needs to recognize the photographic mode as the norm against which we tend to assess the other graphic arts, especially in portraiture. Photography caught on so very quickly because it was seen as a method of producing true portraits, by and large of named individuals in society. Within a couple of years it ruined the profession of miniature portrait painting. When we look at the caricatures of photographic portraiture of the 1840s (see Figure 6.2), where the sitter is shown with his head in a clamp to hold it still, we would be wrong to think these clamps were the invention of the photographers beset by long exposure times. They were the traditional tools of portrait painters in oil, needing even longer 'exposure times' than the early photographers. Portraits had been in demand as a sign of social status for a very long time. They were a well-established and well-understood means of demonstrating and emphasizing a personal and social identity. Sitting for a portrait, however, was both time-consuming and expensive. Photography came as a great boon to the aspiring bourgeoisie: one might say that it almost became a means of achieving social prestige. The powerful new device gave its individual subjects a new status in the cultural firmament through the mere existence of their portrait. The cultural and social dynamics of this practice are still thriving in the activities of today's High Street Photographers.[12]

The photographs in the supplement to *L'Express* are portraits of individuals, a few of them well known to everybody: the President of the Republic is obviously François Mitterrand; the couturier is Jean-Paul

Gaultier. We are given all their names and we do not doubt for a moment that they all have particular and unique social identities. They stare out of the page at us, though the fact that we do not know them personally lends them a kind of fake anonymity. Every photograph has the same neutral beige background so that all these people (except one) are without any visible context. The pointed exception is the President, who is photographed in one of the grand rooms of the Élysée – but in a wide-angle shot showing him seated on a chair placed on the same beige studio background-roll used for all the other portraits, with the infinity curve of the roll showing (see Figure 6.3).[13] The effect of this

Figure 6.2 *Honoré Daumier, from* Les bons bourgeois, *1847. No. 49: 'Position reputed to be the most comfortable for a handsome portrait by daguerreotype'*

neutral background is to give an artificial prominence to the individuals, abstracting them from time and space and inserting them into a cosmic void which works like an aura, emphasizing their individuality in the sense which Walter Benjamin gave to this notion (see Benjamin, 1973). In this they are like the images produced by the studio of Nadar, the greatest of portrait photographers active in Paris throughout the second half of the nineteenth century.[14] (The pictorial convention was in fact borrowed from Jacques-Louis David's portraits, an invention of the 1780s.) It is important to note that the images of the original *Français peints par eux-mêmes* are represented also without background, though the effect is not to endow them with aura and thus an intense kind of individuality, as in a photograph, but to universalize them as what we now call 'types'. There is room to question whether such photographs can in fact give a sense of 'type' at all.

Of course, this grand assemblage of characters makes no pretence to scientific coverage or significance. It is a piece of journalistic entertainment, and a good one, rewarding the reader with lots of insights and explanations: especially interesting to a foreign Francophile always

Figure 6.3 *President Mitterrand sitting for* L'Express *photographic portrait, 1993*

fascinated to turn over new pieces of any jigsaw, but particularly so to see where they might fit into the picture we have of French people, and doubly so when they show us the picture French people have of themselves. Not systematic, of course, in the sense of a scientific system, but as surely systematic in the semiological sense as anything could be. Its very pretension, however tongue in cheek, to a system of six categories – this is an indicator of the real import of such a collation. Journalistic entertainment this may be, but that makes it a prime example of *la vie médiatisée*, life as mediated by our organs of communication, and as such almost as much an enyclopaedia of mythology as Hesiod's *Theogony* at the dawn of recorded antiquity. The way to approach this kind of material which promises the most interesting perspective is that kind of analysis of which Roland Barthes was a distinguished proponent and exemplar. We are looking at signs and at myths, but in the modern and analytical sense of those words, where certain kinds of cultural construction can be seen as the constituent elements of a rhetoric signifying an ideology. If we cannot get very far in this short treatment, we may yet point to a field worth exploring.

Some precedents

Where did this kind of representation come from? By 'kind of representation' we should understand any collection of units representing humans in any systematic framework, abstracting them from their context of life (even if referring to it) in such a way as to emphasize their membership of the collection rather than their presence in a real life. Frequently, these units are subjected to some rule of category which points to a 'meaning': their place in the system. After all, real life enmeshes people within a web of intersecting connections which may obscure, or even conceal, the systematic reality defining the ultimate rules governing relations within that system. Escaping all the confusions or distractions of context may be the best way – the only way – to see a meaning not otherwise to be understood or even perceived. We are talking about all those lexicons or storehouses of significant units, alphabets, codes of representations of human beings, selected on any given principle. Some maps of the sixteenth and seventeenth centuries would assemble a range of exemplars around the edge, to show the kinds of people to be found in the place represented. C. Visscher's perspectival map of Paris of 1618[15] depicted *Le Roy de France* and *La Royne*, a *Gentilhomme Parisien* and a *Gentille femme*, a *Bourgeois de Paris*, a *Femme bourgeoise*, a *Villageois du Paris* and a *Villageoise*; these French terms are actually offered as translations of Latin terms (*rex, nobilis, civis, rusticus*) (Figure 6.4). They are all in the appropriate costume and they clearly represent – even if somewhat perfunctorily – the full range of human beings as recognized within the feudal order. We find a similar set surrounding Hondius's *Nova Totius Europae Descriptio* of 1595, this time offering images of all the main nations of Europe, representing each by a *nobilis* and a *mercator*, except for one solitary Norwegian *habitus communis*. This categorization is informative to us by its very strangeness. It defines a mind-set fundamentally different from our own.

A rather more interesting and altogether richer tradition of representation was in the printed images of city street vendors known as 'street cries' in English, or *cris de la ville* in French.[16] The oldest of these have been dated to Paris around 1500, and they developed as a staple production of printing shops wherever printing spread. They were usually woodcuts printed on cheap paper to be sold by street sellers, *colporteurs*, stall-holders at occasional markets, etc. But in the seventeenth and eighteenth centuries in Paris in particular there were several etched sequences made by artists of reputation, perhaps the best known being that by Edme Bouchardon. Published from 1737 to 1746, the title of his five suites was *Études prises dans le Bas Peuple ou les Cris de Paris* (Figure 6.5). The phrase *bas peuple* would suggest that the construction of this set comes from the élite culture of the period and is addressed to the privileged members of society. Vincent Milliot (1994: 5–28)[17] has shown that the development in the eighteenth century of a sophisticated level of production and consumption of these images relates stylistically to the taste for inversion among the privileged. The convention had developed of representing shepherds and shepherdesses as children of nature, and this had become an ideal – so much so that Louis XVI even created a fully equipped rustic theme park for Marie Antoinette in the grounds of Versailles. The variety of ways we might describe those royal diversions points to the crucial problem of interest here: why would people who had everything pretend to be people who had nothing? Was it for fun? Is there not a truly significant identity game going on here? Royal diversion it was, of course: a game for the ladies of the court. They could really milk the cows, dress in rustic garb (or at least a travesty of rustic garb) and pretend to their heart's delight that this ideal was truly real. They were identifying with a lifestyle wholly at odds with the actual life of a lady at court. It was pretty much at odds with life on an actual farm, too. But, of course, it was only playing. I am suggesting that there was also an identity game under way with the pictures of street sellers. A similar rhetorical device

Figure 6.4 *Images from the border of C. Visscher's map* Lutetia Parisiorum, *1618*

Figure 6.5 *Title page from Edme Bouchardon's* Cris de Paris, *Suite 4, 1742.*

as that of Bouchardon was used by François Boucher around 1737 in twelve drawings (engraved by Ravenet) for his *Cris de Paris,* converting a tradition of lower class grotesques into a new convention of picturesque urban forms of life for courtly consumption. The crucial thing we have to remember here is that in the dominant ideology the civilized people of the élite were perceived as normal, whereas the real peasants and urban street sellers were 'ordinary' in the old sense, perceived as coarse, deformed and indeed grotesque.

The concept of the grotesque requires a few remarks in this context. It is a notion which has caused much confusion, owing to the differing meanings it carries in different speech registers and indeed in different critical traditions. For Victor Hugo it was the key to the modern spirit, the essence of the Romantic as he defined in his *Préface de Cromwell,* in 1827:

> Dans la pensée des Modernes ... le grotesque a un rôle immense. Il est partout; d'une part, il crée le difforme et l'horrible; de l'autre, le comique et le buffon. Si du monde idéal il passe au monde réel, il y déroule d'intarissables parodies de l'humanité. Ce sont des créations de sa fantaisie que ces Scaramouches, ces Crispins, ces Arlequins, grima-çantes silhouettes de l'homme, types tout à fait inconnus à la grave Antiquité.[18]
>
> (in Furst, 1980: 106–7)

More recently, Mikhail Bakhtin has used the notion of the grotesque as the key to understanding representations of the common people and their tastes. In the framework of his path-breaking study of Rabelais, the grotesque is linked to the carnivalesque so closely that the words become coterminous. This is significant because the character of cele-bration, and especially of communal celebration, is becoming so al-tered by our contemporary media experience that older forms have become remote from us to the point that we may fail to recognize them. Although Bakhtin was not concerned with the history of caricature or of illustration as such, his study of the popular-literary origins of the *cris de la ville* shows they enjoyed a clear identity as a genre of popular entertainment long before the emergence of a visual genre with the arrival of printing (Bakhtin, 1968).[19] Bakhtin's overall parallel between the body of society and the body of the human animal is of course derived from Rabelais, and the celebration of bodily needs and func-tions is directly related to the old social order. When we see a nineteenth-century sequence produced at Épinal[20] with grotesquely distorted features and bodies, say, with snot dribbling in giant gobbets from their noses, we should know exactly where we are in the social system: at the bottom (Figure 6.6). The point of interest is that this is not a celebration, no longer an idealization; it has become a repudiation. If children were entertaining themselves with this, in the last quarter of the nineteenth century, it was surely *not* to identify with the subjects of these pictures.

There are several features of the street-cry tradition that deserve emphasis here. Firstly, there is the unmistakable fact that the people who are depicted in the *cris de la ville* are situated at the humblest level of economic life in pre-industrial society, though not the wholly destitute. It may be asked how they came to be depicted at all. What was the market for them? What the interest? Who would want to buy such pictures and what kind of use or pleasure or instruction was to be found in them? It is very difficult to believe that those depicted ever bought the pictures. Secondly, it is clear that they were always created in sets, as a codified system of signs, and that many of the figures became standard ones with a known profile of expectation; they even became bywords, such as the *Gagne-Petit*, or *Rémouleur*, a knife and scissors grinder who was usually associated with penurious honesty. Thirdly, the fact that many of these sets, from the seventeenth to the nineteenth centuries, were printed with legends in two or sometimes even three languages points to an international market for such images. (This was not true of the *images d'Épinal*.) Fourthly, a sea change occurred in the nineteenth century when the *cris* came to be equated with *petits métiers*, and the genre was extended to become much more self-consciously a general view of the working class. Fifthly, the fact that they continued being produced through the nineteenth century in all the print media from woodcut to photography, from *images d'Épinal* to Atget's *Petits métiers de Paris*, brings the tradition so close to our own day that we might marvel it could disappear – or be transmogrified – so speedily. We might wonder whether changes in ideology wrought this transformation, or changes in rhetoric – and if both, which came first.

A more useful explanation may be that technical developments in visual representation interacted with market conditions to promote differentiation. None of the older techniques actually disappeared; they were just joined by new ones, often with a certain cachet of novelty, while the old ones continued, perhaps with a new audience or clientèle as they found themselves shunted down-market by the sheer attraction of the new. Images which may have been purchased for a gentleman's collection with a certain edifying motive at a particular time and in a specific medium may have been thought suitable as a kind of education

Figure 6.6 Alphabet des cris de Paris, *Imprimerie Olivier-Pinot, Épinal, 1840*

or entertainment for children when acquired, perhaps in a different medium, in the following generation. The main technical inventions concerned were wood-engraving and lithography.[21] The former was reinvented in Newcastle in the workshop of Thomas Bewick and imported to France in the 1830s, becoming immensely popular. The great virtue of this medium was that it could be easily integrated with letterpress printing to make possible and economic the great explosion of illustration in nineteenth-century book or journal publication. Lithography had also been imported to France slightly earlier, from Germany. A lithograph is so powerfully autographic that the image has all the appearance of a drawing, with a capacity for subtle shading and fine manipulation of the brush, the pen, or the greasy crayon. Its disadvantage is that it cannot be combined with letterpress in a single process. Both wood-engraving and lithography could produce long print runs of many thousands of copies. Although both were imports, there is a case for arguing that they achieved their greatest impact in France rather than in their countries of origin perhaps largely because of the character of the market for illustration. There was a demand for images in the French social and political context which was met by an elaborately varied supply – and perhaps the official censorship played a rather more creative part in these developments than is usually credited.

There is no space here to do justice to the great production of caricature in the 1830s and 1840s. In addition to Daumier and Gavarni, who were seen at the time as the best and most productive artists in the media of lithography and wood-engraving, any decent account would have to recognize Charlet, Traviès, Devéria, Monnier, Trimolet and countless others.[22] The point that does need to be made here because it has not been emphasized enough is that the reimposition of political censorship of the press by Louis-Philippe's regime on 29 August 1835 had an important effect with ideological consequences not perhaps foreseen. Charles Philipon, the crucial producer behind so much of this new trade in images, rechannelled the focus of the production of caricature away from political comment lampooning the government of the day to social comment satirizing the behaviour of people ... under that government. Philipon had conceived of a new way of being political which could not be censored: through *la caricature de moeurs*. He commissioned Daumier to do the drawings for what was to become a series of 100 lithographs on the doings of 'Robert Macaire', a trickster figure originating in the popular theatre (Figure 6.7). Daumier did the drawings and Philipon wrote the (overlong) legends to this series,

Figure 6.7 *Honoré Daumier,* Robert Macaire agent d'affaires, *1837*

which took the public by storm. The series shows Macaire in dozens of different situations to do with making money by means of trickery or dishonesty or exploiting people's weaknesses. Sometimes he is a lawyer, sometimes a businessman, sometimes a go-between; he is a cheerful, ever resourceful exemplar of the Guizot principle 'Enrichissez vous!'.[23] The series is a devastating criticism of the prevailing culture, achieving its effects through a mythical figure who could not be imprisoned (as Daumier had been) and who rapidly achieved archetypal status.[24]

Philipon and Daumier went on to produce many other major series, most of them identifying a social class or group and exploring a full gamut of situations to be experienced by such characters. *Les gens de justice, les gens de médecine, les bons bourgeois, locataires et propriétaires, les bohémiens, les bas bleus, les divorceuses*[25] – just starting to list the range of subjects gives an inkling of this remarkable analytical purview of French society in the mid-nineteenth century. Nothing comparable to these great series of social comments, organized encyclopaedically in sets, was produced in any other country in Europe, despite the availability of the image technology, the approximately similar social circumstances and the existence of markets for images. In England at the same time very little of this new visual social comment came into focus. What there was, say, in *Punch* (of which the subtitle acknowledged a debt to Philipon by calling itself *The London Charivari*) did not offer any systematic framework for the images.

Conclusion

Finally, we come back to *Les Français peints par eux-mêmes*. Originally it was conceived as a serial publication of two eight-page fascicles per week for 24 weeks. Each fascicle consisted of an essay and a full-page, wood-engraved illustration, with a few vignettes and tailpieces decorating the text. The full set of 48 could be bound as a volume (and was made available in this form).[26] It was simultaneously published in English in a bound edition under the title *Pictures of the French, a series of literary and graphic delineations of French character* (Figure 6.8). The English version did not continue past the first volume. The titles of the fascicles then became effectively chapter titles, and in the bound version (in both English and French) there was a list of contents which introduced the novel practice of inserting against each title in the list a tiny engraving of the original full-page version (Figs. 6.9 and 6.10). These icons are a striking graphic innovation of the period, showing the

Figure 6.8 *Title page for* Pictures of the French, *London, 1840*

printing house exploiting the possibilities of wood-engraving to enhance communication – but also to augment the mnemonic power of these images, impressing them upon the minds of the readers.

The series was so popular in France that it went on to make up 423 fascicles, published in eight substantial volumes with the subtitle of *Encyclopédie des moeurs contemporaines.* Five of the volumes were on Paris, and three on the provinces. The final volume on Paris included several useful sections giving analytical overviews over the entire subject matter, including a substantial statistical study by Alfred Legoyt on *La*

THE LAW STUDENT, by E. DE LA BEDOLLIERRE		.	.	25
Portrait	.	GAVARNI	LAVIEILLE	25
Headpiece	.	Id.	Id.	25
Letter	.	Id.	Id.	25
Tailpiece	.	Id.	Id.	32
POLITICAL LADIES, by COMTE H. DE VIEL-CASTEL		.	.	33
Portrait	.	GAVARNI	LAVIEILLE	33
Headpiece	.	Id.	Id.	33
Letter	.	Id.	Id.	33
Tailpiece	.	.	.	40
THE LITERARY ADVENTURER, by ALBERIC SECOND		.	.	41
Portrait	.	GAVARNI	LAVIEILLE	41
Headpiece	.	Id.	Id.	41
Letter	.	Id.	Id.	41
Tailpiece	.	Id.	Id.	48
THE MONTHLY NURSE, by MAD. DE BAWR		.	.	49
Portrait	.	H. MONNIER	LAVIEILLE	49
Headpiece	.	Id.	Id.	49
Letter	.	Id.	Id.	49
Tailpiece	.	Id.	Id.	56
THE " RAPIN," by J. CHAUDES-AIGUES		.	.	57
Portrait	.	GAVARNI	LAVIEILLE	57
Headpiece	.	Id.	Id.	57
Letter	.	Id.	Id.	57
Tailpiece	.	Id.	Id.	64
A LEADER OF FASHION, by MAD. ANCELOT		.	.	65
Portrait	.	GAVARNI	LAVIEILLE	65
Headpiece	.	Id.	LOUIS	65
Letter	.	Id.	LAVIEILLE	65
THE PHYSICIAN, by L. ROUX		.	.	73
Portrait	.	GAVARNI	LAVIEILLE	73
Headpiece	.	Id.	Id.	73
Letter	.	Id.	Id.	73
Tailpiece	.	Id.	Id.	80
THE ATTORNEY, by ALTAROCHE		.	.	81
Portrait	.	H. MONNIER	LAVIEILLE	81
Headpiece	.	Id.	GERARD	81
Letter	.	Id.	LAVIEILLE	81
THE FIGURANTE, by PHILIBERT AUDEBRAND		.	.	89
Portrait	.	GAVARNI	LAVIEILLE	89
Headpiece	.	Id.	GUILBAUT	89
Letter	.	Id.	FAGNION	89
Tailpiece	.	Id.	Id.	96

Figure 6.9 *Excerpt from Contents List in* Pictures of the French, *London, 1840*

Population de la France. Other tabular information was supplied to enable the reader to track down every contributor and every subject – clearly intending the work to be treated as a serious contribution to knowledge of the ostensive topic of the entire series, the population of France. It may be a strange eventuality that our knowledge of this series today seems largely to have been the work of art historians seeking to explicate the phenomenon of realism in nineteenth-century painting (see especially Weisberg, 1980). The illustrations are what catch the attention, and there are some remarkable features relating to the realist project of representing the current image of 'ordinary people'. The depiction of individuals out of context, in a blank white space, has the

	Dessinateurs. MM.	Graveurs. MM.	Pag.
L'ÉCOLIER, par M. HENRI ROL-LAND.			134
Type.	CHARLET.	GUILBAUT.	ib.
Tête de page.	GAGNIET.	LAVIEILLE.	ib.
Lettre.	id.	GUILBAUT.	ib.
Écolier.	COUSIN.	PORRET.	136
Type.	GAVARNI.	PERVILLÉ.	138
Souris.	id.	LOUIS.	139
LE COCHER DE COUCOU, par M. L. COUAILHAC.			145
Type.	H. MONNIER.	J. BABAT.	ib.
Tête de page.	ÉMY.	GÉRARD.	ib.
Lettre.	id.	id.	ib.
LE MAITRE DE PENSION, par M. ÉLIAS REGNAULT.			153
Type.	GAVARNI.	GUILLAU-MOT.	ib.
Tête de page.	PAUQUET.	LAVIEILLE.	ib.
Lettre.	id.	LAVIEILLE.	ib.
LE GAMIN DE PARIS, par M. JULES JANIN.			161
Type.	GAVARNI.	SOYER.	ib.
Tête de page.	TRIMOLET.	LAVIEILLE.	ib.
Lettre.	id.	id.	ib.
Deuxième type	CHARLET.	PORRET.	ib.
Cul-de-lampe.	GAVARNI.	BRÉVAL.	170
LA DEMOISELLE A MARIER, par Madame ANNA MARIE.			174
Type.	GAVARNI.	GÉRARD.	ib.
Tête de page.	PAUQUET.	STYPULKOW-SKI	ib.
Lettre.	id.	GÉRARD.	ib.
LE PRÉCEPTEUR, par M. STANISLAS DAVID.			185
Type.	GAVARNI.	STYPULKOW-SKI.	ib.
Tête de page.	PAUQUET.	PORRET.	ib.
Lettre.	GAGNIET.	GUILBAUT.	ib.

Figure 6.10 *Excerpt from Contents List in* Les Français peints par eux-mêmes, *Paris, 1841–42*

effect of universalizing the types and, in this assemblage, emphasizing their equal status. However high or low, all are accorded the same dignity. The bourgeois purchasers of *Les Français* could applaud this feature in a book, though they hated to see it on a salon wall. A further point affecting our view of these depictions is that the artist Gavarni, one of the main contributors, did not draw from models but from memory or the mind's eye.[27] One can scarcely imagine a clearer index of ideological representation.

Art historians have perhaps not appreciated some features that the semiologist would notice. The most important of these arises from the claim to an encyclopaedic view of the material. We may have seen in an alphabet of street cries a code-book of human instances, *l'intégrale du genre*, laying claim to totality, exhaustiveness. What then is the appropriate view of the complete *Les Français?* It does not matter that a line had to be drawn somewhere in order to end the project. The editor and publisher, Curmer, says in his conclusion that more than 3000 contributions were submitted, though only about 400 were used. The point is surely that what is offered is a systematic codification of instances of what then constituted 'The French'. The collection is intended to establish a new sense of the community of French people. It is no longer based on the old feudal hierarchy of the *ancien régime* (though some such figures are included), nor on *métiers* (though many are represented). It is still haunted by notions of character, in the Bruyère sense (Figure 6.11). But there is a new sense of human typology at play. The catalogue to the Musée d'Orsay exhibition makes an interesting point about the use of the word *type* here to identify these characters. It was essentially a completely new usage of the period. The word had, of course, existed for a long time, in both English and French. But just as the word 'illustration' had acquired a new meaning in both sides of the Channel during the 1830s, so also with 'type'.[28] Ségolène Le Men (1994) argues that the use of the word in the list of contents actually referred to the print at the head of each fascicle, not to the character as such. Her argument is supported by the fact that the English translators of the time used the word 'portrait' to translate *type*. This would suggest that the new meaning was just emerging in this very usage, which was to become so familiar that the term entered colloquial speech to mean 'character', or even just 'person'.

Les Français peints par eux-mêmes was codifying the range of social types emerging in the art and literature of the proclaimedly bourgeois culture of the July monarchy. In so doing it gave final form to the concept of social type as we now understand it. There is little doubt but

Figure 6.11 *Four 'types' from* Pictures of the French (Les Français peints par eux-mêmes): *the Speculator, the Physician, the Political Lady, the Monthly Nurse*

that Curmer in his concluding remarks had some sense of what he was doing – and that it had a function, moreover, in *les fastes de la nationalité* (the public celebrations of the nation) (*Les Français*, Province, tome 3: 458). He refers to 'cette galerie physiologique', using this latter term in the sense fashionable in the 1840s, based on the genre of popular literature known as 'Physiologies'. He emphasized the ephemeral nature of the latter ('aussitôt mortes que nées') (gone the moment they appear), while claiming that his own weighty encyclopaedia was 'amusant pour le présent, instructif pour l'avenir' (amusing for the present, instructive for the future). This sense of instructing the future seems a very pregnant phrase when looked at with the hindsight of 150 years. We might find in *Les Français* the best lexicon of the nationalist conception of the French people. The *types* which make the most interesting reading today are perhaps the marginal ones, seen as outsiders or even as intruders, such as *l'Algérien français, le Juif, le Nègre, le Bohémien.*[29] These texts have not been studied as a source for the construction of nationalist ideology in French culture, though I hope I have shown, at least *prima facie*, some reasons for thinking that this would be a rewarding thing to do. That, however, would have to be another story.

Notes

1. I am grateful to Laurence David of St Etienne for drawing my attention to this – and for sending me a copy.
2. The Republic, the Family, the Mind, the Street, the Business World, the Countryside.
3. The Career Officer, the Village Mayor, the CNRS Researcher and the President of the Republic respectively.
4. The Single Mother, the Homosexual Couple and the Doltomaniac.
5. Respectively: the Repairman, the Football Fan and the Chef.
6. Graffiti Artists, Teenagers, Prostitutes.
7. The Business Woman, the Thrusting Manager.
8. The *Pétanque* Player, the Country Priest, the Bobby, the Ecologist.
9. The concept is of course also important in literary study, perhaps especially in 'popular literature'. A very useful compendium was produced by Aziza, Oliviéri and Sctrick (*sic*) (1978).
10. Wechsler (1982) is the most accessible treatment of the physiognomic theme.
11. Reference may be made to Rouillé (1989), a useful source for accessing contemporary opinion.
12. The meaning of the professional portrait photograph has been analysed and re-evaluated by new streams of critical thought following Walter Benjamin, Roland Barthes, Jo Spence and others.
13. The infinity curve is achieved by ensuring a smooth curve in the transition

between the vertical background and the horizontal floor. The photograph will then show a dimensionless background.

14. Gosling (1976) produced a selection of Nadar's portraits of the famous, with brief biographical notes. The Centre Culturel de la Communauté Française de Belgique mounted a major exhibition in Brussels in 1994 covering the full range of Nadar's work: as significant caricaturist, as an illustrator and visual entrepreneur, as an aviator, as well as the most prominent (and long-lived) photographic portraitist of the era. See Peeters (1994) written to accompany the exhibition.

15. *Lutetia Parisiorum Urbs, toto Orbe Celeberrima Notissimaque, Caput Regni Franciae.* The copy available to hand has been given new currency as a complimentary gift to celebrate the Bicentenary of the Revolution by Paris Travel Service.

16. See Massin (1985), which concentrates on French material. A wider conspectus of material is to be found in Beall (1975). The editorial matter here is dual-language German and English. Both are very substantially illustrated. Berrouet and Laurendon (1994) reproduce a selection of materials, predominantly photographic.

17. I am grateful to my colleague, Dr Alex Cowan, for drawing my attention to this article.

18. It is particularly interesting and relevant to refer to the translation Furst offers for this text (1980: 104). The word *type* is not translated by the English word 'type'. 'In the thought of the Moderns ... the grotesque plays an immense role. It is everywhere; on the one hand, it creates the horrible and the misshapen; on the other the comical and the farcical. Moving from the ideal to the real world, the grotesque unfurls endless parodies of humanity. Among the creations of its fantasy are those Scaramouches, Crispins and Harlequins, grimacing outlines of man wholly unknown to solemn Antiquity, yet emerging nonetheless from classical Italy.' It would be tempting, perhaps, to use the word 'archetype' to translate *type* here. Hugo is using the word in its older sense. See also my comments on the use of this word in my closing section, pp. 94ff.

19. The chapter 'The language of the marketplace' (Bakhtin, 1968) is especially useful, and street cries are discussed in detail pp. 181–7. His reference to Abraham Bosse's *cris* seems to suggest that he did not realize how rich the visual tradition was.

20. *Alphabet des Cris de Paris*, Épinal, no. 652 (Pellerin), 1840, 1880; given in Musée Carnavalet (1990: 100). I am puzzled by the note that this was designed around 1840, but published after 1880.

21. For an excellent concise account, see Le Men (1994). I am leaving out of my account all reference to steel engraving because it does not impact on the subject matter or illustrative genres at issue. However, it clearly forms an important part of the overall development of illustration.

22. See Wechsler (1982). The most recent work to make a serious scholarly contribution to this field is ten-Doesschate Chu and Weisberg (1994), especially the contributions of James Cuno and Michael Paul Driskel.

23. Of course, this is quite unfair to Guizot, who actually said 'Enrichissez-vous par le travail et par l'épargne!' ('Enrich yourselves through work and saving'). Unfortunately for Guizot, it was – and is – rarely quoted in full.

24. Readers who would like to look at the Robert Macaire series should consult Adhémar (1979). Reprint by Editions Michèle Trinckvel. *Daumier – l'oeuvre lithographique* (2 vols), 1978 (Paris: Arthur Hubschmid) or 1977 (Munich: Verlag

Rogner and Bernhard) does give all of Daumier's lithographs, but in rather small reproductions.

25. Respectively, lawyers, doctors, the middle classes, tenants and landlords, bohemians, 'blue stockings' and women agitators for divorce.

26. The French edition is dated 1841–42, though the English edition published by William S. Orr and Co. of Paternoster Row shows 1840 on its title page. It is clear that the same woodblocks were used in both editions.

27. The concluding remarks by the editor and publisher of *Les Français*, L. Curmer, included a tribute to Gavarni in the following terms: 'Gavarni, par exemple, modèle d'élégance et de distinction, trace sans étude, et de mémoire, ses plus frappants portraits, privilège merveilleux du talent le plus délicat et le plus profond de ce temps-ci' ('Gavarni, for example, model of elegance and distinction, traces without preliminary studies and from memory his most striking portraits, the marvelous privilege of the most delicate and profound talent of our times') (*Les Français*, Province, tome 3: 459).

28. *The Oxford Dictionary of English Etymology* and *Le Robert: Dictionnaire historique de la langue française* concur with this claim. There may be grounds for fine argument on points of precision since, for example, Daumier's *Types parisiens*, produced by Philipon in 1838, may well be using the term in the new sense rather than the old.

29. The French Algerian, the Jew, the Negro, the Gypsy.

References

Adhémar, J. (ed.) (1979) *Daumier: 'Les Gens d'Affaires' (Robert Macaire)*. Paris: Editions Vilo.

Aziza, C., Oliviéri, C. and Sctrick, R. (1978) *Dictionnaire des types et caractères littéraires*. Paris: Nathan.

Bakhtin, M. (1968) *Rabelais and His World*. Cambridge, MA and London: MIT Press.

Beall, K.F. (1975) *Kaufrufe und Strassenhändler: Cries and Itinerant Trades*. Hamburg: Hauswedell.

Benjamin, W. (1973) 'The work of art in the age of mechanical reproduction' in H. Arendt (ed.) *Illuminations*, translated by H. Zohn. London: Fontana.

Berrouet, L. and Laurendon, G. (1994) *Métiers oubliés de Paris. Dictionnaire littéraire et anecdotique*. Paris: Parigramme.

L'Express (1993) 'Les Français', Supplément gratuit au numéro 2184, 13–19 May.

Français (1841–42) *Les Français peints par eux-mêmes*. Paris: L. Curmer (8 vols). The set consulted is in the Bibliothèque Nationale at shelfmark 4°2 Le Senne 1392.

Furst, L.R. (ed.) (1980) *European Romanticism: Self-definition*. London: Methuen.

Gosling, N. (1976) *Nadar's Portrait Photographs*. London: Secker and Warburg.

Le Men, S. (1994) 'Book illustration' in P. Collier and R. Lethbridge (eds) *Artistic Relations: Literature and the Visual Arts in Nineteenth Century France*. London: Yale University Press.

Le Men, S. and Abélès, L. (1993) *Les Français peints par eux-mêmes. Panorama Social du XIXe siècle*. Paris: Editions de la Réunion des musées nationaux (exhibition catalogue).

Massin, P. (1985) *Les Cris de la ville. Commerces ambulants et petits métiers de la rue*. Paris: Albin Michel.

Milliot, V. (1994) 'Le travail sans le geste. Les représentations iconographiques des petits métiers parisiens (XVIe–XVIIIe s.)', *Revue d'Histoire moderne et contemporaine* 41: 5–28.

Musée Carnavalet (1990) *Paris raconté par l'image d'Épinal*. Paris: Paris-Musées (exhibition catalogue).

Peeters, B. (1994) *Les Métamorphoses de Nadar*. Auby-sur-Semois, Belgium: Marot.

Rouillé, A. (1989) *La Photographie en France. Textes et Controverses: une Anthologie 1816–1871*. Paris: Macula.

ten-Doesschate Chu, P. and Weisberg, G.P. (eds) (1994) *The Popularization of Images: Visual Culture under the July Monarchy*. London: Princeton University Press.

Wechsler, J. (1982) *The Human Comedy: Physiognomy and Caricature in 19th Century Paris*. London: Thames & Hudson.

Weisberg, G.P. (1980) *The Realist Tradition: French Painting and Drawing 1830–1900*. Cleveland: Cleveland Museum of Art and Indiana University Press.

7.

Two women filmmakers speak out: Serreau and Balasko and the inheritance of May '68

BRIGITTE ROLLET

TRANSLATED FROM THE FRENCH BY D.W.S. GRAY

The starting-point of my research was to look at modifications in the treatment of the family by French women film directors. It seemed to me that the theme was in fact often a recurrent one in 'women's films'. What interested me most particularly was the way in which the inheritance of May '68 was or was not visible in these changes. Coline Serreau is a filmmaker who cannot be ignored when examining these issues. The release on 8 February 1995 of Josiane Balasko's film *Gazon maudit* (*French Twist*) and the multiple references to the films of Serreau (and most particularly to her first full-length feature film, *Pourquoi pas!*) led me to consider the possible links between two filmmakers of the same generation. With respect to Balasko's film, the statement by a critic that 'ce Gazon ... est une sorte de *Pourquoi pas!* au féminin, quinze ans après'[1] (Lavoignat, 1995: 31) set me thinking that besides the similarities (and differences) in the treatment of the 'family' and the 'couple', one could compare the two directors on other levels, above all because their personal careers have followed similar paths. What I want to show here is that (despite numerous similarities which will also be considered) the differences which do exist between these two go far beyond their treatment of the same situations: the family and/or the couple. In fact, these dissimilarities reveal not only a different approach to sexual rôles and to the body, but reveal also (and the two are connected) two ways of dealing with the inheritance of May '68, since both belong to that generation. I will be focusing here mainly on the feminist movements and influences arising from May '68. In fact, *Gazon maudit* has very often been seen as a 'feminist comedy', a term which until now has been reserved for Serreau's films. The questions I started with were thus the following: is Balasko in 1995, with *Gazon maudit*, the Serreau of 1977? And if the answer is yes, what has become of the latter? At issue above all will be the theatrical and cinematographic careers up to and including two full-length features of the directors: *La crise* by Coline Serreau (1993) and *Gazon maudit* by Josiane Balasko (1995). These will not be treated in detail, but will serve to illustrate my case.

Before embarking on the study of the actual directors and films, it seems necessary to take a step back for a quick general consideration of the treatment of the family in French films. May 1968 seems in this context (as in many others) to be a key moment. Until the end of the 1960s (or even in the early 1960s) what was dominant was the existence of a traditional family structure, made up of two biological parents of the child, and of one or more children, not forgetting the lover or the mistress (which suggests, to say the least, a caricature of the title of Le Chanoix's film *Papa, maman, la bonne et moi*, made in 1954).

These facts would be considerably modified during and after May '68. The modifications would affect the couple above all. I use this word keeping in mind Françoise Audé's distinction when she speaks of the 'métamorphoses du couple' (the 'metamorphoses of the couple'). She emphasizes that 'l'emploi du terme "couple", lorsqu'il se substitue à celui de "mariage" (l'institution) ou de "ménage" (la cellule sociale de base, gestionnaire du foyer où s'épanouit la famille), c'est déjà la modernité par opposition à la tradition'[2] (Audé, 1983: 80). What we will find, besides a majority of films continuing to present the classic structure mentioned, is a form of 'redefinition' of the couple, and above all of the rôles and expectations of the partners. That this coincided with the arrival of women filmmakers should not be very surprising. Even though women did not only tell 'women's stories', a tendency was still to take shape with certain directors, if only in the choice of different, stronger heroines, as far removed as possible from the 'petites bourgeoises séduisantes et volages'[3] of the 1950s of whom Audé writes (Audé, 1981: 111). The choice of themes reveals a desire to say things hitherto kept quiet (the 'speaking-out' of May '68), whether about feminine sexuality, contraception, abortion or rape. Even though women have not always chosen fiction to express their desires and wishes for change, it is no less true that certain filmmakers were putting 'fiction in the service of the feminist cause', to take up the phrase used of Agnès Varda's film, *L'une chante, l'autre pas* (1976).

Coline Serreau was one of those who started in documentary, before definitively choosing the fiction film. Her first film, *Mais qu'est-ce qu'elles veulent?* (1973–77), is a feminist documentary (considered by some women as *the* feminist documentary *par excellence*), in which, in the filmmaker's own words, it was a matter of making 'un film sur l'utopie dans lequel les femmes auraient décrit très concrètement la société dont elles rêvaient'[4] (in Lejeune, 1987: 196). The film is therefore composed of a series of conversations with lots of women from various social, geographic and professional backgrounds. I mention Serreau's remark on Utopia here, since it will be at issue in much of what follows. In fact, her first full-length feature film illustrates perfectly the Utopian tendency of the period. In her article, Audé classes it among the 'subversions du deuxième type [et les] audaces du nouveau'[5] (Audé, 1982: 80). If we keep the distinction offered by Daniel Serceau, it is an example of Utopian realism, which is to say the brand of realism to be found in filmmakers who, 'donnant plus ou moins libre cours à leur imagination, réalisent leur désir dans la représentation. Leur film anticipe la venue d'un monde qui reste cependant à faire. La "révolution" paraît achevée dans la fiction, à défaut de l'être dans le monde objectif'[6] (Serceau, 1983: 123). That can also be read as the 'soft' approach, as opposed to the radicalism of other filmmakers. What Serreau was presenting in *Pourquoi pas!* was a sexual community. In connection with Faraldo's *Bof!* (1971) Lefèvre would go on to speak of 'communisme sexuel familial' (sexual family communism) (in Cheval-lier, 1983: 39), a definition which could just as well be applied to Serreau. The choice of the word 'communism' is all the more appropriate in that the filmmaker declared in 1978 that her principal concern was 'la jonction entre féminisme et marxisme' (the joining of feminism and Marxism) (Beylie, 1987: 90). This does not prevent the choice of revolution advocated by Serreau in *Pourquoi pas!* from being rather uncritical: in the end she does not radically challenge the model she had set out to overturn. Even though it is true, as Audé emphasized, that 'l'enjeu [du film], c'est l'abolition des rôles hérités' and that 'la marginalité a aujourd'hui conquis un certain droit à l'existence' it is less certain (at least as far as Serreau is concerned) that 'la différence est tolérée et parfois revendiquée'[7] (Audé, 1983: 84–5). Nor should we forget the etymology of the word 'Utopia' invented by Thomas More – 'having no place' – and the impossibility therefore of putting it into practice (as Fourier and Cabet found out through painful experience).

In the same period, on the other hand, the place among others where a much more radical protest was to be found was in the *café-théâtres*,[8] which were proliferating before, during and after May '68. This leads us to Balasko. Rather than compare the cinema with the *café-*

théâtres, I wish on the one hand to emphasize the ever closer connections between the two means of expression in the French context, and on the other hand to consider how in the same period women could voice their demands; and above all how, having both started their careers on the stage and sometimes in similar company,[9] two women, Serreau and Balasko, came to 'speak out'.

Far from the Utopia of Serreau's films or of certain of Faraldo's films,[10] the *café-théâtre* companies, mainly that of the Café de la Gare, and later that of the Splendid, would be characterized by the desire for subversion and transgression by means of caricatures based on all levels of the French bourgeoisie. What is more, the *café-théâtres* would offer comediennes the opportunity to express themselves on taboo subjects. According to Da Costa in his *Histoire du Café-Théâtre*, 'la mode, l'actualité étaient-elles au féminisme? le café-théâtre immédiatement présenterait des spectacles "féminins" ... Les thèmes d'alors: la libération des femmes, la dénonciation de leur "aliénation", leurs grossesses, leurs menstruations, leurs orgasmes, l'avortement, le contrôle des naissances'[11] (Da Costa, 1978: 199). The influence of publications like *Charlie-Hebdo* or *Hara-Kiri* would be quite perceptible and strong in both tone and theme. In other words, what was being expressed on the stages of the Café de la Gare and the Splendid, to mention only two of them, is strongly reminiscent of carnival and of carnival laughter as described by Bakhtin, for whom 'carnival laughter ... is, first of all, a festive laughter [and] it is the laughter of all the people' (Bakhtin, 1968: 11–12). So, through the presentation of the body and its physiological functions, 'grotesque realism' would be rediscovered by *café-théâtre* actors (both male and female).[12] Other characteristics of carnival seen by Bakhtin are also useful when thinking of this women's humour. Thus 'the celebration of the grotesque, excessive body, and of the "material bodily lower stratum", the valorisation of the obscene and of "marketplace" speech in language [and the] rejection of social decorum and politeness' (Stam, 1989: 94) are easily identifiable in *café-théâtre* productions. These places were to become the few where women not only mounted their one-woman shows based on scripts they mostly wrote themselves, but could also flout an established order. The transgression was both sexual and social.

The birth of women's comedy dates from that period (with Sylvie Joly, a former barrister turned comedian, and Zouc, the Belgian comedian, leading the way). Balasko was to join the Splendid company in 1976, where she replaced Valérie Mairesse.[13] She was one of those actors who moved back and forth from stage to screen. Her first main role in the cinema was in Poiré's film *Les hommes préfèrent les grosses*, for which she wrote the screenplay. Furthermore, she was to say about this feature film that 'c'était la première fois qu'une fille tenait un premier rôle sans être une fille superbe'[14] (in Lejeune, 1987: 78). Until her latest film as a director, she was to play in almost 30 films (sometimes with the company from the Splendid, sometimes using scripts which had first been played on stage, and/or written by her). Well known to the public for her many collaborations with the Splendid company, Balasko moved behind the camera in 1985 with *Sac de nœuds*, and carried from stage to screen her persona of a rather gauche woman, with a physique which in France would be politely called 'difficult'. This confined her to ungainly-but-funny rôles of girls or women far from the canons of traditional beauty, and rarely a sexual object – except when the man was drunk, as in *Nuit d'ivresse*. This is not to forget her part in Blier's film *Trop belle pour toi*, where she 'seduces' her boss, played by Gérard Depardieu, married for the occasion to top model Carole Bouquet. Looking at the list of parts she has taken, we can see a certain pattern. To some extent she could be compared with Annie Girardot, if only in the way she puts over a different body image and has succeeded in the cinema despite the unofficial censorship operating on French screens against women who are not sex symbols. Girardot's qualities as described by Audé could just as well be applied to Balasko: 'active, énergique, victorieuse même dans ses échecs. Avec les hommes, elle instaure des relations de camaraderie ou de compagnonage ... elle est simple et saine. Sa sexualité de quadragénaire n'est ni passive ni redoutable'[15] (Audé, 1981: 192).

Moreover, Balasko uses as justification for moving into film direction the difficulty of finding filmmakers who want to adapt her scripts and the rarity of offers of interesting parts for women actors. It is true that she appeared on screen at the beginning of the 1980s, at a time when the cult of the perfect body was dominant, when a kind of 'dictatorship' of the firm young body (far removed from the 'grotesque body'), with a tendency to promote Lolita-like actresses, was being established. Before 1980, however, one of the demands of women after May '68 was the wish to transcend outer appearances to show the inner side of things, summarized by Audé in these words: 'les comédiennes, des personnages, des femmes intéressantes par leur intervention au plan socio-politique ont remplacé le mythe'[16] (Audé, 1981: 219; Martineau and Hennebelle, 1979). Women of more ordinary physique were to occupy a new space, first of all on the stage, and sometimes on the big screen, since many of the plays mounted by the Splendid company were to become films. Speaking out was to acquire a new meaning here. I am stressing the physique, the importance of the body, because Balasko and other *café-théâtre* women actors were using theirs and the physiological functions associated with them as the subject matter of their plays and/or films.

Thanks to the success of a former member of the Splendid, Michel Blanc, who directed *Marche à l'ombre* in 1984, Balasko did not have too much difficulty in financing her first film in 1985, *Sac de nœuds*, which was a critical (and commercial) failure in the same year that another woman film director was beating all box office records with a story of babies and cack-handed fathers. Serreau is the only woman to figure in the list of the 20 most popular films since the start of the Fifth Republic, reaching third position with *Trois hommes et un couffin* ... but perhaps not for much longer, if Balasko's comedy keeps going – audience figures reached three million within two months of the film's release. Serreau proved several things with her success (besides the success itself): on the one hand, that women can make an audience laugh, and can make films which make audiences laugh; until then, comedy was a field reserved for men, as much on the screen as in the distribution of parts; on the other hand, she proved that some ingredients are funnier than others. In this case, in a country which advocates a rise in the birth rate, choosing the idea of the family (even if she 'subverts' it) was not *a priori* taking much of a risk. With other subjects, in *Trois hommes et un couffin*, and then in *Romuald et Juliette* (even though she introduced, in Firmine Richard, the actress playing Juliette, a female character who did not conform to traditional criteria), Serreau was to continue the line of Utopias which characterized her beginnings, though it was now in some ways a much more widely acceptable Utopia, making fewer demands than in the early days. Audé emphasizes in her critique of the film that 'le cinéaste s'interdit ... le sarcasme et les caricatures façon café-théâtre'[17] (Audé, 1985: 79). In fact – and the tendency is confirmed in what follows – we are in the realm of vaudeville and light comedy. From 'subversive' cinema, Serreau moves to an 'establishment' cinema, to take up the distinction drawn by Jeancolas (1979). Women in *Trois hommes et un couffin* are few and are (or seem) more or less mere caricatures. Speaking out has changed its target. It is no longer the couple, nor the people making up the couple, who fill that space, it is the child.

In this, Serreau has moved absolutely with the times. The child becomes the one whose point of view is favoured, and this is to be found in autobiographical or semi-autobiographical accounts (see Kurys's films up to *La Baule les Pins/C'est la vie*) in the context of mainland France and in the colonial context, as Susan Hayward (1992) emphasized (for example, with *Chocolat*, by C. Denis, *Outremer* by B. Rouan, or again, *Le bal du gouverneur* by M.F. Pisier). So the difference from the period before 1968 is that the 1980s and 1990s films tend to put the child at the centre of the story. In Serreau, not only does the child become a fundamental given fact, while it was non-existent (in terms of visibility) in *Pourquoi pas!*, but the domestic space (women's) takes pride of place. Furthermore, the community which was marginal in her first film gives way to bourgeois families, white and middle class. However, it is true that she introduces the idea of interracial relations, or 'inter-social' ones. From the Utopia of her beginnings, the director has moved to the *fable sociale* (moralizing tale) whose structure recalls that of the fairy tale as envisaged by Vladimir Propp – especially with *Romuald et Juliette*. In other terms, the demands have disappeared, making way for comedies more and more classical in form and appealing to wider audiences in content. Serreau's strongly idealized sexual community in *Pourquoi pas!* is much watered down in what came after it. From *Trois hommes et un couffin* to *La crise*, the director was to modify perceptibly the tone and tenor of her comedies. What is in crisis in *La crise* is the family, and no longer just the couple. In this (family) unit, the infant reigns supreme. It is no longer a question of constructing or reinventing the couple and the relationships within it, but of organizing life around the children. The wish to change the couple has gone. It is the cocooning, the making safe which carries no risk, which has taken place. The final statement of *La crise* is summarized in the last scene where the family unit is re-created by the mother's return to the home. Daddy, mummy, a boy, a girl – it is almost an advertising image of happiness for both family and individuals. Despite a few reminders of her past beliefs, Serreau presents happiness as if it inhered in the traditional family, seen as a closed space, where a certain reticence is predominant.

Numerous elements also suggest the absence (or the loss) of the director's original demands. Choosing to make comedies in the vaudeville style on the screen as well as on the stage,[18] Serreau chooses a conventional, bourgeois form of expression. This is also expressed in the choice of casting for *La crise*. In secondary rôles next to Maria Pacôme, the queen of light comedy and bourgeois vaudeville,[19] and Yves Robert (director of *La gloire de mon père* and *Le château de ma mère*, to cite only the most known and recent ones), we find Vincent Lindon, whose name is closely associated with the royal family of Monaco.[20]

Referring to the male actors in Serreau's films, Ginette Vincendeau emphasizes that 'they share striking physical similarities [and] they are perfect specimens of the average (bourgeois) Frenchman' (Vincendeau, 1994: 28). Returning to Bakhtin's distinction, we could almost speak here of the 'classical body'. The connection is all the more tempting in that Serreau introduces into *La crise* a 'low Other' in the person of the 'proletarian bum', a part taken, moreover, by the *café-théâtre* actor Patrick Timsit. He is the 'grotesque body' personified, whether in physical appearance or in the insistent reference to his bodily functions (eating, drinking, vomiting).

Even though Balasko has opted for a similar film genre, there are many points of difference between her and Serreau. Ignored by 'serious' criticism (her first films have not had much success with either critics or public),[21] with *Gazon maudit* she seems to have achieved in full measure the enviable position of a fully-fledged *auteur*, if the critics of *Cahiers du cinéma* are to be believed (Strauss, 1995: 60–3). Although her film was produced by TF1[22] (and Claude Berri), which *a priori* could have reduced its effectiveness and taken the edge off its bite, Balasko has succeeded with a comedy which has echoes of the finest days of the *café-théâtres*. Starting with a worn-out genre (vaudeville) she has managed to go beyond its narrow limits. It is no longer the husband, the wife and the lover, but the first two plus the wife's mistress. Balasko has in fact produced the first French lesbian comedy. She takes the part of Marijo, a lesbian on holiday, who, when she has a car breakdown, meets Loli, the Spanish wife of an estate agent who is a womanizer and a homophobe. An idyllic relationship develops between the two women, much to the despair of the betrayed husband, who falls from the frying pan into the fire when his wife, after having discovered the countless infidelities of her spouse, decides to install Marijo in the conjugal home (and the marital bed). (This is reminiscent of Faraldo's *Les Fleurs de Miel*, where in order to re-establish a balance, a wife forces onto her unfaithful husband not only the knowledge of her own infidelities, but that they took place in the conjugal home.) Taking pity on her husband's misery, Loli decides to set up a rota system, and so shares her nights between her husband and her mistress. After the more or less forced departure of the latter 'in exchange' for a sexual relation with the husband seen solely as 'inseminator', Loli and her husband find Marijo pregnant in Paris, where she is working as a disc jockey in a lesbian disco. (The scene is actually shot against the real background of the Privilège, a night club run by Elula Perrin, one of the few lesbians who have come out in France.) In the shock of meeting again so suddenly, Marijo begins to feel the first pangs of contractions. The final scenes show Marijo at Loli's with her child in a room where the biological father comes to kiss his daughter before going out to look at a house for his enlarged family, where he gets seduced by a handsome Spaniard who owns the place. The following shot shows Marijo and Loli in bed with the baby between them.

Besides Serreau, the points of reference in *Gazon maudit* are quite numerous. Some critics speak of *Jules et Jim*, of Feydeau and/or Bertrand Blier. A comparison with Blier could also establish a similar forthrightness of language (which is doubtless more pardonable in him than in her; this takes us back to carnival and to a form of transgression – here linguistic). About this she declares 'on m'accuse de vulgarité! C'est vrai que j'ai une présence provocatrice qui dérange'[23] (in Lejeune, 1987: 78). On the other hand, the diatribes delivered by male characters against women, which are customary in Blier (and most particularly here against lesbians), are expressed differently, not because it is a woman putting these words in the mouth of a man, but because Balasko makes it so repetitive in her male character that it is him that we laugh at and not the woman he is getting at. She remains faithful here to an intention affirmed since her first film, to break with certain tendencies: 'Ce que j'aime ... c'est prendre les clichés, les archétypes et les démolir'[24] (Lejeune, 1987: 78).

In addition to that, an element which reveals a lot in her way of turning things upside down is the casting. Balasko plays against Victoria Abril and Alain Chabat. The name of the first has been associated for several years with that of the Spanish filmmaker Almodóvar, which is not entirely chance. Her presence in the rôle of the abandoned wife and mother of a family beginning a love affair with a passing lesbian can also be explained by the difficulty in thinking of a French actress who could accept and carry the part. Balasko mentioned Simone Signoret at 40 years of age (!) (Pascal, 1995: 62). Even though the world conjured up by Almodóvar's films is even more outrageous than Balasko's, there remain none the less some perceptible connections between the two filmmakers.[25] Chabat's name – and this was his first major rôle in the cinema – is associated with the TV channel Canal+ in general, and with the *Nuls* programme in particular; which is to say, with a tone and a humour new, to say the least, in the somewhat amorphous French broadcasting scene. The disrespect and derision of the *Nuls* team is also reminiscent of the caustic tendencies of the Splendid and the Café de la Gare. In other words, the actors and actresses of the film already connote outrageous satire, and an influence very much of the 1970s.

As for the content of the film, Balasko does not avoid stereotypes altogether.[26] This can be explained by the chosen genre, comedy functioning principally with stereotypes and their exploitation. Her radical transformation of vaudeville, to put it mildly (and one critic dubbed it 'Feydeau on Lesbos'), is expressed at once in the casting, but also in the many changes of tone and situation in which she puts her characters. This is where we can come back to my opening comparison with *Pourquoi pas!* To some extent Balasko is miles away from Serreau's Utopia or Utopian realism. It is, however, true that a sexual relation is established between all the members of the trio (even though in the case of Marijo and the husband it is somewhat constrained and forced). The harmony of the house in the suburbs of *Pourquoi pas!* is missing from Loli's sunny house. It is not the shining city that Audé was speaking of with regard to Serreau's film. Balasko would instead use a sometimes jarring realism, where the male characters are somewhat overdone.

Where the film is more ambiguous is in the intervention of the conventional element that I was speaking of above: the baby. It would seem almost that 'lorsque l'enfant paraît' (when the child appears), to borrow the title from Laurence Pernoud's best seller, the obstacles become less distinct. In other words, one could easily believe that Balasko is erasing the differences by coming back to a vision of the woman as mother above all, whether she is gay or straight. The child (and thus both maternity and paternity) is seen as what brings people together. Now, the summaries offered by most of the critics omit mention of the ending, though the epilogue turns everything upside down. We might wonder how far this omission could only be justified by the wish to maintain the 'suspense'. The closing scenes of the film, where not only does the family unit get bigger, but the sexual identities are no longer as strictly defined as they were at the beginning, take *Gazon maudit* not only towards the Utopian tendency considered above, but also towards a Utopia which has been cross-bred with the radicalism of the *café-théâtres*, pulling no punches in its provocation.

Concluding this overview of the stage and film careers of Serreau and Balasko, the differences which distinguish the two are numerous. Summarizing rather crudely, we can emphasize Balasko's tendency to opt for satirical, provocative comedies with a jarring realism and an often black humour, in which a certain desire for subversion is expressed (even if done in a roundabout way in a commercial film). For Serreau's part, she chooses rather the comedy of manners and/or the moralizing tale, where most often the conventional humour aims at acceptance. Without doubt this last represents in its own way the end of Utopias and of the militancy of its beginnings, illustrated by her declaration where she refuses the label 'women's films': 'Je ne suis pas une femme qui fait du cinéma: je suis quelqu'un qui fait du cinéma.'[27] Balasko, despite the fact, as emphasized by Vincendeau, that she 'is by no means a conventional feminist (and has been ignored by feminist criticism and women's film festivals alike)' (Vincendeau, 1994: 26) seems by contrast to put into practice in her own way a feminist agenda which is visibly out of fashion. Elected 'patron' of Gay Pride in 1994, the director declared: 'Ce que je fais sur scène ou au cinéma c'est quelque chose, pour l'image de la femme, de beaucoup plus important que tous les discours'[28] which one critic translated by writing that the filmmaker 'aura plus fait pour élargir les esprits de nos contemporains que Monseigneur Gaillot et les féministes réunis'[29] (Riou, 1995: 58). In a very personal way she has also reappropriated the feminist demand from the 1970s for a 'right to dispose of one's own body', in using her own body in acting to transgress interdictions and taboos. In this perspective, and keeping Bakhtin's distinction in mind, we might wonder how far, besides the differences already mentioned, these two directors situate themselves at opposite ends of the 'body spectrum'. In fact, in Serreau's and Balasko's films, whether it is in the humour, in the choice, the use, the presentation of the body and the language, we find the polarities 'high/low', 'official/popular' and 'classical/grotesque'.

Notes

1. 'This *Gazon* ... is a sort of women's *Pourquoi pas!*, 15 years later.'
2. 'The use of the term "couple", when it is substituted for that of "marriage" (the institution) or of "household" (basic social unit, management of the home where the family develops), is already part of modernity as opposed to tradition.'
3. 'fickle and seductive little *bourgeoises*.'
4. 'a film about Utopia in which women would describe in very precise terms the society of their dreams.'
5. 'Subversions of the second type [and the] audacities of the new.'
6. 'giving more or less free rein to their imagination, realize their desire through representation. Their films anticipate the arrival of a world which, however, still has to be created. The "revolution" seems to be achieved in fiction, for want of being so in the objective world.'
7. Even though it is true, as Audé emphasized, that 'the issue [of this film] is the abolition of inherited roles' and that 'those who have been marginalized have nowadays won a certain right to existence' it is less certain (at least as far as Serreau is concerned) that 'difference is tolerated and sometimes demanded'.
8. The nearest English equivalent of the *café-théâtre* was (and is) the 'theatre work-

shop' [trans.]. See Chapter 8 for further exploration of the *café-théâtre* and its forms.

9. Serreau began in the theatre and *café-théâtre*, even playing in 1971 in a play by Coluche, *Thérèse est triste*. At the same time, Balasko was also working in *café-théâtre* with the same Coluche, M. Blanc and G. Jugnot.

10. Interestingly enough, Faraldo took comic actors from the Café de la Gare such as Miou-Miou, Coluche and Patrick Dewaere, and put them into his second film *Themroc*, made in 1973.

11. 'If the fashion was for feminism, the *café-théâtres* would present "feminine" plays ... The themes of the moment were women's liberation, denunciations of their "alienation", their pregnancies, their menstruations, their orgasms, abortion, birth control.'

12. The humour of Poiré's film *Les visiteurs* very much reflects this tendency.

13. If we stay with careers, the latter was one of the heroines of *L'une chante, l'autre pas* by Varda. Following this thread, we can see that this film was released at the same time as Blier's most misogynistic one (*Calmos*), that same Blier, according to Jill Forbes (1992) whose *Tenue de soirée* had been influenced by *Pourquoi pas!* and with whom Balasko was to work in *Trop belle pour toi*, and who was to find the title for *Gazon maudit*.

14. 'It was the first time that a girl took the star part without being gorgeous.'

15. 'active, energetic, coming out on top even in her failures. With men, she establishes relations of friendship or companionship ... she has a straightforward, healthy outlook. At 40, her sexuality is neither passive nor threatening.'

16. 'Women actors, personalities and women interesting for their contribution on a socio-political level have replaced the myth.'

17. 'The filmmaker refrains ... from sarcasm and caricature in the style of the *café-théâtres*.'

18. Serreau plays the main female rôle in a comedy (written by her) at the Théâtre de la Porte Saint-Martin, *Quisaitout et Grobêta*, still running in autumn 1995 and winner of four 'Molières' in 1994 (best comic play, best director for Beno Besson, best costume designer and best set designer). The play is described in the *Officiel des spectacles* as 'un conte moderne, une fable philosophique bizarre sur la quête fatale du bonheur éphémère d'aimer et d'être aimé' (a modern story, a bizarre philosophical fable on the fatal quest for fleeting happiness in loving and being loved).

19. This remains true even though in 1977 she also played in Dolores Grassian's 'feminist comedy' *Le dernier baiser* with Annie Girardot in the main part as a taxi driver.

20. To the point where in October 1995, a French weekly (wrongly) announced the marriage of the actor with Princess Caroline of Monaco.

21. When *Ma vie est en enfer* was released in 1991, she was reproached among other things for slipping into the scatological, which brings us back to the 'grotesque body' and the 'lower bodily stratum'.

22. The commercial channel belonging to the 'roi du béton' (the 'king of concrete', a leading industrialist in the construction industry), the late Francis Bouygues, whose reputation for seamy schedules and programmes of often dubious and scabrous taste no longer needs demonstration, did not hesitate to exploit the success of the comedy in a surprising way. Thus, on the evening of 22 June 1995,

it scheduled *95 plus, et alors?*, a programme presented by Régine, with invited participants Josiane Balasko, Victoria Abril, Alain Chabat and the *café-théâtre* comedienne Laurence Boccolini. The set chosen was that of the Kat-Privilège (with the 'Gaudian' columns recognizable to anyone who had seen the film, even if they had not actually been there). The theme suggested by the title ('95 plus, so what?') was of generous and well-endowed bosoms (95 cm = 37.5 in).

23. 'I am accused of vulgarity! It's true that I have something provocative about me which disturbs people.'
24. 'What I like ... is to take clichés and archetypes and demolish them.'
25. The choice of Miguel Bose as the handsome gay hidalgo can be read in the same light, as the Spanish actor played a male transvestite in Almodóvar's *High Heels*, where, impersonating the mother of the character played by Victoria Abril, he seduces and has sex with the latter.
26. It goes without saying that the film poses many questions relating to the sexual orientation of the characters and as such deserves a much more profound analysis than the outline given here.
27. 'I am not a woman making films: I am someone who makes films.'
28. 'What I do for the image of women on the stage or in film is something much more important than any speeches.'
29. She 'has done more to broaden the minds of our contemporaries than My Lord Bishop Gaillot and the feminists put together'. Gaillot became famous for his television appearances in which, for example, he advocated the use of condoms in the fight against AIDS, and for which he lost his bishopric.

References

Audé, F. (1981) *Ciné-modèles, cinéma d'elles*. Lausanne: L'âge de l'homme.

Audé, F. (1983) 'Métamorphoses du couple et glissements progressifs vers l'utopie?', *CinémAction* 25: 80–9.

Audé, F. (1985) 'Hommes d'intérieur', *Positif* 297 (Nov.): 70–1.

Bakhtin, M. (1968) translated by H. Iswolsky, *Rabelais and His World*. Baltimore and London: MIT Press.

Beylie, C. (1987) 'Le couffin et les moyens (réflexions sur un succès)', *Avant-scène Cinéma* 356 (Jan.): 89–91.

Chevallier, J. (1983) 'Révoltes tous azimuths pour vivre autrement', *CinémAction* 25: 30–42.

Da Costa, B. (1978) *Histoire du Café-Théâtre*. Paris: Buchet-Chastel.

Forbes, J. (1992) *The Cinema in France: After the New Wave*. London: Macmillan/BFI.

Hayward, S. (1992) 'Women filmmakers in the 1980s: now you see them, but then you don't'. Unpublished paper given at the University of Birmingham.

Jeancolas, J.-P. (1979) *Le cinéma des Français. La Vème République*. Paris: Stock Cinéma.

Lavoignat, J.P. (1995) Review of *Gazon Maudit, Studio* (Feb.): 31–3.

Lejeune, P. (1987) *Le cinéma des femmes*. Paris: Atlas Lherminier.

Martineau, M. and Hennebelle, G. (1979) 'Des étoiles de pacotille ou les stars en douze stéréotypes', *CinémAction* 9: 18–19.

Pascal, M. (1995) 'Feydeau à Lesbos', *Le Point* 1168 (Feb.): 62.

Riou, A. (1995) 'Lesbos People', *Le Nouvel Observateur* 1578 (Feb.): 58.

Serceau, D. (1983) 'Du messianisme prolétarien à la transformation des consciences', *CinémAction* 25: 118–29.

Stam, R. (1989) *Subversive Pleasure: Bakhtin, Cultural Criticism and Film*. Baltimore and London: Johns Hopkins University Press.

Strauss, F. (1995) 'L'Empire des sens' (followed by an interview with Balasko), *Les Cahiers du cinéma* 489 (March): 60–3.

Vincendeau, G. (1994) 'Coline Serreau. A high wire act', *Sight and Sound* (March): 26–8.

8.

The people's filmmaker? Théâtre populaire[1] *and the films of Bertrand Blier*

SUE HARRIS

Although Bertrand Blier's work has included a few flops, most notably *Calmos* (1976) and *Notre histoire* (1984), the extent of his success in France is in little doubt: *Les Valseuses* was the third most popular film in terms of box office receipts in 1974, *Tenue de soirée* was the sixth most popular film of 1986 (beaten only in terms of French production by the hugely successful nostalgia vehicles *Jean de Florette* and *Manon des Sources*), *Merci la vie* was the fifth most successful French film of 1991, behind a string of popular French comedies, and *Trop belle pour toi* was the biggest grossing French film of 1989, not seriously rivalled by any other French film that year.[2] This commercial success has been matched by peer recognition, with Césars awarded for *Buffet froid*, *Tenue de soirée* and *Trop belle pour toi*, and the Oscar for best foreign film awarded to *Préparez vos mouchoirs* in 1979. Nevertheless, in critical and academic circles, Blier tends to be one of the least well regarded of contemporary French filmmakers, his work being frequently denigrated for its 'bad taste', 'triviality' or 'lack of seriousness'. Critical reaction has inevitably focused on the more sensationalist elements of his work, notably verbal vulgarity, nudity, uninhibited sexuality and non-standard language, elements which have indeed made Blier a difficult director to reconcile with a conventional, aesthetically valuable reading. Although individual films in the Blier canon have lent themselves to useful analysis, reconciling Blier's evident popularity with these distinctive referential elements of his work across the corpus remains problematic to critics and scholars. Indeed, attempts to account for the popularity of films like *Les Valseuses* have produced interesting results, with one reviewer in *Écran* suggesting that 'le succès du film classe aussi son public'.[3]

There is, then, a sense of artistic inferiority linked to Blier's work, and a tendency to view his methods and products as populist, rather than popular: he is seen as using certain 'shock tactics' to incite curiosity and notoriety, and his popularity is all too often perceived as some sort of by-product of this. Furthermore, the recurrence of certain 'tasteless' elements has frequently been seen as evidence of Blier's embracing of a politically and morally unsound discourse, most generally misogyny. He is indeed a difficult director to categorize: he is difficult to situate in what one critic has termed 'a moral, social, political and aesthetic context' (King, 1993: 100), easier, one might argue, to ignore than to explore. But given his genuine popularity in France, it has become increasingly difficult to continue to ignore Blier's presence in contemporary French cinema simply on the grounds that his work is in some way distasteful or politically 'incorrect'. It is therefore the aim of this chapter to reconsider both the presence and the function of some of the more controversial elements in Blier's work. I shall argue that Blier's work is innovative in that it reflects an understanding of the language of popular theatre, and that his work can in this respect profitably be related to that of the major mainstream and alternative theatre groups which came to prominence in Paris in the 1960s, the period when Blier first began working in film.

Precedents for Blier's dramatic style

Blier's engagement with a popular dramatic style encompasses a wide approach to the question of traditional popular spectacle. What we find in his work is a synthesis of a number of trends in alternative theatre of the type exemplified by *café-théâtre*,[4] as well as those in mainstream *théâtre populaire*, and its interpretation of the dramatic forms and theories associated with 'pre-cultural' arts such as carnival, explored formally within the modern French theatrical genre of *création collective*.[5] His dramatic style coincides with that of the major theatre innovators of the 1960s and 1970s, especially Ariane Mnouchkine and the Théâtre du Soleil, Jérôme Savary and Le Grand Magic Circus, and Roger Planchon. The Brechtian dramatic conception of these groups dominated stage and performance theory in France throughout the 1970s, the period of production of Blier's *Les Valseuses* (1974), *Préparez vos mouchoirs* (1978) and *Buffet froid* (1979); their central tenet was the 'récupération critique de la dite sous-culture, considérée au regard des *normes* culturelles, comme négligeable, "vulgaire", "pauvre", etc. (et alors occultée tout naturellement)'[6] (Demarcy, 1973: 312), and their work, from the 1960s onwards, was a reaction to the tradition of denigrating certain types of dramatic forms as culturally inferior. It also responded to the failure of cultural decentralization to create a vibrant and relevant popular theatre in France. Jérôme Savary's reaction to the establishment culture was more artistically provocative than most of his contemporaries: he 'took the logical attitude that if the failure of the decentralization movement lay in having played the game of the establishment, by making the working class swallow bourgeois "high culture", then "high culture" must be fought with the weapons of "low culture"' (Bradby, 1991: 222). This, for Savary, involved a redefinition of the elements of 'low culture' and the employment of various techniques, including the 'deliberate mobilisation of bad taste, nudity and other things calculated to shock middle class art lovers' (Bradby, 1991: 222). His largely semiotic 'Total' theatre was deliberately carnivalesque in its chaotic narrative structure, dominant celebratory tone, and in the sense of *fête* (celebration, festivity) which informed both the action and the production of his performances.

Although they embraced wide ranging and varied dramatic forms within their individual performances, what linked these groups stylistically was 'un jeu particulièrement gestuel, la relation souvent direct au public ... des formes théâtrales étrangères (étranges) donc bien souvent transgressives par rapport à notre culture'[7] (Demarcy, 1973: 314). The re-emergence in modern theatre of a performance style incorporating elements of song, dance, acrobatics and clowning, resulted in the creation of new forms of episodic spectacle, lacking in points of easy identification, but inherently popular in the language of its production. Although this responded to the groups' aim of 'la *subversion* de notre acculturation'[8] (Demarcy, 1973: 317), as in Blier's work, this very much constituted a return to existing devalued popular narrative forms.

In his treatment of the central issue of taste, and in his deliberate problematizing of the nature of judgements, discernment, manners and social and aesthetic conventions, Blier's dramatic conception shows affinities with wider avant-garde theatre, popular and otherwise. The aggressive attitude towards the public, traditions and artistic conventions that we find in Blier's films is also common to the theatre of the absurd (Jacquard, 1974: 52). Jacquard tells us that:

l'avant-garde se définit 1) par sa volonté '*d'opposition et de rupture*' totale, c'est-à-dire par une attitude révolutionnaire contre les traditions reconnues, et 2) par sa révolte contre le bon goût et les bienséances, par son *agressivité contre le grand public* à l'égard duquel elle prend ses distances, au point de le mépriser ou de chercher à l'offenser.[9]

(Jacquard, 1974: 42)

Thus, Blier can also be seen as working within the dramatic tradition of Antoine, Jarry, Beckett, Ionesco and Adamov where an integral part of the redefinition of the dramatic lies in an attitude of aggression towards the audience and the audience's expectations. A rejection of realism and narrative causality are equally fundamental to the form, and there again we see the direct influence of this dramatic genre on Blier's work. As he himself states: 'Il y a quand même une démarche chez moi. Elle consiste à faire des films qui obligent les gens à réfléchir. Je cherche à perturber. J'ai envie de tirer un peu le tapis sous les pieds des gens'[10] (Halberstadt and Moriconi, 1986: 174). His concerted attack on aspects of taste and on cultural icons responds to this. But interestingly, while this has been generally accepted as a contribution to the wider cultural debate in the domain of experimental theatre, these same elements have been criticized in Blier's work.

Blier's dramatic style, however, is most obviously based on the comic mechanisms and theatrical informality of the Parisian *café-théâtre*, and his contribution to bringing to public prominence individual actors and a particular dramatic style associated with *café-théâtre* is now well documented.[11] His association with, and exploitation of, the unambiguously popular performance style which defined this Parisian movement from the late 1960s on into the early 1980s, signals a familiarity with a particular dramatic form emerging directly from *le peuple*. The *café-théâtre* was the training ground for a new generation of actors unschooled in the traditions of the *Conservatoire*, and the distinctive style which they pioneered drew greatly on the amateur nature of their dramatic conception;[12] this resulted in an extremely energetic, spontaneous and largely improvised style, inherently simple insofar as it depended heavily on the verbal and physical qualities of its actors.[13] This theatrical movement had its antecedents in *commedia dell'arte*, music hall, cabaret and *café concert*, all of which similarly expressed the popular consciousness via essentially dramatic forms and, as is the case for these other forms, the *café-théâtre* was in many ways a modern manifestation of the same popular theatrical phenomenon which has its roots in the expression of the carnival.

The active and visual dimensions of traditional carnival give rise to a distinctive system of images and references which function as structuring motifs in Blier's work. Principal features of this are (i) the assertion of masculinity and male sexuality via excessive sexual and physical behaviour; (ii) the use of coarse or vulgar language; (iii) subversive comment, of both an official and a personal nature; (iv) role reversal, and 'nivellement des individus' (equalizing of individuals) (Faure, 1978: 89) apparent in the appropriation of disguise. Blier's dramatic techniques are rooted in the same expression of the common experience of this particularly dramatic art which expresses little sense of the individual, or of individual psychology, and concentrates instead on the holistic nature of the community experience. Its purpose, as an allegorical dramatic form, is to identify the transgressive individual, with a view to reintegrating that individual positively back into the wider society, and, in the carnival, this is carried out by *le peuple* (the common people) in a dramatic environment free from the constraints of cultural aesthetics.

Blier's use of language, character, parody and 'festive' action all combine to create an effect of an overwhelming sense of play. This ludic dimension to his work, and the intense focus on comic types and formulas, associate him very clearly with what Bakhtin terms the 'one culture of folk carnival humor' (Bakhtin, 1984: 4), and even more closely with Bakhtin's allied concept of grotesque realism. Blier works not within the Romantic grotesque tradition that inspires fear, menace or alienation as might seem the case during the opening scenes of almost all of his films, particularly *Les Valseuses, Tenue de soirée, Buffet froid* and *Merci la vie*, but within an unambiguously medieval carnivalesque grotesque tradition where 'all that was frightening in ordinary life is turned into amusing or ludicrous monstrosities' (Bakhtin, 1984: 47). In *Les Valseuses*, a range of dramatic techniques are employed to show the two thugs (Gérard Depardieu/Jean-Claude and Partick Dewaere/ Pierrot), obsessively concerned with their virility, being made to look ineffectual and ridiculous. The *mise-en-scène* of the scenes towards the end of the film, in which the two characters are seen to resemble each other in dress and by a series of parallel actions, conveys a degree of strangeness and a grotesqueness of appearance and behaviour. The expression of their incomprehension at Marie-Ange's (Miou-Miou) achievement of sexual climax depends entirely on the foregrounding of the ludic dramatic elements of the *mise-en-scène*, and this scene effectively underlines the importance of the physical dimension in creating a comic impact in this film.

The carnivalesque grotesque typically shows two contradictory aspects of life simultaneously, and this reading lends a further level of interest to Blier's use of the male duo as seen across the corpus of his work. The traditional symbolic coupling of life and death, youth and age, male and female, all related to the principle of renewal and renascence, is echoed in Blier's films in the dramatic pairing of characters who are perceived to have opposing, and to some extent mutually exclusive, dominant characteristics. In *Les Valseuses*, the male and the female are contrasted and explored in the male characters, the flamboyant and the timid are the focus of *Tenue de soirée*, law and criminality in *Buffet froid*, and the beautiful and the plain are the object of the exploration of the women in *Trop belle pour toi*. The physical grotesque is further highlighted in *Tenue de soirée*, where the subdued transvestism of Antoine (Michel Blanc) in the dance hall is translated into an explicit grotesque parody which is neither wholly male nor wholly female, but a combination of elements of both.[14] Yet there is frequently a progression involving these characters which results in not only a narrative *rapprochement*, but also a dramatic one. As is clearly the case in *Les Valseuses*, the two male characters are gradually perceived to grow closer until they seem to be more two parts of one whole, indissociable, than two individual beings. The same effect is gained in *Préparez vos mouchoirs* where, although the male characters are not so obviously different in their construction, they are contrasted as opposites in their attitude to a given situation. What emerges in these two films is a certain grotesque quality to the comic paralleling of their actions. Duality of this kind is a fundamental concept of the bodily system of images of popular culture as identified by Bakhtin, and in Blier's work the extension of the concept to a dramatic synchronization of male behaviour intensifies the carnivalesque expression of community experience: there is little sense of an individualized image.

Blier's characters

Blier's characters, particularly those incarnated by Depardieu and Dewaere across a range of films, and latterly by Anouk Grinberg, are deliberately disturbing and somewhat grotesque both in physical and psychological nature. As such they frequently resemble the clowns or fools of the carnival, as well as those created by Beckett and Ionesco.[15] The very careful choreography of the actions of two or more characters in the frame is evidence to the spectator of the strangeness and grotesqueness of these characters, of their difference and distance from their society and environment: they are misfits, theatrical constructs whose movement is not naturalistic, and whose actions have relevance primarily as dramatic events. The grotesque focus on the physical dimension of the characters' bodies is forcefully apparent in *Les Valseuses* and *Tenue de soirée*, and is signalled from the outset in *Un deux trois soleil*, where the Swiftian concentration on the magnified mouth of Victorine sets in motion a series of narrative moments with an intense physical focus. This kind of physical grotesqueness is, of course, a recurrent feature of popular imagery, from *images d'Épinal* to *bande dessinée*,[16] through the comic films of Chaplin, Tati *et al.*, and Blier's treatment of it, therefore, recalls a specifically popular iconographic system of reference.

The patterns of characterization which can be noted in Blier's films show affinities with the *commedia dell'arte* style, where character is generally identified by costume or a recognizable mask, indicative of a particular 'type' of character. The physical dimension of the performance is what then adds complexity and consequently dramatic interest to the already familiar. The *commedia dell'arte* exploited formulaic narrative structures and character types, creating a series of *types populaires*, most commonly *le vieillard* (the old man), *le valet* (the servant), *les amoureux sots* (the foolish lovers) and *les savants ridicules* (the foolish pedants). These figures are of course familiar to French dramatic culture through the plays of Molière. All of these types resonate in Blier's films, but the most striking dramatic parallel is in the character of the *zanni*, or *valets* in French, recurrent male comic characters who were often found in pairs, one led by the other, one handsome, one ugly. These were the *rusé* (cunning) or *débrouillard* (resourceful) characters in the plays, with a range of mutual defining characteristics such as egotism, stupidity, vulgarity, wickedness, the same qualities incarnated by Depardieu and Dewaere who are, in Blier's films, to a great extent direct descendants of the traditional dramatic pairing of Polichinelle and Pedrolino. Depardieu and Dewaere as Jean-Claude and Pierrot, or again as Raoul and Stéphane in *Préparez vos mouchoirs*, express the same sense of the ridiculous in themselves and in how others function around them. In *Les Valseuses* and *Préparez vos mouchoirs*, as in traditional popular drama, these traits are most in evidence, and are most dramatically impressive when the characters are together, and their action, verbal and gestural, is co-ordinated.

Characterization generally in Blier's work, as in *café-théâtre* and *commedia dell'arte*, tends towards being schematic or one-dimensional, with characters functioning largely as representative of certain dramatic or social types. The traits of individual characters, peripheral as well as central, are frequently exaggerated to the point of caricature, a device which is used to considerable effect in films as diverse as *Trop belle pour toi* (Florence's beauty) and *Préparez vos mouchoirs* (Solange's passivity). Characteristically, there are defined parameters to roles, with the essential of character behaviour consistent with conventional spectatorial expectations: in *Notre histoire*, the characters identify themselves as the Drunk and the Nymphomaniac; in *Buffet froid*, they are respectively *L'Assassin* (the murderer), *le Chef de police* (the Chief of Police), *le Cambrioleur* (the burglar), and *la Veuve* (the widow); Rémi in *Beau-Père* refers to himself as the pianist, bringing a self-conscious commentary to the action, and there are recurrent examples of references to self in the third person in *Trop belle pour toi*, *Merci la vie* and *Un deux trois soleil*. The actual names of the characters are of secondary importance: what they do in the films counts for more than who they are as individuals. The assigning of roles in this way is at odds with realist conventions, but is common to the popular theatrical experience outlined above, which deals in fixed or recurrent characterization and a parodic style dependent on the exploration of stereotype and popular expectation.

The body

Blier's intense focus on a system of images of the body further links him with traditional popular dramatic forms. He focuses on three major dramatic aspects related to the body: the build or physical comportment of the individual characters, the body in movement or gesturing, and the body in relation to others, all three factors allowing for a certain choreography of movement for dramatic effect. The narrative and stylistic economy of *Les Valseuses* draws heavily on these features. In a scene reminiscent of the circus clowns and their traditional exploding car, the focus falls on the physical action of the characters in relation to each other: Jean-Claude's verbal outburst and active attempt to deal with the problem with the car's engine are comically contrasted by the positioning and relative inaction of Marie-Ange and Pierrot, who do not budge from their kissing pose in the back of the car. The following scene, in which the three characters try to hitch a lift, exemplifies the expressive use of the body in gesture: in a theatrical set piece, the characters' qualities of failure, insolence and daring are intensified in the stylized nature of their gesturing, and in the way in which they sit or lie. The physical type of each character adds to this: the menacing frame of Depardieu, the carelessness and lack of inhibition of Miou-Miou and the comic cheek – facial and physical – of Dewaere are necessarily perceived as a continuum, expressing *ennui* and contempt for their situation. In this scene the proximity and visual realism of actual cars going past is irrelevant; the essence of the scene is contained in the dramatic mechanisms.

There is, in Blier's work, a carnivalesque concentration on the bodily functions, and a Rabelaisian approach to matters of sexual activity, consumption of food and the general physical nature of the body. In *Préparez vos mouchoirs* the focus is on the fertility of the principal female character and the efforts of the males to impregnate her. The desire for sexual consummation is the driving force of *Tenue de soirée*, and *Les Valseuses* concentrates at various points on the physical action of the body related to breast feeding, genital odour and bathing. These are deliberately shocking elements within a system of judgement by late twentieth-century aesthetic standards. However, as Bakhtin points out, scatological preoccupations of this kind with the 'lower bodily stratum' are characteristic of folk humour, and can be situated without controversy in the long established 'concept of grotesque realism' where 'the bodily element is deeply positive' (Bakhtin, 1984: 18–19). The central image of bathing and washing in *Les Valseuses*, which confirms the intimacy of the relationship of the two men, is a carnivalesque gesture which exposes the private dimension of the body, but does so in a typically unselfconscious manner. The nudity of this film has led to comparisons with pornographic films of the kind exemplified by *Emmanuelle*, the biggest grossing French film in 1974 ahead of *Les Valseuses*. However, it is the de-eroticizing of the nude body and the focus on nudity as a natural condition of being, rather than as a condition of attraction, that makes Blier's film more than simply a sex film in the recognized genre. Furthermore, it can be argued that Blier explores and exposes the moral and aesthetic taboos associated with women's physical nature by concentrating on rather banal commonplaces of male sexual fantasy (women's breasts, multiple or willing sexual partners, sex with strangers), whilst refusing the eroticism with which these images have traditionally been invested. As such, he reasserts the intellectual and creative value of the image of the body, essential to and unproblematic within the carnival tradition.

Carnivalesque visual and verbal expression

Blier's subject matter and recurrent images can therefore be read as consistent with those of carnival and its characteristic reduction of the spiritual and the abstract to a material level. Much of the shock value of these images and expressions is derived from the public expression of what is usually relegated to an unspoken level, and this is true with regard both to content in Blier's films, and to its visibility in the medium of mainstream cinema: elements of the visual and verbal expression we find in Blier's early work are disconcerting precisely because they frequently seem more immediately appropriate to pornography and broad comic farce than to *auteur* cinema.[17] The *café-théâtre*, of course, was initially a 'back street' activity, whose content was often *risqué* or subversively satirical in a way that invited censorship: the police are known to have infiltrated *café-théâtres*, and the subversive magazines *Hara-Kiri* and *Charlie Hebdo* were frequently censored. This question of the 'unspoken' or 'unspeakable' dimension brings us back to the question of the common, that is to say the public, experience as related to carnival: in Blier's work there is little place for privacy or the private experience, as this necessarily denies the social aspect of the collective. What Blier develops here is the thesis underlying the narrative of his first film *Hitler, connais pas!*, which demonstrated that cinema, as an expressive medium, is fundamentally unsuited to recording private experience; there is always a spectator, an observer, an outsider who disturbs the privacy of the intimate moment. Blier's adoption of the dramatic grotesque in his subsequent films develops this exploration of the limitations of cinema, highlighting its popular purpose, consistent with that of Brechtian theatre, as a vehicle of mediation rather than truth, as a medium that is 'popular' in that it sets out to acknowledge, rather than deceive, its public.

Blier's clear focus on aspects of life pertinent to the modern social experience, within a framework of carnivalesque observation and commentary acknowledges a fundamental function of the *fête*: 'il est naturel de retrouver au cœur de la fête ce qui était au fond de tous les bouleversements du moment: la remise en cause des inégalités, la contestation de l'ordre social'[18] (Faure, 1978: 90). This associates his work on a further level with the agitprop aims of modern Brechtian theatre. The sense of revival and renewal which Blier's work dramatizes, and the reversal of the rules of social logic and order which the characters express, and by which they function, are central tenets of the symbolic, festive, theatrical carnival. Furthermore, the system of images of the carnival employed by Blier in his highlighting and criticism of specific social phenomena engages fully with a further political dimension of the festival, where the carnival rites are not 'gratuits' (gratuitous) but are in fact indissociable from 'les gestes de la révolte' (the gestures of rebellion) (Faure, 1978: 97).

The presence of the carnival then, in Blier's work, must inevitably be read as an expression of the same 'insubordination populaire' (popular insubordination) (Faure, 1978: 95) of traditional carnivals, and Blier's use of it as a modern structuring motif has, therefore, an unambiguously popular function. His apparently 'revolutionary' approach to aesthetic filmmaking, dialogue and characterization results in the same kind of 'expression spectaculaire des passions populaires' (spectacular expression of popular passions) manifested by the traditional carnival, and recaptured in the productions of theatre groups such as the Théâtre du Soleil.

Conclusion

The popular dimension in Blier's work is then stylistically, theoretically, and to some extent politically consistent with a specifically theatrical concept. In its appropriation of the forms specific to non-cultural (that is non-*high* cultural) theatre, Blier's work can be ideologically and culturally identified: his tendency towards an imitative and demonstrative, rather than a mimetic or realist art, and the concern to highlight external action rather than introspective psychology, defines the aesthetic context of his films. These profoundly Brechtian principles point to Blier's work as an example of a related exercise in the modern theatrical endeavour to combine political and social comment with entertaining spectacle by means of a recuperation of the forms, techniques and structures of the popular dramatic arts. It is my contention that an analysis based on the theatrical origins of Blier's style is one way into a new reading of a filmmaker who has too frequently been dismissed as unworthy of serious critical attention. A rereading of Blier's films along these lines suggests that far from being simply a series of misanthropic challenges, motivated by a need on the part of the director to 'épater les bourgeois' (shock the middle classes) and nothing more, Blier's work is in fact informed by a self-conscious awareness of popular dramatic forms. This very sound intellectual and creative basis of his work is something that has not yet been acknowledged adequately. The subversion of narrative codes and dramatic elements explored by Blier in his films, as by the theatre groups discussed here, fundamentally associates him with historically marginalized, but nevertheless culturally vibrant, traditional dramatic forms. The defence of these elements in Blier's work and his refusal to impose a notion of culture on film, link him directly to approaches and theories in modern French *théâtre populaire*, and the exploration of the language and forms of this tradition is evidence that Blier, contrary to 'popular' perception, is indeed a serious and well-informed *auteur*.

Notes

1. *Théâtre populaire* is politically motivated theatre, informed by a desire to demystify the perceived bourgeois structures and élitist appeal of theatre, and thereby encourage wider cross-class access to this form of entertainment. This vision of theatre as a 'public service' resulted in the creation in 1951 of the state-subsidized Théâtre National Populaire under the direction of Jean Vilar.
2. Figures are taken from *Le Film français* for relevant years.
3. 'The film's success also reveals a great deal about its viewers.' Quoted in additional comments to a review of *Les Valseuses* by Jean Domarchi (1974: 67).
4. *Café-théâtre* is largely improvised theatre with a topical, satirical emphasis which became popular in Paris in the 1960s and 1970s. This took place first in cafés and other *ad hoc* theatre venues, and later in dedicated theatres. See p. 117 for a fuller explanation of this term, and see Chapter 7.
5. *Création collective* is the principle of democratic collaboration in all aspects of theatre (authorship, performance, production, management) of the type pioneered by groups like Le Théâtre du Soleil.
6. The 'critical rehabilitation of the said subculture, considered with regard to cultural *norms* as unimportant, "vulgar", "poor", etc. (and thus naturally eclipsed)'.
7. 'A particularly gestural performance, often direct contact with the audience ... unfamiliar (strange) theatrical forms, which frequently transgress the norms of our culture.'
8. 'The *subversion* of our acculturation.'
9. 'The avant-garde is defined (1) by its desire for *complete "opposition and rupture"*, that is to say by its revolutionary attitude towards established traditions, and (2) by its rebellion against good taste and propriety, by its *aggression towards the public*, from which it endeavours to distance itself, to the point of scorning or trying to offend it.'
10. 'I do actually have a particular approach, which consists in making films that force people to think. I try to unsettle people. I want to pull the rug from under their feet.'
11. See Forbes (1992: ch. 7); Vincendeau (1993); and Merle (1985).
12. For confirmation of the popular reception of this style we need only look at the parallel examples of the work of Jugnot, Balasko, Blanc, Clavier, Coluche, all of whom have known considerable commercial success. See Chapter 7.
13. See Forbes (1992) for a discussion of this style.
14. In this scene, Blanc is bald, wears make up and is dressed in female attire; Depardieu wears a woman's wig whilst dressed as a man. See also the poster of *Trop belle pour toi* in which there are childish pencil markings of 'ugliness' over the face of Josiane Balasko. Her portrayal as a 'grotesque' character in the film is, however, unconvincing.
15. Martin Esslin highlights the interesting relationship between contemporary grotesque incarnations such as those of Beckett's theatre and the *commedia dell'arte* (Esslin, 1972).
16. See Chapter 6.
17. These elements are possibly less disconcerting in Blier's later films, where the collision of visual elements and genres reflects more general mainstream filmic trends.

18. 'It is natural to find at the heart of festival what was at the heart of all social upheaval of the time: the calling into question of inequalities, the challenging of the social order.'

References

Bakhtin, M. (1984) *Rabelais and His World*, translated by Hélène Iswolsky. Bloomington: Indiana University Press.

Bradby, D. (1991) *Modern French Drama 1940–1990*. Cambridge: CUP.

Demarcy, R. (1973) *Eléments d'une sociologie du spectacle*. Paris: UGE.

Domarchi, J. (1974) ' "Les Valseuses" ', *Écran* 25 (May): 65–7.

Esslin, M. (1972) *The Theatre of the Absurd*. London: Penguin.

Faure, A. (1978) *Paris Carème-prenant: du carnaval à Paris au XIXe siècle 1800–1914*. Paris: Hachette.

Forbes, J. (1992) *The Cinema in France: After the New Wave*. London: McMillan/BFI.

Halberstadt, M. and Moriconi, M. (1986) 'Le perturbateur tranquille', *Première* 109 (April): 78–9; 171–4 (interview with Blier).

Jacquard, E. (1974) *Le Théâtre de la dérision*. Paris: Gallimard.

King, R.S. (1993) 'Help yourselves at Bertrand Blier's *Buffet Froid*', *Nottingham French Studies* 32(1) (spring): 99–108.

Merle, P. (1985) *Le café-théâtre*. Paris: PUF [Que sais-je? 2260].

Vincendeau, G. (1993) 'Gérard Depardieu: the axiom of contemporary French cinema', *Screen* 34(4) (winter): 343–61.

9.

Television, ethnic minorities and mass culture in France

JOANNA J. HELCKÉ[1]

Television is today by far the most powerful means of communication. Every day, millions of people sit down to watch television, and this is a moment when different people are brought together as they sit, watching and experiencing the same programmes. This concept of television as a cohesive force within society, binding people from different social, cultural and ethnic backgrounds through a common viewing experience, is certainly very attractive to those working towards the creation of a less exclusive and more harmonious society. It follows, therefore, that in a country such as France, with a large and diverse minority ethnic population, a population that has become the stimulus for an ever more politicized and heated debate, public bodies such as the Fonds d'Action Sociale (FAS), which work towards the integration of these minority groups, share this interest in the possible role of television as a means of aiding and encouraging mutual understanding. Thus, the FAS has had an active policy towards the audio-visual industry since the mid-1970s. Surprisingly, however, no academic research has been undertaken into the ways in which France's ethnically disparate population watches and interprets television messages, and so, many questions remain unanswered.[2] Do all viewers inevitably understand programmes in the ways intended by the producers? If so, can television help to cement society together by creating a common perception among viewers of different ethnic origins? Or, on the other hand, are people shaped by their social and cultural environment to such an extent that they construct their own meanings of television programmes, meanings not necessarily anticipated by the producers? It is these issues that will be discussed here, using the preliminary results from a body of interview work that was carried out in France amongst three population groups: 'native' French people (understood in the present context as those whose parents and grandparents are French), those of North African origin and those originating from Black Africa. The first step will be to give a brief outline of the FAS's policy concerning television and minority ethnic groups. This will be followed by an analysis of the FAS-financed programme used as a stimulus for the interview work. Finally, and most importantly, the results of the interviews will be analysed and some preliminary conclusions will be drawn.

The FAS: 20 years of audiovisual policy

The FAS is a public agency that was set up in 1958 to assist immigrant workers (and later their families) within French society, but it was not until 1975 that it started to turn its attention towards the possibilities that television opened up for facilitating this task. In these early days when immigrants rarely, if ever, graced the small screen, the FAS undertook to finance programmes that catered specifically for the immigrant community, and the best known of these programmes was *Mosaïque*. However, as the immigrant community became settled, the character of this population gradually changed, and so the FAS decided that its audiovisual policy would have to be modified accordingly. Thus, in the early 1980s, *Mosaïque* was reoriented towards a younger, second-generation audience, and simultaneously the FAS began to put an increasing amount of money into mainstream programmes aimed at sensitizing the general public.

The beginning of the 1990s marked the start of a new era of FAS audiovisual policy. After lengthy discussions with journalists, programme producers and television channel officials, the FAS decided that it would now endeavour to address two main audiences: first-generation immigrants so as to facilitate the process of their integration into French society, and the general public in an attempt to sensitize them to the ethnic minority presence in France. This would be achieved through the financing of three types of programme. Firstly, the FAS would continue to finance public-service programmes targeted primarily at the first-generation immigrant population. Secondly, the FAS would increase its expenditure on two types of mainstream programme aimed at sensitizing the general public: one-off documentaries and films, and television series.[3] It is the FAS's most recent series, *Fruits et Légumes*, a 26-part sitcom focusing on a family of North African origin, that was used as a basis for the interviews conducted. The next part of this chapter will examine the making of *Fruits et Légumes*, highlighting the extent to which the various production partners, in particular the FAS, influenced the end-product.

Fruits et Légumes: from script to screen and beyond

The initial idea that eventually developed into the series *Fruits et Légumes* sprang from the success of the 1990 summer soap opera *Sixième Gauche*, which was jointly written by Henri de Turenne and Akli Tadjer, and was produced by Cinétévé, co-financed by the FAS and broadcast by France 3. However, it took three years of fraught negotiating before the four partners finally agreed on the overall structure of the series, and it was not until 1993 that production work was started on *Fruits et Légumes*. Thus began a fragile, four-way partnership, in which competing objectives became apparent as soon as the authors presented the 'Bible'[4] for the sitcom. Whilst the authors, Cinétévé and France 3 were striving to create a series that would be commercially successful, the FAS was aiming to produce a programme that would encourage the French public to identify with an immigrant family, two objectives that are not necessarily compatible. Thus, the FAS found numerous aspects of the 'Bible' unacceptable, and alterations had to be made, as France 3 and Cinétévé were heavily dependent on the FAS for financial assistance. For example, the FAS insisted that it was essential for the sitcom to incorporate a substantial 'native' French presence representing the host community, as 'l'intégration est un processus dont les acteurs sont autant les immigrés que les "gaulois"' ('integration is a process whereby "native" French are as much actors as are immigrants') (letter from the FAS to Cinétévé, 7 Oct. 1993). Accordingly, therefore, a relatively important 'native' French character was introduced. On the whole, however, the changes made were kept to a bare minimum, just enough to appease the FAS.

When they moved on from the 'Bible' and started work on the scripts, these too proved contentious. As a result of heavy criticism by the FAS many alterations had to be made. The most dramatic example of this was the case of one particular episode, *La Perle de Tipaza*, which had to be completely abandoned because the FAS felt that 'it was not possible to treat such a subject' (letter from the FAS to Cinétévé, 17 March 1994), the subject being marriages of convenience. In the FAS's opinion, such an episode would distance French viewers as they would be unable to relate to a situation of this nature, and more importantly, marriages of convenience are illegal in France. This is a clear example of the FAS's tendency to avoid all that is controversial, thus maintaining a rosy harmonious atmosphere throughout the series, in the hopes that this would provide a reassuring image of immigration to the average French viewer.

Despite the many changes made to meet the FAS's requirements, commercial interests were such that a number of the FAS's wishes were not really addressed. For example, the FAS had hoped that each episode would be based on a real-life situation, such as intergenerational conflict, or relations between the immigrant community and the host population. In this way, the viewer would be directly exposed to the process of integration. However, the other partners felt that the sitcom genre was not really adapted to dealing with such issues. When I looked at the end-product, it became clear that the great majority of episodes revolve around situations that are entirely unrelated to the family's ethnicity, and that could occur in any average French household. Indeed, in only one of the 26 episodes, *La Composition française*, does the story-line concern a family disagreement which takes the form of a cultural clash between the parents' Arab–Muslim–Algerian values and the children's values acquired in France. Due to the sensitive nature of the issues raised in *La Composition française*, it is this episode that was used as a basis for the interviews with the three ethnic groups. It was felt that because the family's ethnicity was more prominent in this episode than in most of the others, it would be more likely to provoke varying reactions and interpretations among the respondents. In this episode the French public is expected to identify with a family that is, at least to a certain extent, culturally different. On the other hand, in the majority of the other episodes the Badaoui family comes across as so fully integrated, or rather assimilated, that the French viewer is merely being asked to identify with a family which looks North African, but to all intents and purposes is French.[5]

TV talk: how people perceived the programme

For the purposes of this research, a questionnaire based on the episode was constructed, and a panel of respondents was decided upon. The variables used were age, sex, ethnic origin and level of education. The two age-groups targeted were 18 to 25-year-olds, and those over the age of 40, the aim being to have two generations: parents and their children. This distinction was considered to be particularly important when looking at responses to the programme from the ethnic minority

groups, as the differing cultural environments in which the two generations have been brought up may well influence their perceptions of the
programme. Concerning ethnic origin, three groups were interviewed:
'native' French people, those of North African origin and those originating in Black Africa. With reference to education, the two levels
targeted were those people having done less than a *baccalauréat professionnel,*[6] and those having been to, or those currently at, university. A
total of 70 people were interviewed but for the purpose of this study the
responses of only one section of the panel have been analysed: 18 to
25-year-old women from all three ethnic origins and of both educational levels. Thus, 14 interviews – six with 'native' French women, five
with women of Maghrebi origin, and three with women originating
from Black Africa – have been analysed in depth. Clearly, due to the
relatively small number of people interviewed, the conclusions that
have been drawn in this chapter should only be taken as an indication
of the way in which people interpret programmes.

At a first glance, answers to the thirty-odd questions asked about the
programme appeared to be so varied that attempting to discover a
pattern seemed to be a near impossible task. Scratching beneath the
surface, however, it soon became apparent that a number of dynamics
had been at work, and that not all the interviewees had understood the
programme as anticipated by the producers. Whilst in some cases the
respondents were unified in their interpretations, in many others they
were not, and on further analysis, a number of factors contributing to
these differences of perception were identified. For the purposes of the
present analysis, three main factors will be considered: ethnic origin,
level of education and personal experience. There were, however,
other factors detected, and, moreover, it is expected that once analysis
of the other groups of respondents has been completed, age and sex
will also be found to be influencing factors. With reference to the
interviews analysed here, it was found that in many instances the various
factors were intertwined, and people's readings of the episode were
affected by two, or even three, of the factors.

Ethnicity

Ethnic origin clearly played an important part in influencing the ways
in which the three ethnic groups decoded *La Composition française*. It
was found that frequently, the interviewees saw things through the
socio-cultural matrix of the ethnic group to which they belonged. Thus,
certain incidents or scenes that were deemed important by one ethnic

group did not even feature in the answers given by another ethnic group. In other words, people were subconsciously focusing on those aspects which they could relate to, and identify with. For example, in one scene, a salesman tries to sell pork sausages to the father of the family at the centre of the series, Amar, who owns a grocery shop. As a Muslim, Amar refuses to taste the products but buys them anyway to sell to his predominantly French, Christian clientèle. During this scene, the salesman starts to discuss his private life, telling Amar that he lost his previous job selling ladies' underwear because, as he puts it, '[j'ai] perdu la tête' ('I lost my head'),[7] and he goes on to say that due to this incident he also lost his wife. With regard to this scene, the respondents were asked the open-ended question 'Que pensez-vous de la scène où un représentant de charcuterie essaie de vendre ses produits à Amar?' ('What do you think of the scene where a pork meat representative attempted to sell his goods to Amar?'). It was found that different interviewees concentrated on different parts of the scene, and that these divisions were along ethnic lines.

All those of North African origin discussed the religious aspect of the scene, and the fact that Muslims do not eat pork. That they all focused on this is clearly related to their personal experience as second-generation North Africans living in France: they are all Muslim, none of them eats pork and in many cases this is the only part of the religion that they practise, and so it has an important role in the make-up of their identity.

On the other hand, only two out of the six 'native' French women mentioned this part of the scene, and it is interesting to note that of these two, one was Jewish, and could, therefore, relate to the religious issue, whilst another had a Muslim boyfriend of Comorian origin. Three of the remaining four 'native' French respondents dwelt on the issue of the salesman's previous job selling underwear. This part of the scene had no ethnically Maghrebian dimension, and concerns everyday life in France, in other words, jobs, unemployment, husband–wife relationships and so on. It would seem, therefore, that their answers to the question centred on this aspect of the scene because it was the part that related most closely to their lives.

All the interviewees of Black African origin spoke of the religious aspect of the scene. Although none of them was Muslim, it is likely that they related to this part because it highlights differences between the host population and part of the immigrant community. Being different from the main population is something that those of Black African origin can identify with as it is something that they too experience.

Clearly, ethnicity played an important part in the way all the respondents perceived this scene, with the two ethnic minority groups identifying with the Maghrebian ethnically marked part of the scene, and the 'native' French respondents relating to the non-minority marked aspects of the same scene. In conjunction with ethnicity one can see how personal experience also influenced the answers of the Jewish 'native' French woman, and of the interviewee with the Muslim boyfriend.

A second example indicating the significant influence of ethnic origin on people's responses is when the interviewees were asked whether or not they liked Amar, and why. In this case, however, it was the 'native' French and the Black African respondents who perceived things in a similar way, whilst those of North African origin stood apart in their interpretation of Amar's character. Altogether, twelve people liked Amar, and only two – both 'native' French – did not. The fact that such a high proportion of the respondents found him pleasant is not surprising because he is the main character in the series, and is, therefore, meant to be likeable.

Of the six 'native' French people, four liked him, a result that would probably please the FAS. However, if one looks at the reasons given by two out of the four for liking him, this result is less encouraging. They both define their liking for him in terms of the fact that he is not too 'Algerian'. As one young woman puts it, 'il essaye d'évoluer pour ses clients' ('he is trying to adapt for his customers'). In other words, they like Amar because he has made an effort to 'de-ethnicize' himself, thus making himself less different and more French. Of the two others who liked him, one found Amar agreable for reasons unrelated to his ethnic origin, and purely based on his personality. Clearly, this is a step forward in comparison with the two other respondents. However, the most interesting and positive result is that of the fourth 'native' French interviewee because she acknowledges Amar's cultural differences which she clearly slightly disapproves of but then goes on to say that she still likes him as a person:

> le père, je trouvais qu'il était assez drôle, très fier de son pays, qu'il était un petit peu intolérant aussi vis-à-vis des gens parce qu'il veut pas que sa fille soit française ... mais en même temps il est humain et il fait des erreurs.[8]

In this way, she has accepted cultural and ethnic differences, and likes Amar not only because of his personality but also because of his cultural specificities. This is an example of what FAS officials were hoping to achieve when they said during the making of the series that they wanted *Fruits et Légumes* to 'favoriser l'évolution des mentalités du public français pour une meilleure acceptation de la différence' ('to encourage the development of the French public's attitudes, so that there is greater acceptance of differences') (letter from the FAS to Cinétévé, 17 March 1994). Concerning the two 'native' French respondents who did not like Amar, one of them gave reasons unconnected to his ethnicity, whilst the other did not like Amar because of his attitude towards his daughter, an attitude which she saw as directly related to his religion, Islam. On this subject she said: 'le fait qu'il interdit à sa fille de penser, pour moi ça c'est musulman' ('the fact that he forbids his daughter to think is, to me, Muslim behaviour'). In this case, therefore, the respondent does not like the father precisely because he is too culturally different. All in all, therefore, three out of the six 'native' French interviewees judged whether they liked Amar or not on criteria related to ethnicity, and it is interesting to note that these three had all done less than a *baccalauréat professionnel*, whilst the three having had a university education all formulated opinions on him based purely on personality. Thus, educational level also appears to have played a part. As in the previous example, therefore, different, intertwining factors are found to influence people's responses.

In the case of the respondents of Black African origin, all three liked the father, but two of them liked him because his behaviour was not too 'Algerian' and not too 'Muslim', the same reaction that was found among two of the 'native' French respondents discussed above. For example, one of the women of Black African origin says 'oui, oui [je l'ai aimé] parce qu'il est modéré ... il est modéré, c'est ça que j'apprécie beaucoup' ('yes, yes, [I liked him] because he is moderate ... he is moderate, and that is what I particularly liked'). Once again, therefore, a liking for Amar has been explained in terms of his not being too different.

It is clear from the above analysis that the 'native' French and the Black African origin samples have very similar reactions to Amar, and that this is because they are 'outsiders' looking at someone who comes from a different ethnic origin and who has a different value system from them. The North African origin respondents, on the other hand, explain their liking for Amar in a very different way, in a way that is related to their position as 'insiders'. All five North African origin interviewees liked the father, and three of them defined their liking for him in terms of the fact that he has retained his cultural differences, and has not become too French. Thus, one of the women says '[je l'ai aimé] parce qu'il était gentil, puis en même temps il était, euh, il était quand même dans le vrai. Enfin, il a quand même ses racines qu'on voit, qu'on ressent, quoi' ('[I liked him] because he was kind, and at the same time, euh, he was realistic. I mean, he still has his roots that one sees, that one feels, you know'). So whilst two of the 'native' French people and two of the Black African origin people liked Amar because they felt that he made an effort to tone down his cultural differences, the North African origin respondents perceived Amar in quite the opposite way: they liked him precisely because he had *not* lost his cultural specificities, because he had not sold out. In other words, although the three ethnic groups all watched the same programme, it is as if the 'native' French and those of Black African origin had watched something quite different from what the Maghrebi origin respondents had seen.

From these two examples, one can see how ethnicity has played an important part in the respondents' interpretation of the programme. Moreover, one can see the way in which, at different moments throughout the episode, certain ethnic groups are brought together in a common perception of the programme. Thus, in the first example, the two ethnic minority groups related to the part of the scene which was ethnically marked, and the 'native' French to the part that was not. In the second example, on the other hand, the 'native' French and the Black African origin respondents were brought together by the fact that both groups were 'outsiders', whereas those of North African origin were 'insiders'. Finally, this analysis also highlighted the fact that the three factors – ethnic origin, level of education and personal experience – influencing people's interpretations are so closely linked that, often, they are impossible to separate.

Education

Despite the fact that the three factors are interconnected, a number of instances were found where level of education played a decisive role in people's perception of the episode. For example, one of the very first questions that the interviewees were asked was 'C'était à propos de quoi cette émission?' ('What was this programme about?'), and there were three categories of response to this question. Firstly, there were those who spoke of the underlying themes in the programme, such as immigration and integration. The second category grouped together those who saw the programme literally, and merely described the general story-line of the episode. Finally, there were those who saw the programme in terms of it being specifically about an Algerian family.

All together, six respondents fell into the first category of answer, and four of these were people who had had university education. Thus, all the 'native' French who had been to university spoke of the underlying themes in the programme, and of the two university-educated respondents of North African origin, one of them also described the programme in this manner. On the other hand, the two interviewees – one 'native' French and the other of Algerian origin – who saw the programme in literal terms had both done less than a *baccalauréat professionnel*, and it would seem probable that the level of education was the determining factor in this case. In contrast, in the case of the third category one can see the influence of ethnic origin. Four out of the five Maghrebi origin respondents fell into this category, and it would seem likely that this is because they, like the central characters of the programme, are North African. It can be seen, therefore, that although level of education had a notable influence on people's responses to this question, ethnic origin was an important factor too.

The influence of educational level can also be seen in the responses to a scene where Yoyo, the youngest son in the family, introduces a Bosnian classmate to Amar. Yoyo tells Amar that the little girl is Muslim like them, and the father is greatly surprised and says 'Musulmane? Mais elle n'a pas l'air d'une Arabe' ('Muslim? But she doesn't look like an Arab'). The respondents were asked to comment on the father's reaction. Two main types of response were found among the interviewees: firstly, those who saw the father's mistake and pointed out the fact that one does not have to be Arab to be Muslim, and secondly, those who were unaware of the father's mistake because they too believe that all Muslims are Arab. Of the six interviewees having had a university education, four of them commented on the fact that the father had confused Arab with Muslim, whilst a fifth one said that the father had not been following the Bosnian issue, an answer which does not make clear whether she was fully aware of the father's mistake or not. On the other hand, three out of the four who saw things in the same way as the father had the educational level of less than a *baccalauréat professionnel*. In the interpretations by the other interviewees of this scene, one can, once again, see the influence of the two other factors: ethnic origin and personal experience. For example, two out of the three Black African origin women see the father's mistake because they know that some of the states neighbouring their own countries of origin are Muslim. However, they did not appear to know that there are Muslims who are neither Black African nor Arab. As one interviewee of Zaïrean origin put it:

non, c'est pas seulement les arabes, les Sénégalais aussi, les Maliens c'est des musulmans. Ah, mais je me dis qu'il [Amar] a dû dire que c'est une Arabe [the Bosnian girl] parce que les autres ils sont noirs à part les Arabes.[9]

To a certain extent, therefore, she is seeing things in the same way as the father because she is 'reading' the scene within the confines of her ethnicity. As with the others who were unaware of Amar's mistake, her level of education is less than that of a *baccalauréat professionnel*. Only one 'native' French interviewee with less than a *baccalauréat professionnel* recognized the fact that Amar incorrectly saw Arab and Muslim as synonymous, and this is probably due to the fact that her boyfriend is Comorian, and is, therefore, Black and Muslim. In other words, personal experience was the influencing factor in this case.

Personal experience

It is clear from the above analyses of the effects of ethnic origin and educational level that the influence of personal experience is something that is always present. The reader will remember, for example, that the fact that one of the 'native' French women had a boyfriend of Comorian origin clearly influenced the way she interpreted many aspects of the episode. However, due to the very fact that it is of a personal, individual nature one cannot – as with the two other factors – see a distinct pattern based on personal experience emerging. In other words, the interviewees' personal experiences tended to divert them from interpreting the programme purely from within the confines of their ethnic group. In one particular case, however, it was possible to see the way in which a common experience had brought together all three ethnic groups in their understanding of a scene.

In the scene in question, Yoyo, the little boy, asks his Uncle Aziz who was the leader of the Franks who halted the advance of the Arabs at Poitiers. Aziz does not know the answer to the question but manages to bluff his way out of an embarrassing situation by saying that he does not know because when he arrived in France he did not come via Poitiers, and he was not stopped by the ticket collector who merely checked his ticket. The respondents were asked what they thought of the uncle's reply, and all but one said that Aziz did not know the answer to Yoyo's question because of his lack of schooling, or alternatively, because of his cultural differences. What one is seeing here, therefore, is the unifying effect of the respondents all having been through the French education system. Thus, what Yoyo learnt at school is something that all the interviewees have studied at school too. It will be of interest to analyse, at a later date, the results of the interviews with the first-generation minority groups, as they have not experienced the French education system, and different interpretations of the scene are likely to be found. With regard to the one person who did not perceive the scene in the same way as the others, she was one of the 'native' French respondents who came from a particularly sheltered and wealthy background, and in her opinion the uncle was only joking, and actually knew the answer to the question. The reason for this interpretation was that from within her very protected and upper-middle-class world she could not conceive of someone not knowing the answer to this fundamental aspect of France's history. Thus, she could not even begin to visualize mentally society outside her own world. Concerning Aziz's answer she says:

> je sais pas si c'était ironique ou alors si . . . si sérieusement il a pas compris la question. Je sais pas, j'espère que c'était ironique [laughs]. Peut-être que, non, je sais pas. Je me rends pas compte, quoi, j'arrive pas à me mettre à sa place. [C'était] ironique, non?[10]

In this case, therefore, it is her total lack of personal experience that influences her interpretation of this scene. All in all, therefore, one can see that personal experience played an important part in shaping the different ways in which the respondents understood the episode.

Conclusion

How far are people shaped by their social and cultural environment in their interpretation of television programmes? From these preliminary results, people do appear to view television through a cultural matrix constructed on the foundations of ethnicity, education and personal experience. The three ethnic groups may have sat down and watched the same programme but what they actually *saw* was very different. The role of ethnicity was strong. Whilst the 'native' French person sat in front of the programme and saw the French aspects, the person of North African origin was seeing all that was Maghrebian: two people being sent the same intended television message, but unravelling it in different ways. In the meantime, the person of Black African origin sat in the middle, sometimes seeing things in the same way as the person of North African origin, at other times joining forces with the 'native' French viewer, and still other times interpreting things within the specific Black African cultural framework. Thus, meaning was constructed at one end by the programme producers, only to be reconstructed at the other end by the viewers.

It would be foolish, however, to conclude that because of these diverse readings of the programme, television cannot encourage a *rapprochement* among viewers of different ethnic origins. Television certainly appears to be able to do the opposite: to feed the widespread negative stereotype of France's ethnic minority population, and in particular the North African community. That two of the respondents commented on the fact that *La Composition française* is unrealistic[11] in comparison with the usual range of programmes broadcast on the subject of the North African community, is an indication that they may have interiorized the negative images that television sends out. Moreover, that these two respondents come from two different ethnic origins – one 'native' French and one Black African – suggests that these negative stereotypes of the Maghrebian community have been absorbed across the ethnic divide. If television has contributed towards this less than positive end, uniting two ethnic groups in their disapproval of a third, why should it not be possible to reverse this trend and use television to encourage mutual understanding amongst France's ethnically diverse population? It is true that the respondents did not decode the programme in the same ways, but is this surprising when *Fruits et Légumes* is but one small dot on France's audiovisual landscape?

Notes

1. The author wishes to thank Professor Alec G. Hargreaves for his invaluable advice on the writing of this chapter.
2. For an example of research undertaken in Britain in this subject area, see Morley (1980). For a more recent example in the United States, see Hunt (1993).
3. For further information on FAS audiovisual policy see Humblot (1989) and Hargreaves (1993).
4. The 'Bible' is the initial document produced by the authors outlining the main characteristics of the series.
5. For further information on the making of *Fruits et Légumes*, see Hargreaves and Helcké (1994).
6. The equivalent of the British BTec.
7. Taken from the episode *La Composition française*.
8. 'I found the father quite funny, very proud of his country, also a little intolerant towards people because he does not want his daughter to be French ... but at the same time he is human and makes mistakes.'
9. 'No, it's not only the Arabs: the Senegalese, the Malians are Muslim too. Ah, but I think that he [Amar] must have said that she's [the Bosnian girl] an Arab because apart from the Arabs, the others are black.'

10. 'I don't know whether it was ironic or whether he seriously didn't understand the question. I don't know. I hope that it was ironic [laughs]. Maybe not, I don't know. I have no idea, you know. I can't put myself in his shoes. [It was] ironic, wasn't it?'
11. Concerning this, one of the interviewees says 'ça [*La Composition française*] m'a étonnée parce qu'en général, quand ils font des films comme ça, ils sont vraiment proches de la réalité. Là, ils me paraissent à côté de la plaque'· ('It [*La Composition française*] surprised me because usually when they make films like that, they're really realistic. Here, they seem completely beside the point').

References

Hargreaves, A.G. (1993) 'Télévision et Intégration, la politique audio-visuelle du FAS', *Migrations Société* 5(30): 7–22.

Hargreaves, A.G. and Helcké, J. (1994) '*Fruits et Légumes*: une recette télévisuelle mixte', *Hommes & Migration* 1182: 51–7.

Humblot, C. (1989) 'Les émissions spécifiques: de *Mosaïque* à *Rencontres*', *Migrations Société* 1(4): 7–14.

Hunt, D.M. (1993) 'The Los Angeles fires of 1992: discussion and viewer decoding' (unpublished communication to the American Sociological Association).

Morley, D. (1980) *The 'Nationwide' Audience: Structure and Decoding*. London: British Film Institute.

10.

Articulating identity from the margins: Le Mouv' *and the rise of hip-hop and ragga in France*

CHRIS WARNE

In his study of the young people of France's socially marginalized outer city housing estates, the sociologist François Dubet (1987) describes a shadowy world left by the collapse of traditional working-class culture, whose inhabitants lead fragmented lives, too shattered by their experience of *la galère*[1] to constitute a meaningful community or assemble themselves in purposeful collective action. Meanwhile, they drink the dregs of an impoverished bourgeois culture, which retains sufficient power to maintain them in dependent stupor.

Within four years, Dubet had tempered this judgement. The emergence of a dynamic youth culture, based around the music of hip-hop and ragga, from the very same estates described by Dubet as cultural deserts, led him instead in 1991 to announce the reinvention of French popular culture. He compared these new movers to *chanteurs populaires* (traditional songsters), articulating identity for and the concerns of a social class that was the most rootless and the most lacking in identity. He regretted however that they had thus effectively constituted an ethnic subculture: a French version of the American ghetto was nearer fruition.

Dubet's judgements, coming as they do from a left-sympathizing intellectual, shed considerable light on the stakes surrounding recent developments in French popular culture. Firstly, it illustrates how much its forms are either denigrated or misunderstood by intellectuals of both Left and Right. Dubet's notions of admissible culture appear to mean that when 'on the ground' he dismisses youth cultural forms as superficial and irrelevant in constituting the *acteur social* (social agent).[2] Only when these forms are rendered 'significant' via massive media attention does he assess their political potential, and then rather noticeably from a distance.[3] He is not alone amongst France's intellectual élites in distrusting recent popular culture. While conservatives might seek to defend France's national culture from Anglo-Saxon 'corruption', those on the Left often subscribe to notions of universal republican values that view the development of subcultures as a threat to national unity and to coherent collective action. Thus, this powerful movement (referred to by adherents as *Le Mouv'*) has met opposition not only from cultural conservatives, but also from those who might be presumed sympathetic. Most French rappers, street dancers or graffiti artists can tell of obstacles faced, often created by community leaders, fearful of Americanization and the threat to traditional cultures, or by well-meaning social workers fearful of encouraging a social and cultural ghetto.[4] The rap group IAM provide further illustration of the ambivalent reception of French hip-hop and ragga. Unable to perform in their home city of Marseille for some time because of a municipal ban on rap concerts (for fear of associated violence, fears more imaginary than real), they were accorded all the plaudits, including a champagne reception at the town hall, by the same municipality, following success in the 1995 national music awards.

In this sense, therefore, French hip-hop finds itself more than ever at the margins. Simultaneously, it has resonated the most amongst young inhabitants of the world so bleakly described by Dubet – faced with the failure of traditions (either of working-class culture and political activism, or of the cultures of their immigrant parents), these young people have been forced to invent their own. However, in doing so, they raise important questions for cultural activists of both Left and Right as to what constitutes 'Frenchness', as to who decides its parameters, and more generally about the role of popular culture in France. Part of this movement's force lies precisely in its socio-economic origins, emerging as it does from a section of French society that in other contexts (drugs, gang warfare, delinquency) has been the object of considerable media and political debate. The importance of *Le Mouv'* is that for perhaps the first time it allows such groups to be the subject, rather than the object of debate. At its heart, the movement addresses notions of identity, what it means to belong or to be on the margins. In order to understand how it does so, it is essential to consider the socio-economic conditions that produced the movement. However, as much has been said elsewhere on the nature of *l'exclusion sociale*, particularly as it affects young people of both French and foreign origin,[5] I shall concentrate instead on a brief outline of the history of hip-hop and ragga in France. This is followed by a closer look at the form that these cultures have taken in the city of Marseille, with special interest in how the theme of identity has been articulated by two groups from that city.

History of hip-hop and ragga in France

The history of French hip-hop divides into three phases. The first coincides with initial media enthusiasm for the first wave of American hip-hop in the early 1980s, which secured a significant following in the *banlieues*,[6] due as much to pioneers who established links with New York as to any media coverage of or fascination with the latest American fad. This phase was most visible in the Smurf fashion, and the accompanying dance craze. Already, impromptu contests were occurring between dance groups, and it was at such gatherings that the first French rappers and DJs made their débuts.[7] It was also at this time that the French chapter of the Zulu Nation was established.[8] Despite its deliberately low profile,[9] there is little doubt that it was pivotal for the pioneers of French rap, particularly in spreading its philosophy and a certain political consciousness that is such a feature of rap.

With the apparent passing of Smurf, the second phase of French hip-hop during the mid to late 1980s was not prominent in the media. This phase is, however, when many of the currently established artists first became active, practising on primitive equipment, organizing low-key gatherings or broadcasting on community or pirate radio. Not until 1987 did hip-hop make its second impact, and then via related, or perhaps misrelated, activities: firstly, and particularly in Paris, in the sudden proliferation of graffiti and tags, and subsequent high-profile attempts by the RATP (Régie autonome des transports parisiens) to deter practitioners; secondly, again more particularly in Paris, in the widespread coverage accorded the so-called re-emergence of gang violence. Whatever the connections between a fluid and indeterminate Parisian, suburban gang culture and French hip-hop, the former's spectacular media treatment undoubtedly served artists struggling for recognition, particularly as hip-hop could be presented as the positive side of *la banlieue*. Thus a third phase began with the emergence of some leading artists, able to secure chart success and contracts from the major record companies. This process culminated in the celebration of MC Solaar and IAM at the 1995 national music awards. However, it would be misguided to equate the French hip-hop movement with these better known figures. A more interesting fourth phase is developing, in reaction to the perceived dangers of entrapment as the record companies' latest product. Behind the success of some artists lies a proliferating network of fanzines, groups, small-scale club nights or concerts and especially dance groups, who are receiving their own form of mainstream recognition.[10] Recently, the first autonomous record labels have appeared, serving as a focus for a range of independent creative activity in the realms of fashion, video and street art. In a way that rock never was, hip-hop, ragga and their related cultures are *the* expressive cultures for significant numbers of young people growing up in *la banlieue.*[11]

While an understanding of the socio-economic conditions behind the emergence of hip-hop and ragga might partly explain why the question of identity is foregrounded to such an extent in their French forms, no one has yet explained why these particular cultures should be privileged as the vehicle for articulating such concerns, while others (e.g. rock) are neglected, sometimes vehemently rejected. The answer is not found in some culturalist explanation of the inherent 'blackness' of hip-hop – *Le Mouv'* is characterized by racial and ethnic diversity. More credence might be given to the attraction of its marginality. However, answers can be found within the structural patterns of the culture itself, which make it susceptible to articulate those concerns prevalent amongst *les jeunes exclus* (young people living on the margins) in France.

There are several reasons why hip-hop and ragga actually represent a radical break with the development of Western rock and pop culture.[12] Each of these offers an explanation for why young French people in search of identity should so readily embrace cultural forms that at first might seem alien. Firstly, the music finds its origins deep in the collective event of the rave, dance party or jam. Whereas some features of rock culture are equally communal (the festival, the concert), rap and ragga music has a closer connection to a specific locality, a particular community or to a self-proclaimed nation or tribe. Consequently, it travels pretty badly from this specific context. A rap, and more especially a ragga, record denotes as much the absence of the live event, a disconnection from the movement and communal celebration that it should provoke. It is not music for detached aesthetic contemplation, and attempts to treat it as such are usually unsuccessful. Rock music perhaps makes this transition more successfully.

A second related distinction is concerned with the status of the artist. Rap and ragga music more easily allows a redefinition of the relationship between audience and performer. It is difficult to play the star if the audience contains someone ready to 'outperform' you. Whereas recent attempts to market these forms as rock music have led to the creation of 'stars', at the ground level, the relationship is much more ambiguous. Rap and ragga are cultures demanding participation, even competition, and a less hierarchical audience–performer relationship. It is precisely this aspect and its attraction that emerged in conversation with members of the group Massilia Sound System: ragga was presented as a culture used to stimulate participation, to counteract passivity and resignation.

The final distinction arises from the direction that the music has taken, representing a profound break with classic forms of the Western pop song. Rap music emerged from the extension of 'breakdowns' in 1960s' and 1970s' Black dance music (funk, jazz funk), and from these forms it inherits and perpetuates a two or even single-chord structure, built upon a repeated bass 'riff'. It is significant that ragga has similarly 'stripped down' the chord structures of the reggae music from which it derives. The variety of the musical form derives not from the traditional chord progressions of Western popular music, but, instead, a hypnotic tension is created in the movement between two root notes. The dynamism of the form arises from sudden breakdowns, or from the lyric content and its energetic delivery. This structure also permits exploration of non-Western musical traditions for sampling, a trend noticeable in French forms of rap.

It is possible then to consider rap and ragga as distinctive, separate cultural forms. Certainly, in France, they have outlasted individual fads and fashions occurring within them. This is why they are important to sections of French youth: cultures which they can recognize themselves in, but sufficiently flexible to allow expression of their own concerns, including the search for meaningful contemporary identity. Given the proliferation of these cultural forms in France, what can be said more specifically about how they have served to articulate feelings of exclusion, *déclassement*,[13] and the need to create identity? To answer this question, I will undertake a closer examination of their emergence in the city of Marseille.

Rap and ragga in Marseille

Marseille's common image is of a racist city, a power base of the National Front. This is supplemented by images of danger and clandestinity: supposedly the seat of the French Mafia, Marseille is also considered the key point of illegal immigration into France. An economic base heavily dependent on overseas trade and an industrial sector heavily dependent on cheap labour from France's colonies were severely affected by the crises of the 1970s, and by difficulties in adapting to changing relationships with those former colonies. Other profound changes belong to the 1960s, the most notable being developments in the urban landscape resulting from the massive programme of low-cost housing in the city's northern sections. These have acquired the image of the concrete jungle, with its associated problems of high unemployment, concentration of immigrant populations, rising crime levels and drug abuse.[14] However, above all Marseille is France's 'immigration city'. Each wave since the 1930s has constructed its own relationship to the town. Currently, several fairly autonomous communities coexist, with dialogue via community leaders, official or otherwise (Wievorka, 1992: 111–26), a model for race relations that is diametrically opposed to prevailing French notions of national unity, integration and cooperative citizenship. Such a development would help explain why for many Marseillais, the city has been *la maudite* (cursed) in relation to the rest of France. More recently, the local authorities have attempted to stress via various publicity campaigns that this ethnic diversity is the city's strength, making of Marseille a model for the rest of France. It is interesting that this concern to validate Marseille as it already is, as well as what it might become, was recurrent for those young people I met. This aspiration has emerged specifically in two distinct but interrelated youth cultures, focused around rap and ragga music. Given Marseille's status as a city in search of identity, it is perhaps unsurprising that these cultural forms should flourish there, and such success can be seen to typify their general attraction for young French people.

The ragga scene is dominated by a group from the Belle de Mai quarter of the city, centrally located, but traditionally working class. Starting in the mid-1980s by organizing concerts and sound system events, Massilia Sound System established their own record label, Roker Promocion, in 1990. More recently they created an 'anti-fan' club, the Chourmo, which is an attempt to encourage emulation. It currently counts about 400 members, drawn from the region, with *Français de souche*[15] predominant. Massilia have established a network throughout southern France, with connections in Italy, and are associated with groups like the Fabulous Troubadours from Toulouse, the Black Lions from Vitrolles, and Hypnotik Gang, also from Marseille. That these groups have English names marks the extent of that language. For Massilia, ragga is a vehicle for expressing their own identity and regional culture, as stated by two of its group members:

TATOU: le rap et le ragga sont des musiques folkloriques ... enracinées qui parlent aux gens. Les Jamaïquains racontent une histoire qui se passe au bout de leur rue, et ça intéresse le bout du monde ... On a voulu faire la même chose avec notre culture provençale et occitane (et) on est allé rechercher les troubadours occitans ...

JALI: ... Nous ne voulons pas l'occitan que pour les occitans. Nous pensons au contraire qu'il faut posséder la culture occitane, niée tout au long de l'Histoire, pour comprendre la culture française.[16]

(in Leclère, 1994: 24–6)

This concern leads them to talk of a 'Linha Imaginot', stretching from Genoa to the Caribbean, 'mais qui ne passe pas par Paris'.[17]

The rap scene in Marseille is more diffuse, but most prominent is the group IAM, whose most recent album sold significantly at national level, and who are currently being consecrated as saviours of French song. Its members of West African, North African and Italian origin reflect the fact that, in Marseille, support for rap music is more diverse than that for ragga, cutting across any ethnic separation. At one Cultural Centre,[18] rap music has provided the focus for a dynamic and creative project encompassing video, music, poetry workshops, street art, dance and street sports. Its co-ordinator Patrick Loir was candid about the failure of a similar project based around rock music, and stressed the participatory, motivational and autonomous features of hip-hop culture. It is for him a vitally important means enabling the children of immigrants' self-expression and the creation of independent culture.

Looking at how these cultural forms have emerged in the hands of Massilia Sound System and IAM, I will concentrate on how the theme of identity is articulated in their work. Of particular concern is the lyrical output of the two groups, but it is important to recognize that this is to take the word from its original context, which may not do it full justice. It should further be stressed that song lyrics represent only one feature of much more diverse and widespread cultural activity.[19] The material under consideration is from 1991, a moment for both groups representing a certain finality in developing specific themes and concerns, and coinciding with the 'second appearance' of French hip-hop and ragga.

The first theme to address is that of creating new identity, or identities. Both IAM and Massilia reiterate an attachment to Marseille and the locality of their upbringing. In contrast to this specific rootedness, both groups self-consciously create semi-mythical tropes in constituting identities that differentiate them from (implicit) notions of Frenchness. All members of both groups adopt pseudonyms. However, these names for themselves do not bear a single, delineated identity, but are adopted and discarded at will, according to the demands of the situation. Their multiplicity conveys dynamic, not static notions of identity. Indeed, for IAM, apart from the reference to a divine supreme being in the group's name (the logo has been designed to read as *Allah* in Arabic when inverted), it can also be considered as a polyvalent abbreviation: *Imperial Asiatic Men, Invasion Arrivant de Mars, Indépendantistes Autonomes Marseillais*... The similarity is with cartoon superheroes, who, via name-change, adopt superhuman qualities. In fact the hidden identity is the more 'true', and enables resistance to threats posed by forces of chaos and disorder. In Massilia, each member has several names, the use of an individual name normally being accompanied by an assertion of the magical powers of the MC. In the track 'Violent', group member Jali (Moussu J) states his claim to identity:

> Je tchatche pour les français, je tchatche pour les occitans
> Les africains, les antillais et ceux du Moyen-Orient
> Je ne suis pas chrétien, je ne suis pas athée, je ne suis pas musulman
> Mes idées je ne vais pas les chercher dans la bible ou le coran
> Je n'ai pas besoin de croix, d'étoile, pas besoin de croissant
> J'ai ma propre liturgie et mes propres sacraments
> A l'office du rub-a-dub, je suis un MC permanent[20]
>
> (Massilia Sound System, 1991: Track 6, 'Violent')

It is firstly based on the ability to speak (*tchatcher* is an Arab word for chatter, verbal confrontation). The verbal duelling of ragga was, according to Massilia, a feature of medieval troubadour poetry, and one they self-consciously adopt. This discourse is however not exclusive – it is outward looking, turned towards and produced on behalf of the other. The MC rejects ideology (both religious and secular) in the search for identity: in fact ragga itself becomes a religion, with the MC compared to the priest-intermediary between truth and the audience. This new religion necessitates an explicit rejection of past (divisive) models.

The playful nature of articulating identities evident here is reflected in the fake political party created by Massilia, a scam sustained for a couple of years. The PIIM (Parti Indépendantiste Internationaliste Marseillais) is an affectionate pastiche of regionalist separatist movements of the 1970s, whose ideas they have to an extent adopted via the Fabulous Troubadours at Toulouse, who introduced them to the philosopher Félix Castan. In press interviews and conversation, Massilia constantly refute the notion that such assertion of Occitan identity is

necessarily exclusive, and distance themselves from its separatist manifestations. They glorify instead popular traditions of Provençal inde-
pendence and strong-mindedness, as seen in the fake political party's
theme song (Massilia Sound System, 1991: Track 13 'PIIM part 2'). It
expresses a desire to participate in a revolution encompassing the
quartiers du monde entier (localities the whole world over), a recurrent
idea that it is up to marginalized communities to find their own identity,
using whatever tools are available to turn the tables on the powerful. For
Massilia, ragga music is one such tool. The Chourmo is another (the
name comes from the Occitan for galley slave). The Fabulous Troubadours organize *repas de quartier* to encourage rediscovery of the local
social space through participation in an outdoor meal. The sense is of
perpetuating traditions of *fête populaire* for which Marseille and the
south were once renowned.

For IAM, identity originates in the African nation, now deemed
world-wide in scope (the Black Atlantic). Unlike American rap groups
who stress the Zulu character of this nation, IAM incorporate their
North African origins, featuring Egyptian hieroglyphics in their art-
work. The group members' pseudonyms reflect this concern: Shurik'n,
DJ Khéops, Akhénaton. They have also constructed a mythology
whereby Marseille was once an Egyptian peninsula, before becoming
detached and floating across to France. Unlike Massilia, traditional
religious identities are not rejected – indeed syncretistic references
recur, to Allah, Egyptian deities and Chinese philosophies. However,
this building of new mythology has political consequences, seen in the
song 'I A M concept', which denounces the falsification inherent in
Western portrayals of the African as the Primitive (IAM, 1991: Track 5
'I A M concept').[21] This concern to valorize the experience of the
oppressed and launch an attack on the oppressor also features in the
song 'Planète mars':

Nous allons déclencher
Une énorme offensive de la cité de Phocée
Tout le monde crie, tout le monde trace
Devant l'attaque des poètes venus de la planète Mars ...
Eille, elle même
A subi des tentatives d'invasion française
Des hordes ténébreuses lors des élections ...
Je m'en rappelle ce jour là, la peur
Quand 25% ont collaboré avec l'envahisseur
Maudits soient-ils avec le rap je l'oppresse[22]

(IAM, 1991: Track 2 'Planète mars')

Marseille, the Phocaean city, is being invaded not, as the National Front has it, by African and Arab immigrants, but by the colonizing French, led by 'un blond, haineux et stupide à la fois' (a man with white hair, full of hatred and stupid as well), clear reference to Le Pen. The lyrical dynamic of rap enables IAM to subvert the former's discourse, by reversing its terms and portraying the French supporters of extreme right-wing groups as the real barbarians.

Oppositional discourse, using the lyrical skills of the MC to counter the conventional, oppressive language of politicians, is equally a feature of Massilia's work. It relates closely to the much recurring theme in French ragga and hip-hop of language as a weapon:

> Je dis la vérité, ce que je dis je le sais …
> Mon attitude est guerrière et mes mots sont meutriers!
> Mon arme c'est ma bouche: canon scié 12mm[23]
> (Massilia Sound System, 1991: Track 10 'Connais-tu ces mecs?')

The words of the MC or rapper are the weapon used to expose the lies of those opposing the free movement of the subject. They replicate the action of a gun in the rapidity of their delivery, and the action of the bullet in their devastating impact. The empowerment of this idea comes because if the subject has nothing else, at least the ability to create personal discourse remains: even when encountering outside pressure and control, it can be a powerful weapon if carefully honed and judiciously targeted.

The motif of opposition to those that would impose restriction reappears in a third theme connected to the articulation of identity. Much of the frustration and anger expressed in both rap and ragga music arises from a sense of restriction, of being hemmed in, by politicians, by the system, by the state. In response, the paradigm for building identity is that there should be *movement*.

> Je veux que tous et toutes dans le rhythme s'électrisent …
> S'angoisser n'est pas une attitude qui me séduise
> Je ne veux pas qu'ainsi les ennuis m'immobilisent![24]
> (Massilia Sound System, 1991: Track 11 'Quelle culture')

There is a valorization of all that is energy, reflected in the verbal fireworks of the music, which is primarily *dance* music. Movement and fluidity are foremost in the related cultures of street dance, but equally so in the fashion accompanying the music. Clothing is dominated by the sporting aesthetic – trainers, loose-fitting sports clothes, the ubiquitous baseball cap. There is a practical and symbolic assertion of the desire to be in constant motion. This paradigm is also reflected in the practice of tagging, the signing of a pseudonym in the form of a stylized signature on blank public spaces. This is not simply a method of marking territory, or even of announcing the subject's existence. Rather, tagging is a practice that constitutes a statement of having passed through, investing the intermediary space between destinations with meaning and significance. It is no coincidence that it is the young who tend to fill such spaces while much of society is evacuating them. Occasionally such movement might be experienced by others in the city space as invasion, as being swamped. In Marseille, that space increasingly equates with the major pedestrian sites surrounding the main thoroughfare of La Canebière. Traditionally sites of popular festival, even carnival, recent initiatives from the municipality on behalf of the tourist have attempted to discourage this rather dangerous image of the centre. Both Massilia and IAM recount momentous times in song when they reclaimed this and other sites of popular merrymaking, to the consternation of more sedate users.

Conclusion

The question of French identity has been at the forefront of both academic and general debate in recent years. The emergence amongst marginalized sections of the population of a vibrant youth culture deriving from rap and ragga music has been informed by and contributed to this debate. The articulation of identity central to these cultural forms appears to revolve around three strategies. First is the need to assert identity by embracing and thereby subverting conventional binary opposition between outsider/insider. Second is the aim to oppose those denying this newly valorized identity, with the weapon of language, acquired by hard work and exercised in verbal dexterity. Finally comes the expression of this identity through movement and the expending of energy, finding its outlet in the rejection of all that restricts, annihilates or disperses. In some respects, these strategies will be acceptable to or easily incorporated within existing notions of French identity. In others, they will be less easily assimilable, and in fact provoke a certain disruption of these notions. Whatever the case, it is to be hoped that this particular response to the problematic of French identity, coming as it does from the margins, is not ignored in the more general clamour advocating closure and exclusion.

Notes

1. Literally, French for a galley or prison ship, but used to describe the hell of growing up in the suburbs. More recently it has taken on a positive connotation of having to strive to achieve one's goals.

2. Describing various youth cultures, principally characterized as 'rock', Dubet remarks: 'Ces diverses orientations de l'action constituent-elles un mouvement social? La réponse est négative' ('Are these various behavioural tendencies enough to form a social movement? The answer is no') (Dubet, 1987: 319).

3. Dubet's analysis (1991: 9–18) of social change, as with that of others in the Touraine school, has been criticized for drawing a chaotic picture of the present with reference to a characterization of working-class solidarity in the past that appears idealized at least. While recognizing the strengths of such analyses to explain the constitution of a new social class of working-class and immigrant youth, the dangers of oversimplifying the past should be recognized. Such idealization of a coherent working-class culture existing before the processes of de-industrialization stems partly, in my view, from precisely the kind of prejudices exhibited by Dubet: certain cultures are 'allowed' to be authentically 'popular', while others, particularly those with the imprint of 'foreign' origins, are deemed characteristic of popular culture in decline.

4. Michel Wieviorka (1992: 204–7) describes the dilemma facing social workers when encountering hip-hop culture, torn between recognizing *le droit à la différence* (the right to be different) and fear of encouraging ethnic isolationism.

5. Of particular relevance is the notion of *déclassement* as developed by Galland, Dubet and others, whereby the social trajectory of the family of origin is no longer meaningful or even available for considerable sections of the young French population, forcing them to seek other trajectories. See also Saïd Bouamama's writing on citizenship and identity (Bouamama, 1993).

6. Working-class suburbs – see Chapter 14.

7. One such gathering is described by Bachmann and Basier (1985).

8. A Black consciousness movement founded by New York DJ Afrikaa Bambaataa, to combat gang violence and drug dependency.

9. Consequently, some commentators dismiss the group's importance e.g. Georges Lapassade (1991: 45).

10. Odile Cougoule (1994: 24–5) describes the 'professionalization' of sections of this movement.

11. Its extent is not always visible to the outsider, even allowing for apparent ground-level experience: charged with bringing music to the young in their catchment area, cultural leaders working on an estate on Bordeaux's outskirts organized in 1993 an event based around hip-hop, in hopes of introducing the young to (the more acceptable?) jazz. Subsequently, one organizer stated: 'On découvre qu'il existait d'une manière "souterraine" tout un réseau de rappeurs, des bricoleurs du rap, avec des cassettes qui circulent, des fanzines ... C'est parmi les plus "marginaux" que l'on découvre le plus de motivation. Jusque-là livrés à eux-mêmes, ils comprennent que le rap tel qu'ils aiment demande persévérance, travail et soin ... ' ('We discovered that there existed, in an "underground" way, a whole network of rappers, of do-it-yourself producers of rap, with tapes doing the rounds, fanzines ... It was amongst the most "marginal" that we found the most highly motivated. Left to themselves up till then, they understood that the rap that

they appreciated demanded perseverance, hard work and care ... ') (P. Duval, project director for 'Rap et vidéo dans les cités', and director of the 'Musiques de Nuit' association, quoted in Matheron and Subileau, 1994: 80).

12. These remarks extend to other Black-originated forms of dance music (techno, house, jungle ...).

13. See note 5, above.

14. See Chapter 14 for details of this kind of urban development in Lyon.

15. Literally, French of old stock, designating families who have lived in France for generations.

16. TATOU: Rap and ragga are folk music ... that is rooted, which speaks to people. Jamaicans tell a story that happens at the end of their street, and that is of interest at the other end of the world. ... We wanted to do the same with our Provençal, Occitan culture [and] we sought out the Occitan troubadours ...
JALI: We're not interested in keeping Occitan just for the Occitans. On the contrary, we think that you need Occitan culture, denied throughout history, to understand French culture.

17. *La Linha Imaginot* is Occitan, perhaps best translated as 'the line of creative imagination' but with ironic references to the Maginot Line of France's Second World War defences. It stretches from Genoa to the Caribbean 'but does not go through Paris' (thus rejecting the cultural hegemony that Paris tends to exert over the provinces).

18. L'Association Rock Vallée, Centre d'Animation de Saint-Marcel, Marseille.

19. For a more exhaustive account of hip-hop culture in France, see Bazin (1995); Lapassade and Rousselot (1990); Desse, Massot and Millet (1993); Louis and Prinaz (1990) and Dufresne (1991).

20. I rap for the French, I rap for the Occitans
The Africans, the people from the Antilles and the Middle East
I am not a Christian, an atheist, or a Muslim
I don't need to get my ideas from the Bible or Koran
I don't need the cross, the star or the crescent
I have my own liturgy and my own sacraments
In the rub-a-dub mass, I am a lifetime MC.

21. The group are using their reading of the Senegalese writer C.A. Diop, in particular his *Nation, nègres et culture* (1954, Paris: Présence Africaine).

22. We are going to unleash
A massive offensive from the Phocaean city
Everyone shouts, everyone moves
In the face of attack from the poets of the planet Mars ...
Eille, herself
Has suffered attempts at French invasion
From dark hordes at election time ...
I remember that day, the fear
When 25 per cent collaborated with the invader
A curse on them, I dominate them with rap.

23. I tell the truth, and I know what I say ...
With a warrior attitude and deadly words
My weapon is my mouth, a sawn-off shotgun.

24. I want everyone to be energized in the rhythm ...

Getting hung up is not an outlook to seduce me
I don't want to let my worries hold me down!

References

Bachmann, C. and Basier, L. (1985) 'Junior s'entraîne très fort ou le smurf comme mobilisation symbolique', *Langage et Société* 34 (Dec.): 57–68.

Bazin, H. (1995) *La culture hip-hop*. Paris: Desclée de Brouwer.

Bouamama, S. (1993) *De la galère à la citoyenneté: les jeunes, la cité, la société*. Paris: Desclée de Brouwer.

Cougoule, O. (1994) 'Air du temps: quand la rue entre en scène', *Danser* 126 (Oct.): 24–5.

Desse, Massot, F. and Millet, F. (1993) *Freestyle*. Paris: Massot and Millet.

Dubet, F. (1987) *La galère: jeunes en survie*. Paris: Fayard.

Dubet, F. (1991) 'Les bandes, de quoi parle-t-on?' in Centre de formation et d'études de la protection judiciaire de la jeunesse, *L'Actualité des bandes: journées d'études 4, 5, 6 février*. Vaucresson: CFRES: 9–18.

Dufresne, D. (1991) *Yo! revolution rap*. Paris: Ramsay.

Lapassade, G. (1991) 'Le Hip-Hop, "La Nation Zulu", les bandes "zoulous" et l'insertion des jeunes noirs de la deuxième génération' in Centre de formation et d'études de la protection judiciaire de la jeunesse, *L'Actualité des bandes: journées d'études 4, 5, 6 février*. Vaucresson: CFRES: 42–6.

Lapassade, G. and Rousselot, P. (1990) *Le rap ou la fureur de dire*. Paris: Loris Talmart.

Leclère, T. (1994) 'Aïoli, rap et foot: Massilia Sound System, entretien', *Télérama* 2337 (Oct.): 24–6.

Louis, P. and Prinaz, L. (1990) *Skinheads, Taggers, Zulus & Co*. Paris: Editions de La Table Ronde.

Matheron, C. and Subileau, J. (1994) *Jeunes, musiques et médiation*. Paris: Ville et Miroirs des Villes.

Wievorka, M. (1992) *La France raciste*. Paris: Seuil.

Recordings

IAM (1991) *De la planète mars*. Paris: Virgin/Labelle Noir.

Massilia Sound System (1991) *Parla patois*. Marseille: Roker Promocion.

Part Three

Alternative Voices

11.

La presse SDF[1]: voice of the homeless?

PAMELA M. MOORES

Homelessness has become an increasingly prominent topic of political debate in France over recent years. Yet the inherent nature of social marginalization, compounded by vagueness and variation over questions of definition, makes it impossible to give a precise picture of the number of homeless people in France. Estimates vary from the conservative figure of 202,000 in 1995, according to BIPE,[2] an estimate based on extrapolation from the 1990 census, to the possibly exaggerated figure of 627,000 suggested by the European federation of organizations working with the homeless (Castaing, 1995b). French demographic specialists admit they have no established method of investigation of homelessness and no reliable source of data,[3] but for our purposes the round figure of somewhere between 400,000 and 500,000 people with no fixed address, which is generally accepted by charitable organizations operating in the field, suggests the seriousness of the problem. A SOFRES poll commissioned by the police in January 1994 found that the growing numbers of homeless people in the streets represented one of the most important problems in Paris in the view of 64 per cent of the population (*Le Monde*, 26 January 1994). Over recent years, food banks and soup kitchens have annually expanded their distribution of supplies in an effort to keep pace with demand on the streets (Castaing, 1995b).

During the winter of 1994/95, militant action against homelessness, particularly the highly publicized occupation by squatters of number 7, rue du Dragon, in the fashionable sixth *arrondissement* of Paris, focused media attention on the issue. On 19 December 1994, when Jacques Chirac, Mayor of Paris and candidate for the Presidency, accepted the argument for the requisition of vacant properties to provide emergency housing, this was a landmark signalling official recognition of the gravity of the crisis. Social issues dominated the 1995 election campaigns for presidential and municipal office, which were regularly punctuated by demonstrations in defence of the homeless (for example, 8 January, 8 and 11 April 1995). Yet, in early April 1995, a poll indicated that 62 per cent of the population still felt that the battle against exclusion was not being given sufficient attention in political debate (Castaing, 1995a). On 1 May, on the eve of the debate between second round presidential contenders Lionel Jospin and Jacques Chirac, Abbé Pierre, champion of the homeless, made a solemn, emotional appeal on television for urgent measures to alleviate the problem. Since the elections, homelessness has been high on the agenda for the new government. On 28 August 1995, Pierre-André Périssol, the new Minister for Housing, announced that 30 vacant buildings in the Parisian area, belonging to financial institutions, were to be requisitioned to provide 500 homes (Garin, 1995). Such extreme measures give an indication of the importance which the problem of homelessness has assumed in France.

SDF publications

It is against this background of deep public disquiet and keen media interest in a highly politicized issue that we examine the phenomenon of 'la presse SDF'. By this we mean newspapers specifically concerned with homelessness which are sold in the streets by people 'of no fixed abode', that is SDF – people *sans domicile fixe*. Following the examples of *Street News* in New York, *The Sheet* in San Francisco and especially *The Big Issue* launched in London in September 1991, a stream of SDF publications appeared in France from the spring of 1993 onwards: *Macadam Journal* (11 May 1993), *Le Réverbère* (30 July 1993), *La Rue* (21 October 1993), *Faim de siècle* (8 November 1993) and a year later *Le Lampadaire* (September 1994). Focusing primarily on homelessness, the titles are not in direct competition with conventional news media, but represent a grass-roots initiative, an alternative press reflecting different, often dissident, cultural values. The newspapers are sold by homeless vendors in return for a percentage of the cover price, normally 60 per cent. Their declared aim is not only to provide a source of revenue for the homeless, but also to act as an instrument of social integration, bringing the vendors greater dignity and self-respect, facilitating their contacts with the public, championing their cause and giving them a voice.

Our intention is to consider the contribution of SDF newspapers to advancing the cause of the homeless through a summary review of their history, their methods of operation and range of activities and a brief analysis of their content. However, the inherent difficulties and limitations of this research should first be acknowledged. The recent emergence of the SDF press means that there is no existing body of literature or research on the topic, and cultural snobbery militates against academic interest in the field. Contact has been established with the majority of the publishers of SDF titles, but their limited financial resources, their semi-professional nature and sometimes unorthodox methods result in limited willingness, or simple inability on their part, to respond to detailed enquiries and provide reliable facts and figures. These problems are compounded by the particular means of distribution, via a changing workforce of homeless vendors who are constantly on the move, selling in railway stations, the Metro, and hypermarket car parks, to a changing clientele as opposed to an assured and regular readership. Our analysis is therefore confined primarily to study of the publications themselves, in the light of the claims their authors make for them. The picture is supplemented with information gleaned from reports in the mainstream press, although the latter have sometimes been inspired by surprising ill-will and cynicism. They also rely heavily on rumour and hearsay.

Identity and diversity

The titles of SDF publications reveal something of their identity. While the name of the British newspaper *The Big Issue* suggests a controversial subject of debate (which, ironically, homelessness is much less in Britain than in France), the titles of French SDF publications generally focus on the urban landscape. Whereas *Macadam*, that is 'Tarmac' in English, is resolutely a twentieth-century reference to the material reality of living rough on the street, *La Rue*, *Le Réverbère* and *Le Lampadaire* carry nineteenth-century associations, recalling opposition publications such as Jules Vallès' *La Rue*, and Henri Rochefort's *La Lanterne*. Vallès had a reputation for championing the cause of social outcasts, the marginal and oppressed, and the associations of the title *La Rue* are therefore most appropriate, except for the irony that, in relative terms, today's *La Rue* is the most conformist and institutionalized of SDF publications, in contrast to the image of Vallès, revolutionary and *Communard*. For Vallès, however, the street was also the centre of life, the meeting place, a source of colour and bustling activity, and the title therefore carries the positive connotations of action and solidarity which the present *La Rue* seeks to convey. The street lamps of *Le*

Réverbère and *Le Lampadaire* are obviously intended to represent a source of light, hope and optimism in moments of darkness, and also the aspiration to shed light on the issue of homelessness. Finally, the pun implicit in the title *Faim de siècle* introduces a more jocular, witty note. Although in written form it refers firstly, and literally, to 'hunger of the century' and hence the dramatic plight of the homeless, in sound it evokes the expression *fin de siècle* and notions of decadence, in keeping with the publication's focus on youth culture.

Indeed, what is striking about the SDF press in France, as compared to Britain, is the proliferation of diverse titles appealing to different audiences. In Britain *The Big Issue* was set up by John Bird with the financial backing of experienced business leaders, the Roddicks of Body Shop fame, and therefore had sound foundations. It rapidly succeeded in attracting substantial public donations and industrial sponsorship, and expanded across the country, gradually setting up regional offices and editions, and completely dominating the market. The history of the first French titles, in contrast, was chequered, and this may be one reason for the emergence of competing titles. Potential rivals, observing the problems encountered, felt confident that they could do better, and launched their own distinctive publications. The result is such diversity that it is useful to devote some attention to discussion of individual titles, comparing their profiles.

Macadam

The earliest publication sold in France, *Macadam Journal* is based primarily in Brussels, and sells in Belgium, France and Switzerland. Its first monthly issue in May 1993 sold 100,000 copies in three weeks and, only three months later, circulation had risen to 400,000 copies.[4] *Macadam* is the leading SDF title, with an average circulation figure in 1995 of around 600,000 copies, which is subject to significant seasonal variation. Winter conditions which threaten the homeless also bring greater publicity and sympathy for their plight. Since the winter of 1994/95, in addition to the news-sheet now renamed *Macadam Info*, *Macadam Plus* has been sold through the winter months in response to extra demand. This is a light-hearted publication containing stories and comic strips.[5]

Macadam was originally founded by a Belgian, Jacques Chamut. According to the research of journalists from *L'Evénement du jeudi* (Bellet and Szac-Jacquelin, 1994) he was an incompetent businessman, however well-intentioned. The original design team was apparently not paid, nor suppliers; finances were also inadequately controlled, with the result that there were repeated thefts from the newspaper's depots. Martine Vanden Driessche, former economics columnist of the Belgian newspaper *Le Soir*, and now *Macadam's* editor, persuaded Chamut to sign the directorship over to her in July 1993, but a bitter power struggle ensued and thefts continued. At the end of 1993, French and Belgian accountants found the financial situation so confused that the accounts could not be audited, although the newspaper has since regularized its financial procedures. The official explanation now given for the early problems is that they were a result of involving inexperienced homeless people too extensively in running the paper, and especially in managing distribution depots. However, Vanden Driessche has also been accused of profiting personally from *Macadam*. Her publishing company, MVD Publications, which had been in financial difficulty, produces *Macadam* and sells it to the French company Macadam France at a profit. *Macadam* has therefore attracted repeated charges of profiteering: 'SDF: où passe le fric de Macadam?' demanded *L'Evénement du jeudi* in early 1994;[6] 'Presse S.d.f. Arnaque ou charité?' questioned *L'Esprit libre*.[7] One should never believe all the sensational allegations one reads in the press, and on 3 May 1995 *L'Evénement du jeudi* was ordered by the courts to grant *Macadam* an official right of reply to its accusations. However, it is true that, during its first year and a half of operation, *Macadam* did not live up to expectations created by an enterprise like *The Big Issue* in Britain in terms of financing social projects. A joint charity appeal with the Catholic *Pèlerin Magazine* and radio station France Inter over Christmas 1994/95 may have done something to redeem its reputation. Certainly the paper has made efforts to improve its image, launching training initiatives to remedy the aggressive tactics of vendors, and participating in research to improve sales techniques (*Macadam Journal*, December 1994: 8–9). At the end of 1994, a charity Macadam Urgence was also set up to assist vendors in need. *Macadam* staff are insistent, however, that the newspaper itself is not a charity and runs on commercial lines. It employs professional journalists, and makes a clear separation between their articles and the pages devoted to vendors' profiles and readers' letters, which provide emotional, anecdotal evidence of the paper's importance in the lives of homeless vendors and regular readers.

In terms of content and presentation, *Macadam* is serious, worthy and occasionally very interesting. Coverage is rigorously focused on charitable and humanitarian causes. However, the desire to provide an alternative source of information, reporting on local initiatives which would not attract the interest of the mainstream press, sometimes results in the unfortunate impression of a parochial charity newsletter rather than the general interest news-sheet which *Macadam* claims to be. Printed black on white, on poor quality paper, with highlighting in one further colour, *Macadam* traditionally has a sober air, which does not seem inappropriate given its mission (although some issues in 1995 introduced brighter, more attractive covers and full colour photographs). The paper incorporates practical information (such as addresses of hostels and soup kitchens), related book reviews, substantive articles from experts on social policy and interviews with influential personalities such as Martine Aubry and Jacques Delors. In 1995 there were full statements on homelessness from all the presidential candidates, and interviews with candidates for the municipal elections. However, the paper claims to have no religious or political agenda and, since it rehearses the same themes repeatedly, becomes dull and predictable.

Moreover, some editorials have been effusive, sentimental and self-satisfied. In the September 1994 issue, for example, Vanden Driessche contrasts the distress of thousands of homeless people with the progress made by *Macadam* vendors who no longer have to sleep rough. Their dreams are no longer Utopia. Some have cars, others are in love. The first *Macadam* marriage has taken place, some couples are to have children. All this, we are told, shows how the newspaper has helped the homeless to get back on their feet, and readers are thanked incessantly for their loyalty and for having 'given in' ('cédé') to the vendor's irresistible appeal. The assumption that the reader's ego must be flattered, and that s/he has bought the paper simply through lack of courage to say 'No', says little for the intrinsic interest and value of the newspaper. The implication is that the vendor is selling his or her situation, not the product, which is quite contrary to the philosophy underlying the creation of the street press, namely that the purchaser is not simply giving a charitable donation, the vendor is not begging, but a service is offered which is rewarded and respected. Elsewhere *Macadam* espouses this philosophy, but it has sometimes been guilty of crude, emotional blackmail and trite romanticism.

Le Réverbère

Le Réverbère, a fortnightly publication, is *Macadam*'s closest rival in terms of circulation (although the disorganized and unreliable management of the paper makes it difficult to state figures with any certainty).[8] *Le*

Réverbère was set up by Georges Mathis, a disenchanted former vendor of *Macadam*, who persuaded the printer Gilbert Caron (subsequently associated with the relaunch of the right-wing weekly *Minute*) to print the early issues free of charge. Mathis quickly met with success which has since been repeated abroad with the creation of sister papers *HAZ* in Berlin, and *La Farola/El Fanal* in Barcelona.

Entirely different in character from *Macadam*, *Le Réverbère* is colourful, rebellious and provocative. The editors of SDF newspapers are generally keen to play down competition between titles, given their fundamental ethos of solidarity and reluctance to admit to financial motivation. Mathis, however, continually engages in mud-slinging against his former employers at *Macadam* and against other SDF publications, despite the fact that *Le Réverbère* patently has the worst record for financial and legal irregularities. Social projects financed by *Le Réverbère* are rarely mentioned. Articles in the mainstream press in 1994 even maintained that Mathis had no bank account, and that money was collected in buckets and rubbish bags in the back of a van.[9] This picture of complete disregard for legality or financial propriety has been confirmed by Sophie Crépon (1994), a former editor of the newspaper. Since March 1994, and a new ruling from the Ministry of Social Affairs, registered homeless newspaper vendors have been entitled to social security benefits without paying personal contributions. However, Mathis failed to register his staff systematically, so they forfeited this entitlement. (Many of the paper's vendors are in fact Eastern Europeans with no official papers.) Street vendors are also required to register with the Conseil Supérieur des Messageries de Presse, the body responsible for newspaper distribution, but Mathis dispensed with such formalities. Some of the paper's vendors owed tax from previous activities, and were keen to avoid contact with the authorities. Others were subcontracting sales of the paper, operating in a sordid underworld. Since early 1995, however, *Le Réverbère* appears to have responded to the bad press it was receiving by regularizing the status of its vendors. The front page headline on 16 January announced 'Vendeurs, nous cotisons à la Sécu',[10] and this information has been repeated on the cover of subsequent editions. Mathis has also assumed a self-righteous tone in his attacks on *Macadam*, although his outbursts are so vituperative that it is difficult to take anything he says at face value (see, for example, Mathis, 1995b: 28).

A spirit of nonconformism pervades *Le Réverbère*. The colourful covers of the paper, which are printed sideways so as to open out into a single continuous page, are striking, the titles sensational. An issue devoted to

terminal care and euthanasia, for example, carries the dramatic headline 'Putain de mort!', accompanied by the image of a gun in the
foreground, a red cross behind.[11] Puns and verbal horseplay abound.
Beneath the title stands the witty invitation: 'Si on parlait de toit', that is,
'Let's talk about a roof over your head' or 'about you', punning on the
homonyms *toit* (roof) and *toi* (you). An entire page is often devoted to
jokes and amusing quotations under the heading **SOURCES POUX
BELLES**, good sources of jokes, but with associations of lice (*poux*) and
rubbish (*poubelle*), both unpleasant reminders of life on the streets. The
humour is black, the wit caustic.

In contrast to *Macadam, Le Réverbère* is also outspoken politically. In
1994, in reponse to calls for French nationals to leave Algeria because of
the intensifying political crisis, Mathis suggested it might be a good idea
for Algerian immigrants to go home too ... (reported in Bellet and
Szac-Jacquelin, 1994: 21). In December 1994, whereas *Macadam* re-
spectfully published without comment a long interview with the outgoing President of the European Commission, Mathis wrote an utterly
scathing editorial about the 'brilliant' career during which Delors had
'succeeded' in consigning yet another 35 million Europeans to the
ranks of the unemployed! He was equally disparaging about Delors's
potential candidacy for the French presidency and the prospect of his
replacing the ailing François Mitterrand: 'La France n'a que faire
d'adopter ce vieux machin quand elle arrive à se débarasser du Gisant
du Faubourg'[12] (Mathis, 1994: 3). Chirac too was savaged cruelly,
particularly for electioneering hypocrisy and opportunism in apparently espousing the cause of the homeless:

> Le chéri Chichi, le chouchou des chochottes que les nénettes de 60 ans
> voudraient se 'farcir' et à qui les mecs voudraient ressembler, se veut
> l'emblème d'une certaine France, la Jeanne des sans-abri, lui qui habite
> depuis trois lustres à l'Hôtel de ville, le plus grand appartement de Paris
> (1200 m²)![13]
>
> (Mathis, 1995a: 3)

The cynicism of this reaction to Chirac's rallying to the cause of the
homeless was shared by many commentators, but the sheer force and
vulgarity of Mathis's irreverent, offensive humour are deliberately
provocative. He mocks the inhumanity of the legal system, the compla-
cent indifference of politicians, and the apathy of the general public. *Le
Réverbère* is passionately outspoken, rebellious and militant compared to
other SDF titles.

Unfortunately, its articles are sometimes so partisan, exaggerated and factually inaccurate as to undermine their credibility.[14] Poor standards of literacy, demonstrated in a slapdash attitude to spelling and grammar, are also irritating to an educated reader, but given that *Le Réverbère* explicitly presents itself as 'le cahier des sans-abri et des sans-emploi',[15] and has deliberately involved the unemployed and homeless in the editorial team, this is not surprising. *Le Réverbère* has the image of an entertaining, perhaps well-intentioned, but nonetheless disreputable rogue.

La Rue

In contrast, one of *La Rue*'s priorities has been to act within the law, be publicly accountable and secure official recognition. The paper's founder, former television journalist Anne Kunvari, was inspired by the example of *The Big Issue* when she compiled a report on the British newspaper for French television in January 1993. With fellow journalist Christian Duplan, she researched the project for a French newspaper thoroughly, working in collaboration with the homeless organization Les Compagnons de la nuit, before launching *La Rue* in October 1993 (*Le Monde*, 22 October 1993). The company Big Issue France was set up with British backing, and with *The Big Issue*'s editor, John Bird, as honorary associate and adviser. Established institutions, the Caisse des dépôts et consignations and charities Fondation de France and Secours Catholique, invested a million francs in the founding company which, in turn, financed the creation of *La Rue*. (Hence frequent barbed comments from rival titles to the effect that they are independent and do not rely on public subsidy.) *La Rue* invites readers to subscribe to Big Issue France, and the profits from the paper are used to fund job creation and social integration projects.

La Rue has always registered vendors for official purposes. It is the only street paper to collaborate with the Office de Justification de la Diffusion (OJD) and have its circulation figures validated. It attaches considerable importance to ethical conduct and, in every edition, presents a statement of its objectives: official status for vendors; financial transparency; commitment to reintegrating the homeless; job creation. Annual accounts are audited by Arthur Andersen and published in its columns.[16] After only a year's operation, 25 jobs had been created, six of these officially recognized under the government's job creation and training programme. Arrangements are made for hostel accommodation, legal advice, medical assistance, sports activities; and

education and training are provided for vendors. In short, the magazine is at the hub of a wide range of activities designed to assist the
homeless. A shared philosophy inspires a co-ordinated team effort, with
primarily social not commercial objectives. As regards distribution, for
example, *La Rue* emphasizes that it does not seek expansion for its own
sake; it does not want a relationship of wholesaler to retailer with outlets
in the provinces, but selects partners with the interests of its vendors in
mind.[17] In Kunvari's words, 'Nous ne sommes pas là pour ramasser du
fric, mais pour faire de l'insertion'[18] (Kunvari, 1994: 21). The idealism
and professionalism are constantly apparent.

In the spirit of working with, and not simply on behalf of the
homeless, the latter are invited to workshops where they are encouraged to develop their writing skills and express their views. Samples
of their work appear in the magazine under the heading 'Mots mêlés'.
Workshop organizer Véronique Pétetin talks of her role in terms of a
political and ethical commitment (Pétetin, 1994: 34). There are also
public discussion meetings following the publication of special dossiers
in the magazine. *La Rue* presents itself as a meeting-point: 'un lieu de
dialogue et de rencontre, un magazine grand public ayant pour objectif
de casser le mur de l'exclusion'[19] (quoted in *Le Monde*, 22 October
1993).

As a product, the magazine is attractive, and more up-market and
expensive than its competitors (selling at 15 FF as opposed to 10 FF for
Macadam and *Le Réverbère* in 1995). It is printed on good quality paper,
with colour photographs and cartoons from well-known artists. It covers
similar topics to other SDF papers: eviction, children at risk, AIDS,
unemployment. The quality of the journalism is good except, perhaps
predictably, for occasional mediocre items in the section devoted to
vendors' writing. The frequency of contributions from well-known
personalities demonstrates the degree of public recognition the publication has earned. The anniversary issue in November 1994, for
example, included contributions from priests, philosophers, academics, scientists, who were invited to share with the reader their dreams for
the future. It is also interesting to note that, on 19 October 1994, Day of
National Solidarity in France, it was from the premises of *La Rue* that
Simone Veil, Minister for Social and Urban Affairs, chose to launch the
government's emergency plans to help the homeless during the winter.[20]

Le Réverbère's response has been to ridicule *La Rue* as naïve, and guilty
of complicity with the establishment, describing it as 'une revue lux-
ueuse, bien pensante, qui ne dérange pas et qui, à force d'écrire qu'elle

fait de la réinsertion, en devient ridicule'[21] (Vergely, 1995: 28). The criticism is malicious and unfair. *La Rue* is outspoken in its campaigns, but measured. Over the winter months of 1994/95, a regular item in the newspaper drew attention to vacant buildings in Paris which were considered ideal subjects for requisition orders. After Chirac's acceptance of the principle of requisition, the paper was blunt and cynical about his electioneering, commenting 'A la recherche de voix, le maire de Paris a entendu celle de l'abbé Pierre'.[22] The editorial team also published an open letter addressed to Chirac, making clear it was expecting him to live up to his promises.[23] There is a basic difference in political philosophy between the two papers: whereas *Le Réverbère* is fundamentally anarchical, *La Rue* has chosen to work from within the system, capitalizing on the goodwill of the many public figures who have rallied to the cause of the homeless. It has produced some serious analysis, interesting feature articles and interviews, and even the first opinion survey examining the attitudes and origins of the homeless.[24] It has avoided both the invective of *Le Réverbère*, and the anecdotal monotony of *Macadam*. While its validated official circulation of 80,000 copies per month is still well below that claimed by its main rivals, *La Rue*'s foundations are solid, its reputation is growing and it can provide concrete evidence of the progress it has made in advancing the cause of the homeless.

Faim de siècle

Faim de siècle claims comparable circulation to *La Rue*, but does not enjoy the same subsidies and has been beset by financial and management difficulties. A fashionable product with glossy illustrations, it targets young readers between 20 and 35 years old, interspersing features on the homeless with news about the music scene and entertainment. Items are short and trendy, but lightweight. Nonetheless, its charitable activities have earned respect, particularly a food and meal voucher scheme run in conjunction with bodies such as the Red Cross. The director Marc Thoumyre also joined representatives of *La Rue* in negotiations with the authorities to secure official status for SDF newspaper vendors.

Le Lampadaire

The most recent of the established SDF titles[25] is a very readable but undistinguished weekly, *Le Lampadaire*, set up by Mohammed El Kaddioui. A former editor of *Le Réverbère* who fell out with Georges Mathis,

El Kaddioui accuses the latter of unscrupulous exploitation of the homeless for personal gain (Müller, 1994). The unsavoury squabbling between the two, and their efforts to destroy one another by discounting newspapers to vendors in order to swamp the market and defeat all competition, have served to give the street press as a whole a bad name, belying any noble intentions.

Assessment

What then is our assessment of the significance of the SDF press? Criticisms in the conventional mainstream media have suggested that some SDF titles are simply opportunistic ventures, launched by callous entrepreneurs who see them as potential money-spinners, and are keen to cash in on public sympathy for the underdog. Mathis's departure from *Macadam* to set up *Le Réverbère*, El Kaddioui's defection to set up *Le Lampadaire*, and subsequently Sophie Crépon's departure from *Le Réverbère*, were all followed by savage denunciations of the activities of previous colleagues which give credence to the suggestion that there has been ruthless exploitation of the homeless for commercial gain. On the other hand, a colourful figure like Mathis, profiteer though he may be, has first-hand knowledge of homelessness and unemployment, and has given powerful expression to the experience of marginalization and disaffection, bringing considerable publicity to the issue. Despite their differences in image and appeal, all the street newspapers have, in their own way and to varying degrees, given the homeless an opportunity to express their views, and to communicate with the general public via letters columns, personal profiles, poems and articles, eliciting sympathy for their cause, and modifying stereotypical views of their situation. To this extent, the SDF press can be regarded as the voice of the homeless, even if it is equally clear that the mediating role of professionals remains crucial, both in order to curb mediocrity and monotony at editorial level, and also to ensure the long-term viability of publications through sound management practices.

On an immediate, practical level, the income earned by homeless vendors has also undoubtedly improved day-to-day living conditions for many individuals. Successful vendors in Paris are said to earn the equivalent of £30 to £40 per day. Jobs have also been created within the newspapers' organizations. This may well explain why there is so little evidence of government efforts to clamp down on profiteering and black market activities, since SDF newspapers have visibly made progress in attempting to alleviate the plight of the homeless, whereas government action has been inadequate. Repressive measures from the authorities might well have provoked public hostility.

As to the wider impact of the SDF press, this is difficult to determine. The timing of the emergence and expansion of the street press from 1993 onwards parallels the rise in public concern in France over homelessness. Yet how much its success is a cause, and how much a consequence, of the sense of moral outrage and public solidarity is not clear. Predictably, the newspapers claim credit for raising public consciousness: 'L'apparition de "Macadam Journal" en mai 1993 a braqué les projecteurs sur les SDF et les exclus. Plus personne ne peut les ignorer', claims Martine Vanden Driessche.[26] Over the same period, however, there was a growth in militancy from campaigning organizations such as DAL (Droit au logement), and increased publicity for prominent champions of the cause such as Abbé Pierre, Monseigneur Gaillot and Professors Albert Jacquard and Léon Schwarzenberg. The relative importance of individual voices would be difficult to establish, but they were mutually reinforcing, participating in a general upsurge of interest.

The precise impact of street newspapers in particular cannot be established without greater knowledge of their readership and reception. A purchaser does not necessarily buy the newspaper because s/he actually wants to read it, and values the product for its intrinsic merits. In many instances the purchase may simply represent a symbolic gesture, a charitable donation in return for a bundle of sheets of paper, which salve the purchaser's conscience, but quickly find their way into the waste-paper bin, and might just as well take the form of a candle, a ribbon or any other token of solidarity. One can comment on the merits and shortcomings of individual publications, but to take the argument about influence any further, audience research is required in order to identify who actually reads the newspapers and what they think of them. The newspaper editors are keen to demonstrate that the publications are read, and cite letters received in response to previous editions as proof of their readership, but such evidence is not statistically compelling. In the absence of further research, we confine ourselves to observing that the street press has achieved significant circulation figures, and has fuelled the debate on homelessness and social integration by keeping the problem in the public eye, both through the presence of vendors on the streets and through the insights it has brought into the reality of homelessness. At a time when conventional newspapers in France are experiencing difficulties in maintaining circulation and face financial constraints, this success is no mean feat, and may to some degree allay fears that, in the global context of international multi-media empires, freedom of expression has become the prerogative of the rich and powerful.

Notes

1. For a definition, see p. 158.
2. Bureau d'informations et de prévisions économiques – Bureau for economic data and forecasting.
3. According to Castaing, a working party set up in October 1994 by CNIS, the national centre for statistical information, is currently seeking to remedy this deficiency.
4. Figures taken from *Macadam Journal* 3 (July–August 1993): 3 and 24, and from information provided by staff at the newspaper's head office.
5. *Macadam*'s main competitor, *Le Réverbère*, had set the example for this diversification, launching a comic strip magazine *Cosmiques Tripes* a year earlier.
6. 'The homeless: where is *Macadam*'s lolly going?' (Bellet and Szac-Jacquelin, 1994).
7. 'The Homeless Press: swindle or charity?' (Müller, 1994).
8. The best general source of circulation figures is the information provided by editors to Sophie Crépon (1994: 40–1). According to Crépon, *Le Réverbère* had an average circulation of between 300,000 and 500,000 copies at the end of 1994.
9. Our sources for these accusations are Bellet and Szac-Jacquelin (1994: 21) and Müller (1994).
10. 'Vendors, we pay national insurance contributions.'
11. 'Bitch of a death', *Le Réverbère* 24–25 (1 Aug. 1994).
12. Satisfactory rendering in English of Mathis's colourful, familiar style is impossible, but in loose translation: 'France has no interest in adopting this old fogey when we manage to get rid of the decrepit effigy in post at present [i.e. Mitterrand].'
13. 'Simpering sweetheart Chirac, the darling of la-di-das, who old girls of 60 would love to have it off with, and who blokes want to be like, sees himself as symbol of a certain kind of France, a Joan of Arc saviour of the homeless, Chirac who has lived for the last fifteen years in the town hall, the biggest apartment in Paris (1200 square metres)!'
14. See, for example, Dalençon (1994: 28–34), in which the author refers to the imminent British general election scheduled for early 1995 . . .
15. This description has frequently figured on the front cover. It suggests that the paper belongs to the homeless and jobless, rather than simply focusing on the problem of homelessness.
16. See *La Rue* 13 (Dec. 1994): 33–4.
17. 'Comment *La Rue* choisit ses partenaires en régions', *La Rue* 7 (May 1994): 34.
18. 'We are not here to make a packet, but to integrate people in society.'
19. ' . . . a space for dialogue, a meeting-place, a magazine for the general public which aims to break down the barrier of social exclusion.'
20. Reported in *La Rue* 13 (Dec. 1994): 10–11.
21. ' . . . a glossy, self-righteous, conformist review, which so insists that it is reintegrating people that it becomes ridiculous.'

22. The line is not easily translated since it turns on a pun. 'Voix' refers both to the votes which Chirac was seeking to attract by espousing the cause of the homeless, and also the voice of Abbé Pierre to which he is said to have responded. Source: 'En attendant les réquisitions ... ', *La Rue*, 14 (Jan. 1995): 33.
23. 'Lettre ouverte à Jacques Chirac', *La Rue* 14 (Jan. 1995): 2.
24. See *La Rue* 14, which is entitled 'Ce que pensent les SDF'.
25. Other titles no doubt exist. We are aware of the publication of at least two provincial SDF newspapers: *En-Sortir*, a rather earnest but dull quarterly set up in spring 1994, which covers the towns of Caen and Rouen; and *Réagir*, a monthly launched in Bordeaux in April 1994.
26. 'The appearance of *Macadam Journal* in May 1993 turned the spotlights on the homeless and social outcasts. Nobody can be unaware of their existence any longer': in 'Edito', *Macadam Info* (March 1995): 3.

References

Bellet, R. and Szac-Jacquelin, M. (1994) 'SDF: où passe le fric de *Macadam*?', *L'Evénement du jeudi*, 24 Feb. – 2 March: 20–1.

Castaing, M. (1995a) 'Plus de cent associations manifestent contre l'exclusion', *Le Monde*, 9–10 April.

Castaing, M. (1995b) 'Les zones d'ombre d'une évaluation statistique', *Le Monde*, 9–10 April.

Crépon, S. (1994–95) 'Les journaux de la rue en France: sans toit ni loi?', *L'Echo de la presse*, Dec.–Jan.: 40–1.

Dalençon, H. (1994) 'Angleterre: entre le scandale de la misère et la richesse scandaleuse', *Le Réverbère* 33 (21 Dec.): 28–34.

Garin, C. (1995) 'Le ministre du logement réquisitionne des immeubles parisiens', *Le Monde*, 30 Aug.

Kunvari, A. (1994) '*La Rue* et *Faim de Siècle*: l'insertion en plus', *L'Evénement du jeudi*, 24 Feb.–2 March: 21.

Mathis, G. (1994) 'Eh ... dito. Adieu Jack', *Le Réverbère* 33 (21 Dec.): 3.

Mathis, G. (1995a) 'Eh ... dito. La loi, c'est pour qui?', *Le Réverbère* 34 (16 Jan.): 3.

Mathis, G. (1995b) 'Réponse à une lettre ouverte pour la fermer', *Le Réverbère* 34 (16 Jan.): 28.

Müller, M. (1994) 'Presse S.d.f. Arnaque ou charité?', *L'Esprit libre* 2 (Dec.): 47–53.

Pétetin, V. (1994) 'Atelier d'écriture: "Un acte politique et éthique" ', *La Rue* 5 (March): 34.

Vergely, M. (1995) 'Sondage partiel ou manip?', *Le Réverbère* 34 (16 Jan.): 28.

12.

Financial (self-)identification: the pink economy in France

STEVE WHARTON

The crux of the matter is that in order to establish our identity as gay people we have to have some tangible evidence of a gay community, a community we can't always see but which we know to exist.

(Short, 1992: 20)

A Paris on peut boire, manger, danser, lire, en un mot consommer gai.[1]

(*Libération*, 25 June 1995: 4)

Ce mot [communauté], qui redevient très à la mode depuis le début des années 80, fait peur à une certaine partie de la société française qui voit dans ce terme une américanisation de notre société . . . [2]

(Basque, 1995: 1)

For anyone interested in gay and lesbian studies,[3] be it in France, England or anywhere, these three quotations neatly encapsulate the paradox of the field, demonstrating as they do that the essential desire to discover and investigate is inevitably restrained by the problems of definition. And if definition itself were not enough of a problem, in a French context we must also find ways of dealing with the very monolith that is *La République*, with its desire for uniformity and fear of matters American which does not permit of ease of terminology. Moreover, what is community, and are we talking here of a French or American model? Yves Roussel (1995: 85–108) recently indicated in *Les nouveaux temps* that the question of 'community' can be seen to have direct links to the American situation, but for him, the French gay community or at least the gay liberation movement from which it has allegedly sprung, lost its immediate post-'68 impetus over the 1970s, with only the rise of AIDS serving once more to provide a driving force.

However, what is of interest to us here is the potentiality for resolving the question of definition through an economic paradigm. In this connection, our second quotation can be seen to be a useful indicator, for in the latter years of the twentieth century, the century which has raised the consumer to the status of a god, it is an incontrovertible fact that a person with spending power is a person to whom people will listen. Those with money are courted by marketing people, salespeople and politicians alike – the consumer is sovereign. And so we must ask – can this general truism be extended to the 'gay community', and is a gay person with money therefore able to say that he or she has power? Can this (financial) power be said to extend to the political sphere; and what are its consequences? In other words, does the ability to spend 'pink money', in conferring visibility and identity, also confer recognition? Finally, if these questions can be shown to have validity in America and Britain, do they have equal weight within a French context, or are there subtleties of difference?

We shall attempt here to answer these questions by first examining issues of definition and self-definition (the search for identity) before passing to two specific examples of contemporary relevance: the 1995 Paris Gay Pride and the work of the SNEG, the Syndicat national des entreprises gaies (National Union of Gay Enterprises). Whilst one is more immediately economic in its thrust than the other, the two clearly demonstrate an increasing visibility of the lesbian and gay community in France. Inevitably and for historical reasons, reference in the early part of this work will be to the American situation, permitting later of comparison between this and the French.

(Self-)definition

So what is 'gay identity'? On a general level, Jeffrey Weeks (1990: 88) makes the position abundantly clear: 'Identity is about belonging, about what you have in common with some people and what differentiates you from others.' It was never always thus with regard to questions of an individual's sexuality or sexual identity, something that has only recently been of interest. We can trace a long history of 'homosexual activities', from Sappho's poetry and Plato's *Symposium* to more recent works; but with Sappho and Plato it is the acts that are homosexual, not those carrying them out (Cruikshank, 1992: 5). In more recent times and in line with Judaeo-Christian tradition, penalties have been more severe: in Britain, Henry VIII made sodomy punishable by death, as indeed it was in France until the Revolution. In certain circumstances – boarding schools, prisons, etc. – conditions may lead to homosexual *acts*, but these do not in themselves mark out the person indulging in them as homosexual. This ambivalence of approach and attitude (seeing homosexuality as 'a passing phase') was something that was known and reasonably accepted by society for some time and has, indeed, been used more recently as an argument against the lowering of the age of male consent in Britain (Wharton, 1994: 71–84). It was not until 1869 and the coining of the term 'homosexuality' by the German K.M. Kertbeny, that we see a move towards more active categorization of people. We should note, however, it was *external* categorization which occurred here, and although the gay community used and uses its own forms of language,[4] its members continued to be judged by mainstream standards. It was not until the rise of political movements in the 1960s that we are really able to observe the beginnings of a definite discourse of identity or 'otherness' within the gay community.[5]

But we must return to the question, what is a community? By itself, the term suggests shared values, ethics and conduct. Cruikshank takes Altman's suggestion that the notion of a gay community depends on a gay culture, since homosexuals have no common country or language to bind them. In her eyes:

> 'gay community' refers to the lesbians and gay men who consider themselves part of a political movement. Membership of the community is thus chosen rather than automatic. 'Gay culture' designates the attitudes, values, tastes, artistic and literary works, groups and organizations, common experiences, festivals, special events, rituals, and their sense of a shared history.
>
> (Cruikshank, 1992: 118–19)

Clearly the one influences the other to an extent, but if we take Cruikshank's definition, a modern-day member of the gay community is someone who has made a conscious 'political' choice to be gay,[6] to be open about their sexuality and to see and use it as a positive aspect of their life. In addition to this choice, they may seek to purchase for themselves objects or services which they know to be in some way connected with the 'positivism' they have chosen – clothes and music, for example: 'Because we are not immediately visible to each other', argues Short (1994: 52) 'and because society seems reluctant to acknowledge our presence, we are forced to prove we exist by projecting a gay image or lifestyle.' By extrapolation, purchasing the items which contribute to this image in turn confers visibility – a conspicuous consumption.

The very conspicuousness of the consumption reflects a more recent element in the gay identity debate, the economic. In parallel with the gay liberation movement of the 1970s and 1980s in the USA came an activism and desire to push home the advantages of greater visibility. Activists argued that, in a developed Western economy, economic power translated as political power; and if society could see that gays were economically powerful, then this would have inevitable political consequences. Such an idea was not new, since many groups working for social change have used the economic argument to good effect. In this instance, in addition to activists stamping dollars with pink triangles to show that the money was gay, market research in America set out to show companies that the gay community enjoyed a higher income than the national average. *Out* magazine, for example, claims 350,000 readers with an average income of over $70,000 (quoted in *Homo Economics*, Channel Four, 9 August 1994). Mulryan/Nash, an advertising agency specializing in reaching gay consumers, studied 76 gay magazines and newspapers across America and concluded that the advertising spend was $53 million annually, with bars and clubs comprising 19.5 per cent of the sample, *téléphone rose* services 12.6 per cent, and legal, medical and other professional services 10.8 per cent. Car advertising accounted for about 2 per cent of all spending (quoted in bit.listserv.gaynet, article 11881, 31 May 1994). In the face of such obvious potential profitability to marketing people and companies, the 'buy gay' concept began to emerge in America and the 'gay lifestyle' was promoted, for example with the Toyota Seca Ultima advertisement of 1991 showing two men and their Dalmatians with the caption 'The family car'. It reached the apogee of 'mainstream' acceptability with the Ikea advertisement first shown in America in March 1994 (though after 10 pm). In this, two men explain how they set out to find a table as they embarked upon setting up house together. They bought one with a leaf: 'A leaf means staying together', says one. Despite the transmission time, the advertisement is acknowledged as a signal step: 'Time was, you couldn't get away with a commercial that depicted gay men having a flair for interior decoration. That's progress for you', wrote Phil Rosenthal of the *Los Angeles Times News* (quoted in *Homo Economics*, Channel Four, 9 August 1994). And so in America at least, this rich and predominantly untapped market was being courted. Where they were previously conspicuous by their absence from mainstream images, gays began to appear ever so slightly in advertising as their apparent potentiality for profitability became more apparent.

In Britain, the pace and thrust was a little slower. Although male homosexuality has been decriminalized for some 25 years (though the lower age limit of 18 was only achieved in 1994 and is still not on a par with the heterosexual 16),[7] activism is not as prominent as in parts of America and has tended to concentrate on the political – decriminalizing homosexuality, for example – rather than the economic. As a result, Britain's Castro and Christopher Street are still a long way off, though the rise of Old Compton Street in London and the Gay Village in Manchester over the last five to ten years gives greater visibility to gay spending power. Even here, though, to point to the rise of the club/café scene as a clear indicator of greater political muscle would be erroneous since:

> The pub and club scene is probably only the noisier part of a much larger gay market; and a part which most genuine, high-earning 'A' and 'B' consumers usually move on from. It is surely beyond the bar scene that the 'last untapped market of capitalism' really lies.
>
> (Short, 1994: 52)

And yet paradoxically it is this 'noisy' and visible element which is seen by marketing people as being important. According to advertising executive Peter Duckworth:

> What's changing is the power of the gay community itself, its visibility. . . . Advertisers can see it, they know it's there, and if they think hard enough about it they recognize *it's got a spending power that they want to appeal to.*
> (*Homo Economics*, Channel Four, 9 August 1994, my emphasis).

Put more cynically (by Peter Fressola of Benetton US, speaking on the same programme), by virtue of their income gays 'enjoy *the right to be marketed to*' (my emphasis). Moreover, it is argued by marketing people that since society has given them a rough time in the past, any gay-positive approach will bear fruit in the present as grateful gays buy from their friends. The implications of such 'brand loyalty' are clear, and a 1994 survey showed that any company advertising in the gay press was likely to command greater loyalty from those customers (*Homo Economics*, Channel Four, 9 August 1994). Ultimately, however, it can be argued in the majority of cases that any 'mainstream' commercial interest in the gay community is commercial first and gay-friendly second.

Open any gay magazine and you will see copy for spirits, cars, music, goods and services – not necessarily adapted for the gay market, but there.[8] The market is still ready to hear the siren call of gay = money.

Even so, the present trend in the UK is towards marketing targeted at gay men rather than lesbians. The incorrect perception of lesbians as enjoying lesser financial power than gay men clearly determines advertising strategies. The recently-launched British lesbian magazine *Diva*, for example, has attracted little mainstream advertising whereas a similar publication aimed at gay men, *Attitude*, does not suffer this handicap.

In marked contrast to the American argument, in Britain the accent is more on the trend-setting angle of the gay community. The 'PR spin' is that products popular in the gay market automatically cross over into the mainstream. The last 18 months have seen the rise of so-called 'lesbian chic' in the mainstream – for example, three out of the four main GB soaps have had lesbian story-lines – and it is becoming 'the thing' for straight couples to go to gay clubs.

But what of the situation in France? To my knowledge, no French soap opera character's sexuality has been divulged. On the other hand, we *can* see parallels with the 'mainstream cross-over' marketing argument of the British marketing people. This has certainly been the case with Absolut, the vodka company whose campaigns have been present in the gay press since the 1980s but since 1993 have been more openly 'gay' in their message, with campaigns such as 'Absolut Queen' and 'Absolute Régine'. On a more general level, the first 'gay advertising' can be said to have appeared in the gay press in 1982, for Yves Saint Laurent perfume.

As to the 'gay village' argument, any visitor to the Marais in Paris cannot have failed to notice that this is France's Christopher Street. From the first bar there in the 1980s, called, appropriately enough, 'Village' (Madesclaire, 1995: 48), a thriving bar, club and restaurant community has flourished, also offering such diverse services as laundries, plumbing and electricians. Indeed, such is the popularity of the area that a bar can easily fetch two to three times the asking price for a comparable site elsewhere in Paris (interview with the Syndicat national des entreprises gaies, 31 July 1995). But, according to the SNEG representative: 'le Marais ne s'est pas créé tout seul: il répondait à une urgence: sortir les pédés de leur anonymat, les déculpabiliser.'[9] So here, it is argued, the establishment of a precise geographic location permits lesbians and gay men to be seen together as a group, to make clear that they are many and not few: 'C'est bien cette visibilité qui est au cœur du mouvement actuel et qui sert de slogan à toutes ces marches, ces parades, tous ces défilés.'[10] In other words, the time has come for the lesbian and gay community in France to demonstrate clearly that it exists or, in the words of the famous American slogan, 'We're here, we're queer, we're not going away'.

Our two case-studies provide ample demonstration of how 'we're not going away'. The 1995 Paris Gay Pride and the SNEG give us clear examples of the increased and increasing confidence and solidarity of the French gay and lesbian community. Whilst Gay Pride has no immediate financial or economic bearing on questions of identity, its very occurrence gives precisely the positive imagery and visibility which we have already indicated are necessary in the elaboration of a gay identity. The SNEG, on the other hand, brings together gay businesses in the fight against AIDS.

Case-study 1: Gay Pride 1995

On 24 June 1995, just as gays and lesbians were demonstrating their solidarity in other towns and cities across Europe, Paris became host to a parade of some 70,000–80,000 people from the Rue de Rennes to the Place de la Bastille, all expressing their pride and solidarity in their sexuality. Be it with the large banner 'Fières' unveiled at the start of the march, the one minute die-in[11] on the Boulevard Saint-Germain or the music at Bastille, visibility and commemoration were the order of the day – visibility through the presence of so many, commemoration through the simple slogan 'Nous aurions pu être 14,000 de plus'.[12]

The events of Saturday 24 June had been the culmination of over a week of press and media coverage, with the run-up to Pride '95 and the question of lesbian and gay visibility appearing in *Libération, Le Monde, L'Humanité, Le Nouvel Observateur* and *L'Express,* with Canal+ running a Gay Night on Friday 23 June. And so 'the mainstream' seemed particularly indulgent towards matters this year. At the same time, a new gay magazine *Têtu* had been launched on the Monday preceding Pride:

> Ainsi c'est moins dans le domaine de la revendication directement politique (par exemple, celui des droits des homosexuels) que la 'Lesbian and Gay Pride' marquera cette année que dans la volonté de s'inscrire, voire de transformer la culture générale.[13]
>
> (Lebovici, 1995: 23)

Certainly the participants interviewed underlined their delight in the sheer numbers and the sense of solidarity this conveyed, as for example in the words of Natalie and Muriel, both 30, quoted in *Libération*: 'Cette fête change des autres jours où on est invisibles. Dans la rue et ailleurs, nous ne nous cachons jamais, sauf au boulot'[14] (Prigent and Rémès, 1995: 23).

This last comment serves subtly to remind us of the possibility of discrimination that still exists and indirectly raises another point: if a place such as the Marais can offer positive imagery and a place to go, does it not also by its very concentration in one area offer the danger of ghettoization? As we know,

> Un ghetto est l'endroit où une minorité est séparée du reste de la société. C'est aussi un milieu refermé sur lui-même, dans une condition margin-ale. Le ghetto agit comme une métaphore géographique de la condition des gays, fixant de façon territoriale les limites entre eux et l'ensemble de la société.[15]
>
> (Madesclaire, 1995: 48)

But this vocabulary of *repli sur soi* with its negative connotations does not have to be the only definition of the Marais:

> Forgé par des affinités et une mémoire commune de la discrimination, ce monde homosexuel s'installe dans une ségrégation librement choisie, semblable à celles des groupes moraux qui, selon les théoriciens de l'Ecole de Chicago, foisonnent dans les grandes villes où ils se substituent aux liens sociaux traditionnels.[16]
>
> (Pollack, 1995: 8)

In other words, as we have already noted, ghetto is not the correct term for an area such as the Marais. Rather, it is an area of free association, clearly identifiable yet open to all, providing goods and services to all comers. The sense of community it gives relies much more on Cruik-shank's definition (1992: 118–19) than any discourse of segregation.

There has however been one major occurrence over the last ten years which can be argued to have done more than anything else to crystallize a sense of community, the tragedy that is AIDS. It is felt, for example, that the advent of AIDS is the single most important influence in bringing people together, in giving a sense of 'community' (interview with SNEG, 1 August 1995). In our second case-study, we shall see how the gay community has acted to meet the problem in a way that helps to forge the sense of identity and to work in the economic sphere.

Case-study 2: the Syndicat national des entreprises gaies

Founded in 1990 as an *association de loi 1901*,[17] the SNEG serves to bring together both those who run businesses targeted at the gay community, and those businesses run by gays, helping in the fight against AIDS. SNEG's initial impetus was the defence of gay businesses and individuals and the provision of special services (goods at wholesale prices, etc.). It has some 600 members, individuals and organizations, to whom legal services are provided together with liaison with police stations and local branches.

On the prevention side, liaison work with both the Ministry of Health and the Paris Social and Sanitary department has provided funds to finance SNEG's initial work. For practically the first time since the appearance of AIDS, both government and business were working together to fight the problem. Indeed, the latest government campaign, 'En vacances j'oublie tout sauf le préservatif' (On holiday I forget everything except my condoms) was adapted for the gay community thanks to SNEG's input.

Clearly committed to the fight against AIDS and working effectively with both private enterprise and government and non-governmental organizations, SNEG, although based in Paris, has divided France into six regions, each with a regional delegate to work closely with organizations in the region and ensure that its message is effectively transmitted throughout the country.

Tables 12.1 and 12.2 show SNEG services and recent campaigns. In addition, SNEG has had major input into the summer 1995 posters forming part of the national AIDS prevention campaign. The posters are well designed, simply phrased and clear in their message of condom use and the precautions necessary.

And so SNEG has grown from the desire to help with AIDS prevention and built on the feelings of solidarity that have arisen, harnessing the energies and to an extent the financial goodwill, of gay businesses. What is interesting to note here is that, in the case of France, the SNEG has concentrated on preventive work, bringing together those organi-

Table 12.1 *SNEG services offered to its members*

Service	Details
Legal advice	either on employment or more general matters
Purchasing co-operative	condoms and lubricant (at reduced price when sponsored) for free distribution in bars, etc.
Bi-monthly newsletter: *SyNErGie*	lists information on AIDS prevention, details of legal matters, general information, etc.
Minitel service	Telephone 3615 SNEG for information from the newsletter, together with more commercial information (e.g. property sales, job offers, etc.)

Table 12.2 *SNEG campaigns (1993–95)*

September 1993	Distribution of beer-mats with messages on the use of condoms in all gay bars in Paris, supported by the DASES (Direction de l'action sociale, de l'enfance et de la santé).
December 1993	*Weekend de la glisse* in Parisian saunas, designed to promote the use of lubricant with condoms.
Christmas 1993	300 Christmas trees – *Arbre de l'amour et de la prévention* – distributed in bars and clubs across France, with condoms, lubricant and booklets on AIDS prevention fastened to the branches.
April 1994	Week-end *'Réflexe latex'* in bars and clubs across France, with the aim of promoting condom use.
Spring 1994	Nation-wide tour of 'Hot Show, Hot Safe', a musical performance designed to demonstrate safe sex.
1 December 1994	To coincide with World AIDS Day, SNEG set up *Les Fresques*, areas of canvas in gay clubs where people could commemorate their loved ones in paint (a variation on the AIDS quilt concept). Postcards of these canvases were later sold in aid of charity.
Christmas 1994	Another 300 Christmas trees.
March 1995	An exhibition of the previous December's *Fresques*. New signing for use in gay saunas and similar areas, adapting the universally recognized road sign scheme.
April 1995	Another *Weekend de la glisse*. New beer-mats. Another 'Hot Show, Hot Safe' tour.

zations where the work is most likely to be effective, whereas its British counterpart, the Gay Business Association, serves more to regroup businesses and commercial interests, groups in Britain such as the Terrence Higgins Trust already dealing with the preventive aspects.

Conclusion: financial (self-)identification, sense of community, achievement or manipulation?

Impressive as they are, however, these achievements do not mean that gays and lesbians automatically enjoy equality and freedom from discrimination. Even in the USA where relative economic and political power is much stronger, the fact remains that 'It has very little to do with whether we are free, have equality, [or] can be free from violence and discrimination' (Urvashi Vaid in *Homo Economics*, Channel Four, 9 August 1994).

In other words, and in contrast with the aspirations of the economic activists, any perceived economic gain is not reflected in the decline of discrimination, as was intimated by Natalie and Muriel in an earlier quotation. It could even be argued that within a British and American context the 'political power through economic power' argument has been cynically manipulated by certain commercial interests to call upon notions of solidarity and loyalty within the gay community to further mainstream commercial advantage rather than equality. Ultimately, political activism is more important than consumer activity, although the latter can support the former if used appositely.

What we have been able to observe in a French context is that the tragedy that is AIDS has ironically done more than anything else over the past decade to crystallize feelings of solidarity. At the same time, this has not prevented lesbians and gay men from celebrating their lives and lifestyle with increasing confidence, and doing so with increasing visibility.

The title of this chapter is 'Financial (self-)identification', and yet we inevitably find that it is the question of visibility that is more important than questions of finance when contributing to our understanding of gay (self-)identity. It is surely the case that the current commercial interest in the 'pink economy' is more a trend than a political force – after all, trend-setting has been cited as a marketing tool. No one can deny that the gay community exists and enjoys spending power, but perhaps no more so than any other group; surveys in the USA and Britain have certainly shown this. The first studies of the pink economy in France are only now being undertaken, by the accountants Axes (Rémès, 1995b: 6), and so for now we must perhaps wait and see; but it is unlikely that we shall see any major differences between France and the USA and Britain.

The more important question in identity remains one of visibility, and it is this question of visibility and periodic reidentification, of definition and self-definition, which is more important than apparent questions of political muscle through financial power. Whether 'the pink economy' provides for cynical manipulation of the credulous gay consumer *en quête d'identité* (in search of identity) or not, the most important fact to emerge from the present study is the effect of solidarity conferred by the increased visibility positive gay images can give. This was certainly the message of Gay Pride 1995, and in conclusion, I can do no better than quote Erik Rémès, long-time contributor to gay journalism:

> Pour la Lesbian et Gay Pride, avec la multiplication de ces relais entre la communauté homosexuelle et la société à laquelle elle appartient, la parole des homosexuels va enfin pouvoir circuler, sans tabou ... Ce profond changement de mentalité et d'attitude à l'égard de l'homosexualité que l'on observe en France n'auraient pu avoir lieú sans le courage de ces homosexuels, hommes et femmes qui ont choisi de rendre visible leur homosexualité dans leur entourage. ... Cette Gay Pride appartient donc à tous, gays et lesbiennes et autres, quelles que soient leur apparte-

nances sociale, politique ou religieuse, qu'ils et elles soient cuirs, folles, Queers, techno-queens, séropos, pédés, travs, butchs, ou encore hét-éros.[18]

(Rémès, 1995a: 32)

Notes

1. 'In Paris you can eat, drink, dance, read, in a word consume gay.'
2. 'This word [community], which has become very fashionable since the beginning of the 1980s, frightens a certain proportion of French society which sees in the term the Americanization of our society.'
3. Throughout this chapter, the term 'gay' will be used to refer to both lesbians and gay men. The term 'homosexual' is used as a generic term, with 'gay' indicating a more politically active stance. This chapter is not the place to enter into the 'gay' versus 'queer' debate which I am happy to do outside the parameters of the present work.
4. For example, *Polari* in English, as in 'Vada the bona lallies', for 'Look at those lovely legs'.
5. Those interested in knowing more about the history of the gay liberation movement in France should read Darrier (1987).
6. See my comment in note 3 above.
7. Lesbianism has never been illegal in Britain.
8. Whisky, gin, vodka and port are the most popular spirits in Britain (*Gay Times*, January 1994: 25).
9. 'The Marais did not come into existence all by itself: it answered an urgent need: to bring queers out of their anonymity, to free them from guilt.'
10. 'It is precisely this visibility which is at the heart of the current movement and which serves as a slogan for all these marches, parades and demos.'
11. A tactic elaborated by ACT-UP (the AIDS Coalition to Unleash Power) involving lying down as if dead, blocking the road.
12. 'There could have been 14,000 more of us.'
13. 'And so it is less within the sphere of direct political demands (for example gay rights) than from a desire to speak out or even to transform general opinion, that Lesbian and Gay Pride would wish to make its mark.'
14. 'This "fiesta" is a change from the other days when we're invisible. We never hide, on the streets or elsewhere, unless we're at work.'
15. 'A ghetto is a place in which a minority is separated from the rest of society. It is an area which closes in on itself, which is marginalized. A ghetto works like a geographical metaphor for the gay condition, setting territorial limits between gays and the rest of society.'
16. 'Forged from affinities and a common folk memory of discrimination, the homosexual world sets itself up in freely chosen segregation, one similar to those moral groups which, according to the theoreticians of the Chicago school, thrive in large towns where they take over from the traditional social links.'
17. That is, a non-profit-making organization recognized by the law.
18. 'As far as Lesbian and Gay Pride is concerned, with increased links between the homosexual community and the society to which it belongs, what homosexuals have to say will finally be heard without any taboo ... This profound change of

attitude towards homosexuality which we can observe in France could not have taken place without the courage of gay men and women who have chosen to make their homosexuality visible to those around them. ... This Gay Pride therefore belongs to everyone, gays, lesbians and others, whatever their social, political or religious affiliation and whether they are leather queens, queens, queers, techno-queens, PWAs, gay, drag queens, butch, fem or even straight.'

References

Basque, P.-A. (1995) Editorial in *Exit (le journal)*, 21 July–3 Aug.: 1.

Cruikshank, M. (1992) *The Gay and Lesbian Liberation Movement.* New York: Routledge.

Darrier, E. (1987) 'The gay movement in France since 1945', *Modern and Contemporary France* 29: 10–19.

Lebovici, E. (1995) 'Gay Pride, air de fête et effet de foule', *Libération*, 26 June: 22–3.

Madesclaire, T. (1995) 'Le Ghetto gai: en être ou pas?' *Illico*, Aug.: 48.

Pollack, M. (1995) 'Communauté? Un débat ouvert', *Exit (le journal)* 23: 8.

Prigent, L. and Rémès, E. (1995) 'Je suis un homme simple en robe violette', *Libération*, 26 June: 23.

Rémès, E. (1995a) 'Les Gays de concert', *Libération*, 14 June: 32.

Rémès, E. (1995b) 'Les Gays entrent dans la pub', *Libération*, 18 June: 6.

Roussel, Y. (1995) 'Le mouvement homosexuel français face aux straté-gies identitaires', *Les Nouveaux Temps* 582: 85–108.

Short, B. (1992) 'Queers, beers and shopping', *Gay Times*, Nov.: 20.

Short, B. (1994) 'Redefining gay lifestyles' *Gay Times*, Jan.: 52.

Weeks, J. (1990) 'The value of difference' in J. Rutherford (ed.) *Identity: Community, Culture, Difference.* London: Chatto and Windus.

Wharton, S. (1994) 'Glad to be gay? Newspaper representations of homosexuality in Britain and France' in R.M. Blackburn (ed.) *Social Equality in a Changing Age.* Cambridge: Sociological Research Group.

Television programme

Homo Economics, Channel Four, 9 Aug. 1994.

World Wide Web Usenet group

bit.listserv.gaynet, article 11881, 31 May 1994.

13.

Police and public in France: an overview

SIMON KITSON

In 1942, Adolf Hitler claimed that the French police were the most unpopular in the world (Ferro, 1987: 411). A number of saner commentators have reached much the same conclusion. The police themselves share this belief in popular disdain and ingratitude towards them. In a 1981 survey conducted amongst police officers in Toulouse, 64 per cent expressed the opinion that the force was lacking in public sympathy. Most believed that the public was more hostile to the police in France than in other countries. Of course, perception varied between different categories of officers. Uniformed officers viewed the situation as slightly less catastrophic than their plain-clothed partners. Certain branches such as the Renseignements Généraux were especially prone to a feeling of rejection. Younger members of the force were particularly pessimistic about police/public relations (Jacq and Pons, 1981).

This belief in police unpopularity is in stark contrast to the general findings of surveys carried out among the public. In polls conducted by CSA for the newspaper *Le Parisien*, 83 per cent of those questioned in 1990 claimed to have a good opinion of the police; in 1991, 82 per cent expressed the same claim. In a survey carried out for the *Nouvel Observateur* in 1988, the police came first in a list of institutions to which the public granted confidence, ahead of schools, the *grandes écoles*, the army and the system of justice (Maurin, 1988: 29–32; Gorgeon, 1994: 247). Of course, the reliability of opinion polls can be questioned. Events happening around the date of a particular poll may influence results. The phrasing of questions tends to vary from one survey to the next. It is often not possible to determine exactly which branches of the police are being referred to in the pollsters' questions: sometimes it is specified that the answer should concern the Police Nationale, other times the focus is on the Gendarmerie, but very often the phraseology limits itself to the rather nebulous term 'police' (Maurin, 1988: 22; Gorgeon, 1994: 246). Despite these difficulties a remarkable overlapping of opinion polls can be detected as regards the general question of confidence in the police. However, closer scrutiny of these polls together with the results of a series of studies carried out in France suggest that the relationship between the population and its police is considerably more complicated than this almost unanimous expression of confidence would seem to suggest. Indeed a number of subsidiary questions in these same polls point to areas of dissatisfaction and hope for improvement. Far from being a simple relationship, relations between the police and the public are fraught with areas of suspicion and ambivalence but also with mutual ignorance (Gleizal, 1985: 9).

Ignorance and representations

It may seem somewhat surprising to suggest that the police are ignorant of the public. After all, the police penetrate society more completely than any other service or administration. Considerable amounts of police time are devoted to informing the government of the mood in the country. But the police view is often blinkered and undermined with cynicism. Coming in frequent contact with seediness and corruption, police officers develop a particularly black impression of their human environment. Welded together by the dangers inherent in their duties, they enjoy a high degree of professional solidarity, resulting in an 'us and them' mentality. They often socialize with colleagues, thereby furthering their social isolation (Loubet del Bayle, 1992: 98–110). In many situations, the state will actively encourage this isolation. Examples of this practice can be seen where the state attempts to limit the period during which an officer may be assigned to a particular region, insists that officers be assigned to regions far removed from their place of origin or sends in mobile police units from other regions to ensure public order. These are all means of restricting the affinity of the police for the policed (Loubet del Bayle, 1992: 74–6).

The public for their part are ignorant of many of the technicalities of policing (Cathala, 1971: 15). Citizens often have a limited knowledge of their rights when confronted with the police, thereby opening the way for police excesses. Moreover, in popular perception the police tend to merge into an unspecified mass (Audebert, 1938; Ministère de l'Intérieur, 1983: 27). Individuals are more likely to say that they are being chased by the police than that they are being pursued by the Brigades des Recherches du Commissariat Central. Even in those areas where the public does differentiate between different branches, categorization is rudimentary. The classic example of this is in crowd control policing where the public will shout out slogans against the CRS (Compagnies Républicaines de Sécurité) when the force they are confronted with is in fact the Gendarmerie Mobile (Jacq and Pons, 1981: 43). The police complain that because the public fail to discriminate between one branch of the force and the rest, any excesses committed by one section will cause the rest of the institution to be tarred with the same brush. The police also assume that the public are ignorant of both their real possibilities of action and the difficulties of their profession (Cathala, 1971: 15).

Public ignorance of policing is not just inspired by civic laziness. Sources of information and representation of law enforcement often portray a distorted view and differing sources contradict each other considerably. The difficulty in obtaining reliable information is partly a result of the reluctance of the institution to open itself up to the public gaze. Several factors explain this reluctance. Firstly, the police often operate on the fringes of legality and a revelation of the techniques they use would cause them to lose any claim to the moral high ground. Secondly, police operations require a considerable degree of secrecy if they are to be brought to a successful completion. The fear of breaching this code of secrecy rapidly develops into a phobia of revealing even the most trivial details of their operations. Finally, the success of policing is considered to result as much from a public myth of the power of the police as from the actual strength of the force itself (Brodeur, 1984: 27). Revelations that the institution is in a lot of ways badly equipped and its personnel demoralized are not thought compatible with the aim of perpetuating the myth of police strength. The information the police do communicate to the public about their operations is often in the form of communiqués to the media. These are hardly impartial accounts of police activity. They seek to emphasize police successes, overlooking any excesses committed in the course of arrests, and, where excesses are reported from an independent source, police communiqués will often attempt to blacken the name of the victim of these excesses by stressing any criminal activity in the victim's past.

Besides official communiqués, the public find another source of information in the media: the investigations carried out by journalists. The representation of the police contained in both the press and broadcasting is viewed as unfavourable by the majority of police officers. In the Toulouse survey, 77.4 per cent expressed the opinion that the press were hostile to them. 62.7 per cent made this same claim of radio representations, whilst 63.4 per cent were critical of the coverage given to police questions by television.[1] That the police feel that the media are not on their side is not necessarily a bad thing. It can be seen as a reflection of the media fulfilling their rightful role in a democracy: that of acting as a counterweight to the power of the state. However, the media are certainly not above criticism in their use of this right. Too often the race against the clock causes articles to be written too hastily, to be poorly researched and sometimes misleading.

Another form of representation of police activity occurs in fictional portrayals put across by the cinema or literature. Since Edgar Allen Poe invented the modern detective story with his *Murders in the rue Morgue* (1841), detectives have been a source of constant fascination for fiction writers. Few subjects can claim such a vast representation in film and print (Casamayor, 1973: 19–20). Most police officers view this literary and cinematic representation as favourable. Some recognize, however, that the fictional portrayal will cause the public to be somewhat disappointed when they meet real law enforcement agents. The tough, go-it-alone fictional cop, who disobeys his/her hierarchy, using only personal intuition to solve a case in the public interest, bears little resemblance to the average police officer who relies on a long period of investigation and feels constrained by a code of practice (Cathala, 1971: 16).

The public's perception of the police is also influenced by historical legacy. When Louis Lépine came to the post of Prefect of Police in Paris at the end of the nineteenth century, he found the image of his force tarnished by what may be termed 'a Vidocq syndrome'. The collective memory had retained the image of Vidocq, the criminal turned police chief, and this cast suspicion on Lépine's force (Berlière, 1993: 118). Frequently these legacies are manipulated and exploited politically to point the finger at contemporary institutions. Thus, commemorations of the round-up of the Jews by the French police in 1942 reinforce current accusations of racial discrimination on the part of the police against those of North African origin. The behaviour and presentation of the police sometimes play into the hands of those who choose to portray today's force as a simple continuum of its Vichy counterpart. The speeches of former Minister of the Interior Charles Pasqua calling on his police to terrorize the terrorists and to shoot and he would cover them (Ancian, 1988: 63) recall similar phrases from the mouth of the wartime Milice leader Joseph Darnand. The practice of discriminatory identity controls in the street is incompatible with modern democracy.[2]

Police–public encounters

Beyond representations, public impressions of the police are also influenced by their personal encounters. In a survey conducted by the SOFRES polling agency in 1993, 73 per cent of the Parisians questioned said that they had been in direct contact with the police during the previous year: 43 per cent when asking for information and 35 per cent receiving a ticket for a traffic offence. 34 per cent said they had been inside a police station during this same period (SOFRES, 1994: 8). For most of those questioned these contacts had been favourable. Surveys in Lille and Marseille suggested that around 65 per cent were satisfied with the reception they received in police stations (Moser and Pascual, 1991; Robert, 1992).[3] This still leaves a sizeable minority of about one-third who were dissatisfied with their reception. Reasons for dissatisfaction may be grouped into three categories. The poor organization of police services is a subject of frequent criticism. This involves inappropriate opening times and excessive delays. The second focus of attention is a failure to meet public expectations. The police are considered particularly inefficient when dealing with burglaries. For their part, the police argue that the public are often unaware of the limits on police powers and fail to appreciate that just because certain acts may be considered outrageous or immoral, this does not necessarily mean that they are against the law. Lastly, there was the behaviour of individual officers, too often guilty of rudeness or aggression in reception or insensitivity in their treatment of victims. Because people who are upset are a major source of embarrassment for the police, officers tend to form an emotional shield to protect themselves and often appear to be ignoring the distress of victims (Southgate, 1986: 14, 25–6).

This question of how the police cope with human feelings is a dominant theme in police encounters with the public both inside and outside of the police station. The police and the public approach their encounters with different objectives (Reiss, 1971; Southgate, 1986). For the police it is important to obtain respect and to establish their authority early in an encounter. Called to the scene of a crime they usually have an extremely limited amount of information about those they are encountering. They try to remain distant, believing that those they are treating as victims might turn out to be culprits, requiring a change of tack which would be difficult to negotiate if they had begun the encounter by offering too much sympathy. Moreover, one of the basic principles of professionalism is the requirement that the professionals disengage themselves from personal involvement, lest this involvement cause them to offer favouritism to individuals who appear more sympathetic. For law enforcement agents, contact with the public in the course of their duties is mundane and routine. For the public, for whom dealings with the police are exceptional occurrences, the encounter has much greater significance. It may involve a range of emotions, including anxiety, resentment, distrust, embarrassment, hostility and nervousness. In such emotionally stressful situations, citizens want to be treated as persons, rather than cases. They would like to see the police show some personal concern for their problems. In these circumstances the distant civility required by professional codes of conduct may appear bureaucratic.

Marginalization and exclusion

Not all sections of society receive equal treatment from the police. In this respect immigrants, the young and women are particularly worthy of note. The police as an institution is noted for its racism. In a survey carried out in Lille, 57 per cent of women and 45 per cent of men believed that the police were racially prejudiced (Robert, 1992: 8). A demonstration of police officers in Paris in June 1983 which culminated in a march on the Ministry of Justice and included anti-Semitic chants and cries of 'foreigner go home' directed at the Justice Minister Robert Badinter (of Jewish origin) merely served to confirm suspicions of a racist current in the police (Roach and Thomanek, 1985: 136). The adoption by a government decree of 18 March 1986 of a code of practice which was specifically designed to curb racism in the force provided official recognition of a problem in this respect. But this question is deep-rooted and its causes manifold. The historical precedent of the Algerian war, during which the police were pitted against the Algerians, caused a worsening of relations between the police and the North African community in France (Monate, 1974: 38–44). Moreover, the police are often set a poor example from above. Particularly during Charles Pasqua's periods as Minister of the Interior, North African immigrants were designated as a prime concern for policing. The ability of the government to do this was largely a measure of the limited political clout of immigrant communities (Loubet del Bayle, 1992: 52) but also of the ambiguity of public opinion. Although the public denounce police excesses against individual immigrants, they also call out for greater security and make a direct link between immigrants and insecurity. For a police force which claims to be hugely overworked and under pressure to make arrests, immigrants offer an easy target. Because of the need for work and residence permits, the number of laws applicable to immigrant groups is greater than for the rest of the community. They are therefore more likely to be in breach of the law, and thus immigrants provide an easy way to relieve this hierarchical pressure.

Age is also an important consideration in police/public relations. Two-thirds of young people questioned claim to have faith in the police. However, the number of people in this age group holding an unfavourable opinion is greater than in older sections of the population. Young people are less likely to have recourse to the police than the elderly. This is in spite of the fact that polls discovered a widespread concern for security in this age-group. In the SOFRES sample in Paris, 40 per cent of the 18–24-year-old group claimed that this was an issue of major concern to them (SOFRES, 1994: 4). This is hardly surprising when recent studies suggest that those of this age-group are more likely to be victims of crime than those of any other age category (Robert, 1992; Moser and Pascual, 1991). For many young people, especially in the suburbs of large cities, the police are seen almost exclusively in their repressive role and are viewed as brutal and discourteous (Renouard, 1992: 2). Young people often see themselves as unfairly categorized as objects of immediate suspicion. Indeed, whilst 15 per cent of those from all age categories questioned by the SOFRES claimed to have been asked to produce their identity papers in the previous year, this percentage rose to 27 per cent in the 18–24-year-old bracket (SOFRES, 1994: 8). These poor relations are set against a backdrop of a host of confrontations between the police and young people in the last 30 years, leaving a tense situation where the very presence of the police can be enough to create potential riots.

The relations between police and women are different from those with either young people or immigrants. Crime is a particularly male-dominated activity. Its perpetrators are more often than not men and even today crime-solving is entrusted primarily to men. Recent surveys suggest that men are more likely than women to be victims of crime, owing to the frequency of incidents of physical assault (Robert, 1992; Moser and Pascual, 1991). Yet women are more likely than men to have recourse to the police. At least three explanations can be put forward for this. Firstly, when crimes of a violent nature are committed against women they are frequently more serious than those perpetrated against men. Secondly, opinion polls indicate that women feel more vulnerable than men. Whilst 54 per cent of male Parisians claim to feel insecure in the streets at night, this feeling climbs to 65 per cent for women (SOFRES, 1994: 4). Thirdly, women express greater confidence in the police than men. In the CSA poll, 87 per cent of women expressed faith in the police, compared to 79 per cent of men (Gorgeon, 1994: 245–73). Most women who had dealings with the police claim to have been well treated but a sizeable minority were not satisfied. Sexual assault victims are often treated insensitively by police officers, who sometimes suggest that if they were assaulted it was because they were asking for it.

Police discrimination against women differs in its form from other types of police discrimination. Owing largely to lower female crime rates, women are generally less targeted for police identity controls than men. However, it is not infrequent for arrested women to have to endure sexist comments. When Corinne Marienneau, bass player of the pop group Téléphone, was arrested in a bar in the rue Fontaine in Paris, police officers openly discussed whether they felt sexually attracted to her and made disparaging remarks about the size of her breasts (Ancian, 1988: 250). One area where the police have traditionally enjoyed a free hand to behave much as they please towards a category of women is in the policing of prostitution. This area of policing has always been used as a means of gathering information about political and criminal activities, but the vagueness of the regulations governing it have allowed the police to extend their abuses to sexual favours in return for non-prosecution.[4]

Who controls the police?

One of the most common complaints against the police, beside the discrimination they are seen to exert, is that they are not close enough to the people. Seventy per cent of those questioned in Marseille and 81 per cent of those in the Lille survey expressed this opinion (Gorgeon, 1994: 250). One aspect of this is the tendency for the police to be seen as simply an instrument of state power. In this model, the government needs a means of imposing the decisions it has been democratically elected to take. The police act as faithful servants of the will of the state and change direction according to the political colour of the country's leaders. Both the government and the police have a vested interest in portraying the police in this way. State leaders cling to this vision because it offers the comforting perspective that their decisions will be faithfully enacted. The police shelter behind this version as a means of exonerating their personal responsibility by claiming that they are simply obeying orders. The consequence of the police being portrayed as an instrument of state is that the unpopularity of the government will sometimes rub off on the police, but by the same token, excessive force by the police will affect the government's image. The Chirac administration of 1986–88 was badly affected by its use of police to control student demonstrations against the Devaquet education bill. In particular, the march on the road-block in the rue Esnault-Pelterie on 4 December 1986 resulted in a number of injuries to demonstrators because CRS and mobile Gendarmerie units fired tear-gas grenades into the crowd at ground level. The public was shocked by the extent of injuries suffered by those hit directly by these grenades: a fractured collar-bone, a lost eye, a fractured skull and a broken nose, a severed toe, a severed hand, a fractured jaw and a damaged shoulder blade (Ancian, 1988: 86–93). The government was accused of heavy-handedness.

Although there are a number of areas, such as crowd control, where hierarchical control is tight enough to ensure instrumentality, in a lot of ways the institution is a state within the state. The police have considerable autonomy because of the local contacts established by police officers, their control of the supply of information sent to the government and the impossibility of maintaining close hierarchical control over the bulk of daily police work. The law is supposed to act as a counterweight to this police power but because the law is written in general terms, law enforcement officers have a considerable degree of discretion in its application. Controls of the police become too lax, accusations of police corruption abound, the nature of their duties brings some officers into contact with those in criminal milieux who are in a position to offer interesting supplements to the salaries the police consider inadequate. Another form of abuse is in the use of physical violence on suspects. This type of abuse has become so institutionalized that a special vocabulary has developed to describe it. For instance, the expression *passer à tabac* as a euphemism for 'to beat up' originates with a turn-of-the-century police practice. Parisian police officers were given tobacco as a reward for obtaining the confession of suspects, so the image of converting these suspects into tobacco described the methods with which these confessions were obtained (Bischoff, 1938: 4).

The problem in these circumstances is that the police are seen as unanswerable to the public. Mechanisms of supervising police activity do exist, but are sometimes inadequate. The public exercise one level of control. Since the introduction of uniforms in 1829, the population have been able to recognize at least a certain proportion of police officers. Numbers were sown on these uniforms from 1856 in Paris and from 1942 in provincial France (Ancian, 1988: 31; Archives Nationales, 1942). Although neither the Second Empire nor the Vichy government introduced this provision with public welfare in mind, personnel numbers allowed members of the public to identify the particular officers against whom they had a grievance. The proportion of officers in uniform is now on the decrease as more operations are performed in plain clothes, making recognition difficult. But recognition is only the first stage towards getting an abuse investigated. The next is to find someone competent to investigate the abuse. Politicians and the justice system both receive complaints, but neither has any mechanism specifically designed to investigate alleged police abuses and both are to some degree dependent on good relations with the police. Increasingly the public are addressing their complaints against the police to the institution itself and in particular to its complaints' commission, the Inspection Générale de la Police Nationale (IGPN). Although the IGPN can argue that members of a professional body are most competent to judge the conduct of other members, when investigations are carried out internally there is always the suspicion that their proceedings will be biased. IGPN investigators often know the officers they are investigating and may in any event feel an inherent sympathy with the professional predicament of their colleagues. Suspicion is further fuelled in cases where the punishments it recommends are inappropriate. Patrick Deguin was wrongfully arrested for the theft of a handbag in Paris on 16 March 1986. Whilst in custody he was beaten up by an inspector who insulted him racially and hit him in the testicles with a truncheon, claiming that this would prevent him from having any children. The IGPN investigation revealed sufficient evidence to punish the inspector, but the punishment imposed was simply his transfer to another branch (Ancian, 1988: 43–53).

Possibilities for improvement

Despite the abuses mentioned and examples of discrimination and exclusion, the population at large recognize the need for a police force and believe that without it all chaos would break loose (Gorgeon, 1994: 264; Loubet del Bayle, 1992: 8). Indeed the public continue to demand increased policing (Gleizal, 1985: 29). In a poll conducted by BVA in May 1985, only 22 per cent of those questioned thought that people should resort to their own means for their personal defence, whilst 66 per cent believed that the police should be given greater means (Maurin, 1988: 29). The police, for their part, spurn public opinion but recognize the need for public co-operation. Policing through consent facilitates information gathering but also ensures legitimacy. Both police and public recognize that there are a number of areas of interaction where improved relations are needed.

Any attempt to tackle areas of poor police/public relations would necessarily try to confront both the internal and external causes of disquiet. The police force as an institution must reform itself internally and show that it has public concerns at heart. The institution appears too self-contained. An investigation by *Interface* in 1988 suggested that the lack of openness on the part of the police was a common public reproach. The police must become more visible and open to public gaze by providing more information about their operations. The establishment of a specialist research unit, the Institut des Hautes Etudes de la Sécurité Intérieure, in March 1989 is a step in the right direction as regards research, and further initiatives in this same direction must be encouraged. But this openness should not be limited to encouraging specialist studies of the organization. It must be seen to apply to general police practice which needs to be brought closer to the population. One suggestion which has been gaining ground in recent years and which has seen the beginnings of implementation is the notion of *îlotage,* that is to say foot patrols who are responsible for walking a particular beat and establishing personal contacts in that area. In 1988, 2762 police officers were given over full time to this type of policing and another 1149 occupied with it part-time.[5] However, rather than this task being carried out as at present by groups of law enforcement agents, whose presence is often intimidating, officers must be encouraged to walk their beat in pairs if this experiment is to serve any purpose.

Besides changing the nature and presentation of the police mission, another internal improvement would involve raising the standards of police officers themselves. Since the establishment of police training schools, many of which date from the 1941 reform, considerable progress has been made towards the training of a professional police force. There is certainly still room for improvement in this respect, particularly as 60 per cent of the public questioned in Marseille expressed the view that the police were often badly trained (Moser and Pascual, 1991: 11). Professional codes of practice are necessary in a credible police force, but training officers to be objective in all circumstances should not be allowed to cause them to forget that each encounter with the public is different and that they are dealing with human beings who deserve to be judged on their individual merits. Establishing good personal contacts with the population supposes a lessening of police workload by the removal of some of their more administrative tasks, so that officers have the time to devote to the people they are supposed to be serving. By encouraging popular sympathy for the police and by improving the working conditions of officers, the profession would be made that much more attractive, encouraging a better recruitment and reducing demoralization, making the temptations of corruption easier to resist.

If the police truly wish to act in the interests of the population, their recruitment must be made more representative of that population. This process has begun. In today's cosmopolitan society the police are encouraging people from ethnic minorities to join the force (Loubet del Bayle, 1992: 63). However, the complete absence of specialist research on this question in France is symbolic of the as yet limited scale of interest in this policy. As regards the recruitment of women, the process is at a more advanced stage. The first women entered the police in 1914 as secretaries in the Paris force. From 1935, women began to be called in to do more active police service but their numbers were still infinitesimal (*Paris soir*, 10 April 1935; *Le Petit Parisien*, 10 April 1935): in April 1935 two *assistantes sociales* were incorporated into the Parisian force; in December of the same year two women were brought in in Grenoble and three joined the Lyon force in 1937.[6] It was the Vichy government which first began recruiting women on a larger scale when in 1943 labour shortages forced it into recruiting several hundred women officers (Archives Nationales, 1944a and 1944b). Some of these were removed at the Liberation. The right-wing administration of Valéry Giscard d'Estaing and the Socialist government of François Mitterrand gave a new incentive to female recruitment and since 1974 women have begun to access all branches (Dessus, 1990: 200–21; Marchal, 1993: 24). They still account for a tiny percentage of police officers: 1 per cent in 1981, rising to 5 per cent in 1989 and 6.4 per cent in 1993 (Marchal, 1993: 23). In general the presence of women officers is well received by the public. In an *Interface* survey in 1982, 91 per cent of those questioned viewed the presence of women in the police as positive. Forty-six per cent justified this reaction by reference to sex equality, whilst 19 per cent claimed it would improve the communication powers of the police (Dessus, 1990: 42). Given that women have recourse to the police more often than men and that some women complain of the insensitivity of male officers this recruitment can only be seen in terms of making the police more representative and efficient.[7]

But measures to improve police/public relations should not just come from within the institution. The public also have an input in how a police force is run. Rather than shying off into a passive indifference on matters of policing, the public should let police officers know when they approve or disapprove of police activities. Channels of protest do exist, whether through letters to the police hierarchy, or to politicians, or in more extreme cases through street demonstrations. Negative criticism can quickly become demoralizing for police officers and needs to be accompanied by constructive comments and positive feedback where this is justified. The public must become much more involved and more consulted in the debate over policing in France. Only once the public formulate a clearly defined and coherent set of principles for policing, can a police force in the service of the people begin to become a reality.

Notes

1. This phenomenon of the police considering themselves to have an unfair trial in the media is a fairly recent one. A survey similar to the Toulouse study was conducted with police officers in 1965 and found that the press was thought by 55 per cent to be favourable, 56 per cent considered the radio was on their side whilst 55 per cent thought the same of television.
2. Identity controls were viewed as a fundamental infringement on civil liberties by those interviewed in a survey in Lille (Robert, 1992: 26).
3. See also CREDOC (1993): 199–223.
4. For an interesting account of policing in this respect during the Third Republic see Berlière (1992).
5. According to Minister of the Interior Pierre Joxe at a press conference held on 12 September 1989.
6. Holland was the first country to incorporate women into their police force in the mid-1920s. In 1928, Germany counted around 70 policewomen, whilst Britain had 175 in 1936 (with 160 in London) (Rolland and Reybier, 1947: 7).
7. In Britain similar conclusions were reached (Southgate, 1986: 28).

References

Ancian, J.-M. (1988) *Police des Polices.* Paris: Balland.

Archives Nationales (1942) AN F7 14907 [554] *le Directeur de la Police Nationale à MM les Préfets Régionaux*, n° 454, Pol.I/P.R.circ. 30/7/1942.

Archives Nationales (1944a) AN F7 14896 *Note de la Direction de la Sécurité Publique*, C-PN 1716 n°4, 6/5/1944.

Archives Nationales (1944b) AN F7 14909[1265] *Rapport mensuel sur l'activité des services de Sécurité Publique pendant le mois d'avril 1944*, 23/5/1944.

Audebert, G. (1938) *Organisation et méthodes de la Police Française*. Doctoral thesis, Tours University.

Berlière, J.-M. (1992) *La Police des Mœurs sous la Troisième République*. Paris: Le Seuil.

Berlière, J.-M. (1993) *Le Préfet Lépine, vers la naissance de la police moderne*. Paris: Denoël.

Bischoff, M. (1938) *La Police Scientifique*. Paris: Payot.

Brodeur, J.-P. (1984) 'La police: mythes et réalités' in *La Police après 1984*. Montreal: Presses de l'Université de Montréal.

Casamayor (1973) *La Police*. Paris: Gallimard.

Cathala, F. (1971) *Cette police si décriée*. Saverdun: Champs de Mars.

CREDOC (1993) 'Les Français, la sécurité et l'image des forces de l'ordre en 1990 et 1992', *Cahiers de la Sécurité Intérieure*, 14 Oct.: 199–223.

Dessus, N. (1990) *Police et jeunesse, en quoi les représentations sociales de la police évoluent-elles chez les délinquants mineurs avec l'entrée des femmes dans l'institution?* Diplôme d'Études Approfondies, Paris X.

Ferro, M. (1987) *Pétain*. Paris: Fayard.

Gleizal, J.-J. (1985) *Le Désordre policier*. Paris: PUF.

Gorgeon, C. (1994) 'Police et public: représentations, recours et attentes. Le cas français', *Déviance et Société* 18(3): 245–73.

Jacq, P. and Pons, B. (1981) *Les Policiers et l'image de la police dans l'opinion*. Toulouse: CERP.

Loubet del Bayle, J.-L. (1992) *La Police. Approche socio-politique*. Paris: Montchrestien.

Marchal, P. (1993) *Les Femmes gardiens de la paix*. Mémoire du DUEPS, Tours University.

Maurin, J.-L. (1988) 'La Police et l'opinion française' in J.-L. Loubet del Bayle (ed.) *Police et société*. Toulouse: Presses de l'IEP.

Ministère de l'Intérieur (1983) *Les policiers, leurs métiers, leur formation*. Paris: La Documentation Française.

Monate, G. (1974) *Questions à la Police*. Paris: Stock.

Moser, G. and Pascual, A. (1991) *L'image de la police à Marseille: les quartiers nord et le centre ville*. Paris: IHESI.

Reiss, Albert J. (1971) *The Police and the Public*. New Haven and London: Yale University Press.

Renouard, J.-M. (1992) *Les relations entre la police et les jeunes: la recherche en question*. Paris: IHESI.

Roach, J. and Thomanek, J. (1985) *Police and Public Order in France.* London: Croom Helm.

Robert, J.-P. (1992) *L'image de la police dans l'agglomération de Lille-Roubaix-Tourcoing.* Paris: IHESI.

Rolland, B. and Reybier, H. (1947) *La police féminine, son rôle dans la lutte contre le proxénétisme et la prostitution (vers un nouveau régime des mœurs).* Paris: Cartel d'action morale et sociale.

SOFRES (1994) *Le jugement des Parisiens sur l'action de la police à Paris et l'image de la Préfecture.* Paris: SOFRES.

Southgate, P. (1986) *Police–Public Encounters.* London: HMSO.

14.

Re-creating collective identities in urban France: the case of Vénissieux (Rhône-Alpes)

SUSAN MILNER

Vénissieux, on the south-eastern outskirts of Lyon (France's second largest city), serves as an example of the social and demographic changes affecting France's urban areas. Traditionally a working-class or 'people's town' (*quartier populaire*), its social composition has undergone significant changes in the post-war period and particularly since the urban renewal programmes of the 1960s. The identity of the local community was for many years based on heavy industry and working-class solidarity, expressed largely through support for the French Communist Party (PCF), which dominated local government and political representation. However, the social changes experienced in Vénissieux, which also reflect a breakdown of local socio-economic structures, have weakened collective identities to the extent that Vénissieux tends to be defined – negatively – from the outside rather than through a conscious and positive self-identification. Like other deprived urban areas in France, Vénissieux has moved from being a *quartier populaire* to being perceived as a *quartier difficile* – a town defined by the social problems it contains.

The social engineering carried out in the 1960s and 1970s under the banner of 'urban renewal' created the conditions in which the effects of the economic crisis were later experienced in the *banlieues* or working-class suburbs. National government opened the way for mass building works in prioritized areas, with its 1958 policy of *Zones à urbaniser en priorité* (ZUP). Paris, Lyon and Marseille were the worst affected by wholesale housing reorganization in the 1960s and 1970s, entailing the removal of whole neighbourhoods of people. In the case of Lyon, the result was a massive shift in population towards the 'red belt' of the eastern communes, which received about two-thirds of the net gain in residential units (Grillo, 1985: 85). If the motives of some planners were philanthropic – to create a decent living space in overcrowded cities – many authors attribute more cynical motives on the part of builders and promoters (profit) and local politicians (electoral engineering). The use of mass-production techniques in the construction industry led to the erection of huge tower blocks, four at a time (so as to utilize the full circle of the crane's reach), using the cheapest materials and maximizing coverage of ground-space. The city of Lyon thus concentrated its 'undesirable elements' (the unemployed, the poor, immigrants, those likely to vote Communist) in the outer suburbs, whilst the relatively well-off sections of the population benefited from proximity to work and the commercial and cultural goods available in the city centre (Corbel, 1983: 274; Guglielmo and Moulin, 1986: 42).

The situation in the suburbs worsened in the late 1970s as a result of socio-economic change – specifically, mass unemployment – and also as a direct result of government policy. The new consensus that the high-rise construction programme had been a massive error gained ground remarkably quickly – but too late. In 1973, a new policy attempted to reverse the trend by encouraging private ownership and the construction of individual homes (*pavillons*) – a policy whose positive and negative effects are graphically described in personal accounts in Bourdieu's *La misère du monde* (1993).[1] This U-turn by the state led to impoverishment of the city estates as funds were diverted away from what had become a major embarrassment for government. As a result of this neglect, those who had the means to get out of the *banlieues* did so, leaving behind those at the bottom of the housing ladder (Bidou, 1995: 18).

Changes in the local economic structure in the late 1970s and 1980s exacerbated this social segregation. The concentration of immigrant families in the ZUP increased with new needs caused by the arrival of female immigrants and the founding of families in France. Families in the high-rise ZUP, particularly hard hit by the steep rise in unemployment in the 1980s, were effectively trapped in these areas, unable to leave the 'relegation zones' (Lapeyronnie, 1991). Unemployment in Vénissieux stood at 14.8 per cent in 1990 (and 20.4 per cent of the unemployed had been out of work for two years or more) (INSEE, 1991). Residents 'of foreign origin' in Les Minguettes had a 37 per cent unemployment level in 1982. The relative number of workers within the local active population decreased from the mid-1970s: thus, in Vénissieux it dropped from 55 per cent to 44 per cent between 1975 and 1982, and to 41.42 per cent in 1990. As local companies closed down or carried out mass redundancies, workers had less incentive to stay in the local area and moved closer to their place of work or potential places of work. The declining importance of local employers also reduced the collective identities built up around factories such as the Berliet works at Vénissieux and their political significance. Thus, whereas RVI (formerly Berliet) still employed more than 12,000 people on its Vénissieux-Saint-Priest site in 1982, by 1991 the number was down to 5600 (Leprince, 1991).

Hence, although in the 1970s it was relatively easy to define the social question as work-based class relations, in the 1990s the social problems of urban France are multiple and much harder to treat because they cannot be resolved by integration through work. The new urban policies created in order to appeal to specific sections of the population (especially youth) have responded to this change by shifting the emphasis away from the traditional workerist discourse of the Left, but as a result collective identities have been placed under even greater strain.

Local politics: the end of the 'red suburbs'?

Despite the disintegration of the local industrial base, the Left and particularly the PCF managed to retain a position of relative strength in Vénissieux, although it was severely eroded in the 1980s (see Table 14.1). The question is, how long can it hold out against the trend towards greater fragmentation? In other words, can the local PCF representatives serve as a non-class-specific mouthpiece for a more fragmented local population whilst also providing it with the services it requires in the face of mounting financial pressures? And if the PCF cannot carry out this function, are there any alternatives?

The question of immigration undoubtedly lies at the heart of the sociological changes and their political expression. According to Begag and Delorme (1994: 46), two notable new phenomena characterize the situation in France's deprived urban areas today: the widespread establishment of a parallel economy (usually drugs-based) and the concentration of immigrant populations, leading to what they describe as the 'ethnicization' of social policy. The two phenomena are often conflated. In these conditions, they suggest, urban policy may simply be a code word for immigration policy. In many ways it is wrong to assume that 'old-style industrial society' integrated immigrants through trade unions and other work-based institutions. French trade unions always had problems deciding how to react to immigration and never had

Table 14.1 PCF score in municipal and legislative elections in Vénissieux. 1945–1995 (percentage of registered voters; percentage of votes cast)

a. Municipal

April 1945	Oct. 1947	April 1953	March 1959	March 1965	March 1971*	March 1977*	March 1983*	March 1989*	June 1995*
35.71	35.90	44.85	43.06	56.45	40.30	45.09	32.08	27.83	23.89
49.24	54.45	61.03	63.71	100	61.81	70.24	59.44	58.38	46.36

b. Legislative

Oct. 1945	June 1946	Nov. 1946	June 1951	Jan. 1956	May 1957	Nov. 1958	Nov. 1972
37.84	35.85	38.09	41.78	45.95	38.51	30.16	36.50
47.74	45.16	51.03	53.86	55.63	63.46	43.61	57.87

March 1967	June 1968	March 1973	March 1978	June 1981	March 1986	June 1988	March 1993
47.40	42.80	40.52	38.76	28.65	16.16	19.57	16.74
58.95	51.99	50.77	49.48	47.06	24.66	36.79	27.61

Note: *Union de la Gauche candidates
Sources: Brula, 1993; *Le Monde*, 20 June 1995 for 1995 results

great success in organizing immigrant workers. When they started to make headway in the 1970s, it was on the basis of a recognition of immigrant workers' specific demands (cultural and religious as well as their status as victims of discrimination and racism). Hence what we are seeing is not so much a break with a (mythologized?) past as the exacerbation of problems already inherent in industrial society.

The crux of the issue is the formation of collective identity, which for a time was possible around the working class. Advanced capitalism has accentuated both individual responses and a fragmentation of collective identity (age, gender, race) as work has become scarcer. Recognition of this trend has forced the Left (including the non-aligned anti-racist associations) to change its attitude towards the Far Right. Although a straightforward equation between Communist Party (PC) losses and the Front National (FN) gains is undoubtedly too simplistic, there is an undeniable underlying truth. Electoral gains by the Far Right were among the first signs of the erosion of the 'red suburbs'. The sudden rise of the Front National in 1983–84 was especially marked in the bastions of the Left, notably in the Paris area. The seven communes of over 3000 inhabitants where the Far Right made the greatest gains in 1983 were all Communist-controlled in 1977 (Ronai, 1986: 83). The FN was poaching on the Left's territory: the Far Right vote in 1983 rose according to the level of urbanization of the *département*, the degree of insecurity perceived and the proportion of immigrants. The FN had now become the *other* 'party of the discontented' and was even more able than the PCF to present itself as the outsider because it had not been in charge of the communes where discontent was spreading. An IFOP exit poll conducted after the first round of the presidential elections in April 1995 indicated that 27 per cent of Le Pen's electorate define themselves as workers, 24 per cent unemployed, and 24 per cent as *commerçants et artisans* (the traditional Far Right electorate). When asked to define their social category, 33 per cent placed themselves in the group of 'the underprivileged' (as opposed to 19 per cent of Jospin supporters, 14 per cent of Chirac supporters and 13 per cent of Hue supporters); 19 per cent classed themselves as 'working class' (25 per cent of Jospin voters, 17 per cent of Hue voters and 13 per cent of Chirac voters) (*L'Humanité*, 11 July 1995).

In a remarkable investigation published in *L'Humanité* (11 July 1995), the PCF attempted to get to the root of the FN's attraction for working-class French people. The picture that emerges from interviews with FN voters is one of an accumulation of daily petty harassments and especially the rise of small-scale crime (broken windows, damage to cars, burglaries): in other words, the overwhelming preoccupation with lack of security. The FN itself and its policies are not important to these victims of urban decay: they are concerned above all with their own lives. Another noteworthy feature is the feeling of loss of dignity – often noted in relation to the immigrant 'underclass' – expressed by many of the interviewees: 'On en a marre, on nous prend pour des imbéciles ...' ('We've just had enough, they [the politicians] take us for fools'). As the party which has often in the past allied itself with immigrants, the PCF is accused of defending petty criminals for fear of appearing racist:

> Le PC est devenu trop conciliant avec ceux qui foutent la merde, excusez-moi l'expression; vous les communistes, vous avez un grand défaut. Je sais que ce n'est pas vous qui les avez amenés, les immigrés, c'est Giscard, avec le regroupement familial, mais vous êtes quand même pour les Arabes![2]
>
> (*L'Humanité*, 11 July 1995)

The reporter observes that this population, destabilized in its own habitat, has homed in on the issue of nationality as the focus for its feelings of social disintegration. It is perhaps no accident that the PCF, during its years of glory, also used nationality as a major unifying theme, despite its solidarity with immigrants and anti-colonial wars.

The FN vote appeared in Vénissieux at the European elections of 1984 (15.4 per cent of the vote, as opposed to the PCF's 28.95 per cent). At the six general elections held between 1984 and 1989, it obtained around 14–15.5 per cent of the vote (but the local FN leader M. Joannon scored 19.2 per cent at the legislative election of 1988). In the presidential election of 1988, Le Pen got 19 per cent of the vote. At the regional election of 1992, the FN score went over 20 per cent for the first time (24.5 per cent), coming first among all the parties present (the PCF obtained 22.86 per cent). And in the municipal elections of 1995, the FN came second after the Union de la Gauche, with 29.56 per cent of the vote and seven *conseillers municipaux* (three in the outgoing council). The local council was so worried by the popularity of the Far Right's message that in 1995 it too commissioned an in-depth survey among the FN voters. The survey found that the FN itself was not deeply rooted as a party in Vénissieux, but that its ideas found a fertile breeding ground in the local environment, particularly in local nostalgia for an idealized past. Researchers encountered 'a very strong need [among FN voters] to speak, to communicate, to recreate political and social links' (*L'Humanité*, 26 October 1995).

Table 14.2 *Abstention rate in municipal, legislative and presidential elections in Vénissieux,*
1971–1995 (percentage of registered voters)

		Municipal		
1971	1977	1983	1989	1995
33.05	34.07	43.63	50.57	47.04

		Legislative			
1973	1978	1981	1986	1988	1993
18.87	20.06	38.68	32.52	45.87	37.46

	Presidential		
1974	1981	1988	1995
15.4	38.68	26.13	25.76

Sources: Brula, 1993; *Le Monde,* 20 June 1995 for 1995 results

The other major sign of the weakening of PCF support, and more
generally support for the Left in urban France, has been the rising
number of abstentions. This was the main cause of the decline in
support for the Left at the 1983 municipal elections, and it continues to
grow among the Left's traditional supporters in the 'red suburbs'. In
Vénissieux, the abstention rate rose dramatically in the 1980s, particularly in municipal elections (see Table 14.2).

Another newcomer to the electoral scene was Bernard Tapie. At the
1994 European elections, his Energie radicale list won 12.89 per cent in
Vénissieux as a whole, and 16.98 per cent in the ZUP (Centre d'histoire
et d'études, 1994). Tapie's popularity reflected the disillusionment of
Vénissian youth, including and perhaps especially *beur*[3] youth, with the
established parties. The short-lived Tapie phenomenon pointed to the
extent of the rejection of mainstream politics by younger voters. In
L'Humanité's interviews with FN voters cited earlier, Sandrine (a
28-year-old check-out assistant) is quoted as saying: 'A la présidentielle,
j'ai voté Le Pen au premier tour, Jospin au second. Aux municipales, j'ai
voté Mégret les deux fois. Mais si Tapie s'était présenté, j'aurais voté
pour lui. [Pause] Vous voyez, chez moi, c'est le cafouillage total.'[4]
Sandrine's voting behaviour is now not uncommon among urban
youth. These important changes in voting behaviour point to a breakdown in the relationship between local people and the Left-controlled
council, which traditionally formed the pivot of working-class identity.
Let us now examine more closely the ways in which collective identity
has been affected by socio-economic change, and the response of the
local Left council to them. The question is of course whether the social
problems described are an inevitable product of post-industrial society
or whether they can to some extent be reversed or alleviated by specific
policies.

Working-class culture and collective identity in Vénissieux

Philippe Videlier, who has conducted an exhaustive study of working-class subculture in 1930s' Vénissieux, concludes that, in its heyday, Communism exerted a hold over the commune not just because, along with Villeurbanne, Vénissieux was the most proletarian of the towns in the Lyon area, but also because it provided a 'foyer utopique' (a Utopian meeting-point) in which everyday dissatisfactions could merge with a wider collective project. Class consciousness was a mixture of everyday demands (largely concerning work) and party activism at local level. It was backed up by an informal social network which played a huge part in integrating workers and their families from extremely diverse backgrounds, reinforced in everyday domestic life (Videlier, 1992: 36). Vénissieux's population included a significant proportion of immigrants: 43.9 per cent in 1931! But a strong local identity, at first merely negative (defensive) and passive, developed through this twin action of the factory experience and everyday local life. The later mythologization of the proletariat has all too often hidden the real plurality of working-class existence and its ability to include all categories of the underprivileged, not just the large-scale factory worker. The negative collective identity of the *banlieusard* (an inhabitant of the *banlieue*), forged in relation to the larger urban area, particularly the affluent parts of the city, constituted a response to the perceived inferiority of the *banlieue* and helped to reinforce collective identity. In this way, the local PCF was able to unite diverse nationalities around a common ideal, using the wartime experience to forge a collective identity which was both localistic and intensely patriotic (Centre d'histoire et d'études, 1992).

However, this collective culture was severely destabilized by the upheavals of the 1960s and 1970s. Allowing for an adjustment time similar to that of the early days of Vénissieux's industrialization (ten to 20 years), no new collective identity has emerged to transcend community fragmentation. This is not to say that the working-class subculture has disappeared entirely; it lives on, but alongside other claims to individual identities. The negative identity remains. But the feeling of defensiveness is not by itself enough to unite people, and it also has negative effects in lowering self-esteem unless it gives rise to specific projects. Two particular challenges to collective identity stand out.

The first is immigration. Although Vénissieux was accustomed to welcoming immigrant populations, Lyon's policy of moving immigrants out to the 'red suburbs' in the 1960s was deeply resented. In the 1970s, the new conditions of family immigration together with a context of rising unemployment meant a concentration of poor immigrant families in the commune, especially in the ZUP: 26 per cent of the population were registered as being 'of foreign origin' in 1975 and 29 per cent in 1982. In such conditions, immigrants themselves became a focus of concern and a wedge was driven between the 'foreign' and 'native' populations. The exodus of residents became a major point of concern for the council. A *Charte de la ZUP* (priority area charter) drawn up by the council, following a meeting between councillors and local residents in Les Minguettes in October 1976, called for new efforts to finish the construction work and also for an end to foreign immigration into the ZUP and more equal distribution of immigrant families throughout the Lyon area (Corbel, 1983: 280). The Communist mayor and MP Marcel Houël had already made similar demands in an article in *Le Progrès de Lyon* on 18 December 1975 (Grillo, 1985: 127). Grillo notes that this view was quite widespread among council officials he interviewed. In my own research, direct questions on immigration caused considerable unease; however, in interviews with white residents, including PCF voters, the question of immigration cropped up frequently. In these remarks, a republican standpoint (the need to integrate immigrants) and often sympathy for immigrants mingled with comments about the concentration of immigrant populations. Concern was expressed that too high a concentration of immigrants prevented them from mixing (often this was expressed in nostalgic terms: the claim that children of all races used to play together, but that this no longer happens) and encouraged lifestyles which were unacceptable to the majority population.

The second major challenge to a collective identity is a marked generational break in values. As with immigration, access to the labour market constitutes a large part of the problem. Unemployment in the 18–24 category is significantly higher than for all other age-groups (around 28 per cent), and of course young people from immigrant families are worst hit of all. However, the generational gap is also a wider cultural distance. Whereas the older generations' cultural references revolve mainly around the local area, in the case of younger Vénissians they are more universal and often entail a rejection of the local environment. Sport is one area where a sense of community belonging still prevails. Videlier (1992) notes the significance of *boules* and football for the integration of immigrant men and their families in the 1930s. Today, football is particularly important for youth: local heroes are footballers. However, outside of sport, youth culture generally looks beyond the commune. The generational divide has been noted in research on the use of local commercial space (Corbel, 1983: 285; Bavoux, 1991: 108). Young Vénissians often feel the need to move out of the commune for their leisure activities, and get away from their neighbourhood peer groups. In this context, the 'negative' identity associated with Vénissieux is more likely to lead to a rejection of the local environment, to alienation rather than a sense of belonging.

Politically, the alienation of youth is expressed in an almost complete rejection of 'politics', that is, established parties and 'politicians' (which could well include local figures of authority). As mayor, Gérin has made great efforts to get close to young residents, including young *beurs*. In October 1990, a few days after the Vaulx-en-Velin riots, Gérin held a meeting with several hundred young residents and pledged to set up a continuous dialogue with local youth, leading where appropriate to the provision of specific services. In June 1991, the polling agency SOFRES was commissioned to carry out a survey among Vénissieux youth (a representative sample of some 300 15–24-year-olds). The results confirmed what young people were saying to Gérin in their meetings: they massively rejected politics. Asked what they wanted, they responded vociferously: jobs (Gérin, 1991). Gérin's consultation of local youth raised two key issues which have been put forward as possible responses to the alienation of youth in the suburbs: citizenship (giving a voice) and the provision of specific services to a population lacking resources in certain areas (such as access to the labour market).

Lapeyronnie and other scholars have emphasized the political dimension of exclusion. In post-industrial society, his argument runs, solutions which hark back to the industrial order – employment – do not work any more. Instead, the only answer open is a real citizenship which gives the underprivileged a voice and gives them access to decision-making structures (Lapeyronnie, 1991: 17). Similarly, Kepel's work on the growth of Islam as a defining element of the identity of *beur* youth in France has focused on the problematic issue of citizenship in explaining their rejection of mainstream culture (Kepel, 1994). As Lapeyronnie recognizes, democratization must be accompanied by concrete action, otherwise it becomes counter-productive. When unemployed youth are consulted about their future, they know that only access to the labour market will give them the resources and the social recognition they want, post-industrial society or no. The problem, as Lapeyronnie points out, is that to date the only real chance of concrete action exists at the local level – the mayors and local councils. Thus, within the framework of decentralization laws, the government has given local councils responsibility for employment. But the local councils' real room for manoeuvre remains strictly limited. In this sense local government is caught in a Catch-22 situation. Whilst recognizing this trap, the Vénissieux council has made explicit efforts to move forward on both fronts.

The PCF and municipal policy in Vénissieux

Collective identity does not simply arise from a combination of circumstances; it is actively constructed and shaped. As noted earlier, some of the key actors in shaping a local collective identity in Vénissieux have been the Communist mayors, all originally local workers. Corbel (1983) rightly devotes a major part of his book on Vénissieux to the former stonemason Marcel Houël, who led the commune through the troubled period of the 1970s. Today he is remembered with great affection by Vénissians as a local 'fixer' who provided services for local inhabitants and battled on their behalf with the outside authorities. Particularly for older voters, Gérin (re-elected mayor for the second time in 1995) benefits from Houël's reflected glory. Several interviewees during the course of my research in Vénissieux (including people whose answers otherwise suggested they did not share PCF values) mentioned the PCF's record in providing local services and specifically alluded to Houël's work (and to a lesser extent Gérin's).

The council itself recognizes the central role it has to play in promoting community cohesion. In the new climate where individual, private concerns matter more than collective references, it argues, links between the resident and the council are what matter. Since Vénissians suffer from a negative image and a lack of dignity in their dealings with the outside world, attention must be paid to improving the attractiveness of Vénissieux in the eyes of its own residents and the outside world. This policy, which also aims to lessen the segregation within the commune by improvement of the ZUP, has been at the heart of PCF municipal policy in Vénissieux but has been given new urgency by the recent decline in Communist electoral support.

In January 1969, the commune of Vénissieux along with others in the *agglomération* was incorporated into the COURLY (*Communauté urbaine de Lyon*, now known under the name of *Le Grand Lyon*). Most of the mayors of the suburban communes were opposed to the initiative, since it meant that even very basic services (such as road maintenance or refuse collection) were taken away from them and organized centrally. More importantly, it meant that the centre now had the deciding voice regarding urban renewal projects. Hence, since the late 1960s, the commune has had to work within the strict confines both of national urban policy and of the city. One of Vénissieux council's chief complaints is that renovation schemes have sometimes fallen foul of one or both of these partners. To some extent the idea of the local council battling against the city authorities and national government helps to boost its image as the defender of the local population, but this strategy can only succeed over a long period if some notable victories are gained. In fact, the council has succeeded in managing an urban development policy and gained some notable victories, particularly the extension of the Metro line to Vénissieux. It would appear that the council's more ambitious schemes do not succeed in winning full backing, but often give rise to slightly less costly plans which are agreed. Thus, in 1994 there were complaints that the council's plans for the complete rebuilding of the Démocratie area of the ZUP had failed because the government refused to fund them, but in October 1994 the *Grand Projet Urbain*, agreed by the council, the city authorities, the regional and departmental authorities and the state as well as the Université de Lyon II, was unveiled. The new plan promises the renovation of social housing and the construction of a médiathèque and an Institut Universitaire de Technologie. The demolition of the Démocratie towers was intended to provide space for this project (Gérin, 1994).

The urban development policy has focused on three main areas: renovation of the ZUP, restoration of the old centre so as to recreate a sense of community ('inventer la ville'), and integration of the commune into the city so as to decrease the sense of isolation and abandonment ('désenclaver la ville'). The Metro project, begun in 1987 and opened in 1992, represents the keystone of the latter policy and was the subject of a long campaign between the commune and the city authorities. The second policy involved the restoration of the old centre in the late 1980s and has been successful in transforming the physical appearance of the commune, as any visitor will testify. It also entailed attempts to revive cultural life, with the creation of the Centre culturel communal (Centre Boris-Vian) in 1967 and the Cinéma Gérard-Philippe in the ZUP in 1980. The commune still lacks popular entertainment facilities, however, for which local youth must travel to the city centre. It is arguably the ZUP which has been the most important policy area, nevertheless. Here the commune has been able to call on government funding in line with national policy priorities. A plan for the construction of commercial and social facilities and the renovation of the worst sections of the ZUP in order to increase attractiveness and thereby reduce the number of vacant flats, within the context of a re-examination of city urban policy to ensure a more equitable distribution of the population, was adopted by the council in February 1981 and approved by the COURLY under the government's 'Habitat et vie sociale' programme.

Following the riots in Les Minguettes in the summer of 1981, the government set up the Dubedout Commission, which aimed to encourage a more integrated approach to the *grands ensembles* (high-rise housing estates), associating the improvement of educational and training services and social facilities with the renovation of the physical environment. This programme saw the creation of four *Zones d'éducation prioritaire* (areas with increased funding for specialized teaching posts) in Vénissieux. In addition, three areas of the ZUP were singled out for attention, including Monmousseau, where the majority of flats now stood empty. In the 1980s, the most dilapidated of the towers were shut down and the population rehoused. In October 1994, the ten towers of the Démocratie area (which had been boarded up since 1984) of the ZUP were demolished. By 1994, the ZUP accounted for less than a third of the commune's inhabitants (from around half in the 1970s and around 40 per cent in the 1980s). The council's housing action has shown that it is possible to alleviate some of the worst effects of the high-rise policy of the 1970s and the concomitant segregation of the local population. But there is still a long way to go.

On employment, the council has more freedom in principle but is severely restricted in practice by the priorities of local employers. The decentralization law of 8 March 1982 gave municipal councils powers to set up structures to promote local employment, and in recent years government has re-emphasized local responsibility for employment. In Vénissieux, a joint local committee for employment was set up in 1982, but replaced in March 1983 with a commission on economic affairs reporting directly to the urban policy unit. Originally, the council intended to reserve 1 per cent of its budget for this commission, but was unable to set aside this amount. The commission's budget of 1.3 million francs in 1985 was spent on promotion activities to increase Vénissieux's attractiveness to potential investors, and job creation schemes for young people (Platier, Gobet and Bafounta, 1985). The council's action is subject to severe financial constraints, since social services necessarily account for the lion's share of the budget in Left-controlled councils and cannot easily be cut to make room for new promotional activities. With the economic climate bringing the closure of many businesses, the income from local companies (the local business tax, which in the 1980s accounted for 68 per cent of Vénissieux's fiscal receipts) has declined. Pressure on those companies which remain increases, thus further discouraging investors (the tax rate stood at 11.76 per cent in Vénissieux in 1985, as opposed to only 5.56 per cent in the neighbouring commune of Corbas) (Platier, Gobet and Bafounta, 1985: 66).

The council knows that the only way to retain popular support is to continue to provide services to the community as a whole (social and cultural facilities), to individuals (on a 'drop-in' basis) and also, increasingly, to specific groups. One group which has become particularly important is the young *beurs*, in whose direction the mayor has made special efforts, as we have seen. Kepel (1994) notes that immigrant groups have generally preferred to lobby politicians in power rather than to establish their own parties or field their own candidates. Even with the formation of independent *beur* movements in the 1980s and, more recently, Islamist youth associations, politics tends not to be viewed as an end in itself but a means to an end (specific services and a voice). Vénissieux saw the beginnings of an independent *beur* political movement with the 'Marche des beurs' in 1983, which set out from the commune to march on Paris. In the following municipal elections, the *beurs* challenged the political establishment by attempting to build an autonomous political force. However, their candidate, Mokrane Kessi, scored disappointing results (1.55 per cent of the vote). At the 1993 legislative elections, Kessi stood again and polled 1.87 per cent of the vote. Whereas many other left-wing councils cut their links with Islamist groups in the wake of the Rushdie affair, Gérin has maintained good relations with the local youth associations, and made premises available for the Union des jeunes musulmans for its annual congresses in the 1990s. The danger, however, is that by appearing too conciliatory towards 'foreigners' in the eyes of the 'white' electorate (or that fraction potentially tempted by the Front National) the Left council could lose out electorally. In order to forestall such accusations, the council would have to invest massively and imaginatively in the 'petites choses de la vie' ('little things of everyday life'), to use Françoise Gaspard's phrase (cited by Begag, 1991: 162), to reassure these voters and alleviate their own personal misery.

The relationship between the left-wing council and young Muslim voters raises a wider question about the relationship between citizens and politics. One of the remarkable things about the Vénissieux council is the extent to which it has actively promoted a dialogue with local residents, even in the 1970s before concerns about the erosion of the Communist electorate. Consultation with residents before any decisions about urban redevelopment is systematic. Information is widely available. The council publishes a fortnightly newspaper, *Expressions*, and regularly updates residents with mailshots on different issues. The extension of the Metro line was approved beforehand by Vénissieux residents in a referendum (*référendum d'initiative populaire*). Exhibitions detailing plans for the *Grand Projet Urbain* were exhibited in the town hall and residents exhorted to visit. Many residents are active in local committees, *conseils de quartier*, which formulate residents' complaints and demands and direct them to the local council. However, the issues raised by these residents' associations highlight the difficult position of the council in relation to matters belonging to the COURLY. At the council meeting of 25 June 1993, for example, questions raised ranged from the need for a multiracial police force to the condition of pavements and the need for speed bumps in certain roads (Conseil municipal de Vénissieux, 1993). In these cases, however, residents realized that the council's action could only be one of pressure on the relevant authority.

Conclusion

From our analysis of Vénissieux's experience it would appear that several features of life in the *banlieues* are the result of specific policies and can therefore be tackled, assuming political will and adequate financing. However, in France, the question of the appropriate level of intervention remains salient despite the decentralization laws of 1982–83. As Lapeyronnie notes (1991), the power of local councils to reverse strong underlying trends is extremely limited, and this explains at least in part the search for alternative solutions on the part of a growing number of voters.

In particular, there is the now well-established problem of unemployment. With limited tax funds at its disposal, a local council does not have the means to fight unemployment, particularly when it reaches 14.8 per cent, as in Vénissieux (INSEE, 1991). Job training must be part of the solution, since young Vénissians are markedly underqualified in comparison with their counterparts elsewhere. But why bother to study or to train when local jobs are so scarce? The local approach to employment needs to include the range of relevant authorities across the different levels of administration: municipal, departmental and regional. The question of exclusion needs a much broader, multi-faceted approach involving a fundamental choice: what value does society place on the employment of its youth?

Local democracy is necessary but not by itself sufficient. Although it can do much to give people back a sense of control over their own lives, citizenship in a wider sense is called into question by such pockets of social exclusion. The old republican model of citizenship, through which foreigners, workers and those unable to work were all integrated, has proved its inability to cope (leaving some to look at the past through rose-tinted spectacles). The challenge is now to build a new model of citizenship which recognizes cultural diversity and grants real equality of voice.

Notes

1. See Chapter 4.
2. 'The Communist Party has become too soft on the shit-stirrers, excuse the language. You Communists have one big failing. I know it wasn't you who brought the immigrants over, it was Giscard, with his family immigration policy, but still, you're on the Arabs' side!'
3. i.e. children of immigrants born in France.
4. 'I voted for Le Pen in the first round of the presidential elections and Jospin in the second. In the municipal elections, I voted for Mégret [FN] both rounds. But if Tapie had been a candidate I'd have voted for him. [Pause]. You see, with me it's a complete mess.'

References

Bavoux, P. (1991) 'Rue de la Ré', *Les Temps Modernes* 545/546: 107–24.

Begag, A. (1991) 'Voyage dans les quartiers chauds', *Les Temps Modernes* 545/546: 134–64.

Begag, A. and Delorme, C. (1994) *Quartiers sensibles*. Paris: Seuil.

Bidou, C. (5 April 1995) 'Les politiques du logement au cœur des politiques urbaines', *Problèmes Economiques* 2418: 16–19.

Bourdieu, P. (ed.) (1993) *La misère du monde*. Paris: Seuil.

Brula, P. (1993) *Les résultats électoraux du PCF à Vénissieux de 1945 à nos jours. Une étude statistique* (unpublished working document kindly supplied by the PCF at Vénissieux).

Centre d'histoire et d'études, Municipalité de Vénissieux (1992) *Formation d'un nouvel électorat communiste à Vénissieux?* (unpublished working document kindly supplied by its authors).

Centre d'histoire et d'études, Municipalité de Vénissieux (1994) *Elections européennes du 12 juin 1994* (unpublished working document kindly supplied by its authors).

Conseil municipal de Vénissieux (1993) *Bilan des conseils de quartier. Conseil municipal du 25 juin 1993: Compte rendu intégral des interventions du public et des réponses des élus.*

Corbel, M. (1983) *Vénissieux: du village à la cité industrielle.* Paris: Messidor.

Dubet, F. and Lapeyronnie, D. (1992) *Les quartiers d'exil.* Paris: Seuil.

Gérin, A. (1988) *Minguettes. Challenge pour une ville.* Paris: Messidor.

Gérin, A. (1991) *Jeunes. Une chance pour la ville.* Paris: Messidor.

Gérin, A. (1994) *Quartier Démocratie: lettre d'André Gérin* (council communication to residents).

Grillo, R. (1985) *Ideologies and Institutions in Urban France: The Representation of Immigrants.* Cambridge: CUP.

Guglielmo, R. and Moulin, B. (1986), 'Les grands ensembles et la politique', *Hérodote* 43: 39–74.

INSEE (1991) *Recensement général de la population de 1990 (Rhône).*

Kepel, G. (1994) *A l'ouest d'Allah.* Paris: Seuil.

Lapeyronnie, D. (1991) 'L'exclusion et le mépris', *Les Temps Modernes* 545/546: 2–17.

Leprince, G. (1991) *Le monde du poids lourd. Les travailleurs Berliet/RVI à Vénissieux, 1915–1991.* Paris: Messidor.

Platier, J.-M., Gobet, C. and Bafounta, E. (1985) *L'interventionnisme économique à Vénissieux dans le cadre de la loi de décentralisation* (mémoire de deuxième année, Université de Lyon II).

Ronai, S. (1986) 'La crise des grands ensembles et les nouvelles politiques municipales', *Hérodote* 43: 75–89.

Videlier, P. (1992) 'La construction d'une culture ouvrière', *French Politics and Society* 10(1) (winter): 25–42.

15.

Ecology, political action and discourse

MARC ABÉLÈS

TRANSLATED FROM THE FRENCH BY JOHN J. A. CULLEN

'Marginale l'écologie? Elle est centrale ... Nous devons bien nous convaincre et convaincre autour de nous que la défense de l'écosystème constitue une préoccupation essentielle qui interpellera sans cesse davantage tous les partis politiques ... '[1] These are not, as you might think, the words of a militant ecologist, but those of a Socialist leader, Laurent Fabius (1990). By recognizing the preponderant place of ecological themes in current political debate, Fabius is simply acknowledging a profound change. Within a generation the ideas of a minority, the prerogative of a small circle of enthusiasts, have become, like common sense, widely accepted. We may ask ourselves whether the success achieved by ecological ideas, their progressive dissemination, is not the principal cause of the collapse of the Green Movement that we see today. It is as if political ecology had failed to prove to be a credible force in France, even though it seemed to be gaining ground in a political landscape marked by the weakening of the traditional Left.

In contrast to the German Greens, who have managed to occupy a specific niche between Christian Democracy and Social Democracy, French ecologists have always found themselves caught in an uncomfortable and electorally fragile position between Left and Right. At the outset the Ecology Movement was original in that it advocated an anti-productionist policy which contrasted with the dominant visions based on economic expansion. Similarly, environmental protection was still viewed as a minority interest. The increasing influence of political ecology came during a period of severe crisis marked by disillusionment with progress. Doubts about the economic choices endorsed until then by both Left and Right gained ground among the public at large when the means of industrial and agricultural production, which have long been synonymous with wealth and growth, were blighted by the economic crisis.

The economic restructuring which began in the mid-1980s has shown that the productive model in force till then was no longer viable. The reduction in the number of jobs, the worrying prospect of endemic underemployment: these are the problems which confronted a political class disorientated by new forms of conflict and the difficulty of mastering the effects of the crisis. It is in this context that we can better understand the political breakthrough of environmentalist ideas at the end of the 1980s. In fact it was not a new political movement; the majority of its leaders had already been active for more than 15 years. But it took the deterioration of entire sections of the French economy before we saw the emergence of this political force which, let it be emphasized, did not propose any specific remedy to the very real problems confronting French society.

By blaming the religion of progress and the damage it engenders, ecologists were emphasizing the need to re-establish a harmonious relationship between people and the environment and to rectify the excesses affecting our ecosystem; this is the touchstone of ecological thinking. Criticism of the ideology of production was most acute when it became clear that producing and consuming more was not resolving the social question, as witness the inability of economic projects – both the nationalizations of the Left and the privatizations of the Right – to overcome the crisis. Furthermore, with the movement towards decentralization set in motion by the Left, the question of the environment came to the fore once again. The ecologists always favoured the local and regional dimension over the imperialism of the state. They contrasted the natural arena for the management of society with the administrative inertia which has accumulated throughout history. Their enthusiasm for a Europe of regions in which people are deeply attached to their locality was full of ambiguities – nevertheless it responded to deep misgivings and was offered as an alternative for those who saw the future of Europe as a loss of identity.

By highlighting the anti-central government aspect of the Ecology Movement we emphasize one of the aspects of the ideology which has been able to attract a certain section of public opinion which is not necessarily concerned with environmental questions. The ecologists were seeking their reference points in scientific ideas based on notions such as ecosystems, biotopes, biocoenoses, which conceived of humans as organisms living in close, mutual dependence on nature. There was a search for a global vision which would serve as a background to the political debate. Similarly, the idea that one could make specific local demands based on ecological ideas and also articulate a global critique based on a requirement for rationality and responsibility brought a fresh approach to politics. New parameters were brought into the equation: science, expertise and ethics, which until then were ignored in the political debate.

We would search its political programme in vain for the source of the passion that the Ecology Movement has excited. And it is here probably that the misunderstanding which characterizes the analyses of the Green breakthrough of the 1980s was born. The Greens did not present more original or more credible solutions than the other political parties for solving the problems of French society. It is rather the mixture of scientism with an appeal to a sense of morality, and a rejection of the traditional political battleground, which marked it out. At the moment when President Mitterrand was starting his second term of office, and when the Left, at the height of its popularity, had entered a phase of élitism, the Ecology Movement was able to appear as the main player in the redistribution of the political cards. Between the Right, ill-used by the electorate, and the Left, more and more self-assured the more it seemed to have abandoned all thought of reform, was there not room for a third force? The candidate for that place had to give the appearance of a new and uncompromising force compared to the traditional parties.

The most skilful at playing this role were the ecologists. They were able to pride themselves on having a different approach to politics; until then they had always failed in their attempts to win the argument. We could list all the criticisms they had suffered in the preceding period: Utopianism, tunnel vision which sees only the environment, lack of organization, limited popular legitimacy, etc. Now all these handicaps became trump cards when public opinion lost confidence in the capacity of the traditional parties to influence the fundamental causes of the crisis. With Mitterrand having nothing new to say by way of Socialism than the slogan 'Neither privatization nor nationalization', and with the Right challenging the liberal orthodoxy that it had made its own between 1986 and 1988, it was possible to believe in sailing against the tide of the two major national political forces. The very fact that ecology had never succeeded at the electoral level became a guarantee of rigour and consistency. It was time to turn towards a discourse and behaviour which clearly broke with the past.

The success that the ecologists have had probably stems from this distinctiveness. The Greens' list won 10.67 per cent of the vote in the

European elections of 1989. The ecologists' dynamism reached its peak in the regional elections of 1992 when 14.2 per cent of the votes cast went to the Greens and Génération Ecologie. Although having no elected representative in the National Assembly, the ecologists seemed thereafter to have secured their position since they were involved in the management of the regions and had even won one of them. At the national level, the moratorium on French nuclear testing also seemed a not inconsiderable success. Lastly, the presence of one of their established leaders, Brice Lalonde, in the Rocard government signalled the recognition of ecologist legitimacy by the political establishment.

Reasons for the decline

How today can we explain the decline which has overcome this movement? In my view, it stems both from the way in which the ecologists' discourse has been taken on board by politicians and from the behaviour of the advocates of the movement themselves. The first of these considerations makes sense only if we imagine, in its entirety, the intellectual mind-set which governs the balance of power between political parties. It is this mind-set which experienced major upheaval in the 1980s with a refusal by the electorate to come out in favour of any of the 'ideologies' which were perceived as antagonistic agendas since they were based on serious sociological divisions. Mitterrand's 1981 message was simple; it was a matter, he explained, of giving a political majority to the sociological majority in the country. The idea of an ideological balance of power made sense, whereas by 1988 that idea seemed inadequate and outdated.

There then appears the possibility of a much more fundamental reconstruction of the political landscape in which global considerations become relevant. The willingness to question our relationship with the ecosystem shows also a desire to overcome in-built social divisions and antagonisms. Antoine Waechter's 'neither the Left nor the Right' is its most remarkable political expression. For several years it summed up the Greens' dominant ideology, and this policy unquestionably contributed to the ecologists' electoral breakthrough. The idea of circumventing opposing ideas in order to have a better grip on reality was gaining ground. Humankind must be improved: we must mend our ways with regard to nature. At the same time, society must be improved. Ecology probably offers the first example in history of the incursion of political correctness into political thought in France.

With hindsight we can better understand the enthusiasm for a movement which emphasized an ethical approach to political questions. We must remember that the second new personality of the Rocard government, besides Brice Lalonde, was none other than Bernard Kouchner. With him, the humanitarian theme officially entered the government's political agenda. This double incursion of ecology and humanitarianism marked a turning-point since it was to influence the content of several political debates. Humanitarian and ecological questions became part of every politician's vocabulary without the 'historic' spokespersons for these two concerns being in a position to reap the political dividends from the change. Admittedly Kouchner and Lalonde were credited on the personal level with this innovation – the personalization of politics is undeniable, as the public opinion surveys of the day show – but they were not able to turn this popularity into real political success.

We must, of course, distinguish between Kouchner and Lalonde. The former wanted to be the incarnation of a cause but lacked a party machine to back him. Lalonde, however, has always sought to establish a body of supporters. In other words, he could not be content just to be the mouthpiece of a political message with an ethical slant: he had to promote ecological ideas at the grass roots. With hindsight, it is interesting to note that the ecologist heyday came at a paradoxical time. At the beginning of the 1990s, one of the ecologist leaders was in the government while the other was running an opposition movement. In contrast to the centrists, who under de Gaulle, then under Pompidou, were in a similarly divided position (we recall that Jacques Duhamel was Pompidou's minister whereas Jean Lecanuet led the centrist opposition) and easily managed to turn the situation to advantage, the ecologists seem, on the contrary, to have exhausted themselves in a sterile debate which progressively weakened them. The Lalonde–Waechter *rapprochement* which was to come about later, during the 1993 general election, shows by contrast that nothing fundamental has ever separated the two leaders.

What brought Waechter and Lalonde into conflict can be classed as political infighting: competition for the leadership and disagreements about choice of alliances and tactics. We would search in vain for a serious internal debate which goes beyond these purely circumstantial issues. One of the most striking paradoxes of the ecologists' attitude is to have been the instigators of a new intellectual orientation among politicians by deploying a major idea for consensus which had an ethical resonance while behaving in practice just like traditional politicians. The movement's internal guerrilla war, its strategy, based in large part on an analysis which highlighted the problem of relations with the other parties, no longer allowed it to transform its more and more dramatic electoral results into actual policy changes. It was in this context that public opinion deserted it. Thereafter the ecologists' image was that of a party like any other, but one which was rather less clever at strategy.

Ecology was thus the victim of what it had always claimed to fight: politicking. By playing the game, and by locking themselves into the world of short-term politics, the movement's leaders allowed their adversaries to hijack the main planks of their argument. In fact, it was easy for the Greens' opponents to push them into a corner using the strategy of the game of Go. Becoming a party like the others, the ecologists condemned themselves to being measured by the yardstick of their policies and effectiveness at winning votes. On the first point, they could be credited with only an incomplete approach to problems on account of their obsession with the environment. On the second, they were forever condemned to be marginalized at a time when militancy was no longer successful. In these conditions, it was quite legitimate in the public's view for the mainstream parties to appropriate the novel content of the ecologist argument. Rocard's 'Big Bang' operation was destined to fulfil this role. But it proved to be of only limited worth electorally. In fact the votes brought in by the Socialists were just votes for the Left which had defected to the ecologists and which were coming back home naturally.

In fact the Socialists had gained nothing from this strategy, for it became apparent that the votes garnered by the 'neither Right nor Left' policy either became abstentions or were spread between the various parties. Despite ecologist ideas becoming commonplace and despite the exhaustion of the movement, no traditional party has really profited. Rather, the profound impact of ecology and its precursors must be sought, on the one hand, in the attempts at face-lifting the programmes of the traditional parties and, on the other hand, in the emergence of a current of criticism of politicians which took very different forms according to circumstances. It is clear that this occurred in favour of Bernard Tapie and the Radicals in the European elections of 1994, at the very moment when the ecologists were collapsing. The fact that Tapie was joined by defectors from Génération Ecologie, such as Noël Mamère, and received the vote of Bernard Kouchner, himself a candidate for the Socialist Party, clearly shows that the environmentalist/humanitarian tendency had managed to find a home whereas the ecologists, perpetually at the mercy of internal dissensions, had scarcely any supporters any longer.

The absorption of the ecologists' ideas by the political parties, and the capture of their critical stance by the radical movement, bear witness to the weakness of the ecologists and their inability to bounce back in the face of attacks by the other parties. We may enquire whether this decline was inevitable. In Germany the Greens, without significantly strengthening their position, have managed to hold their own with the major parties. They have been able to win and hold on to regional and local positions, whereas it seems that in France, the ecologists' strategy has not allowed them to maintain their foothold. This raises a question which requires more than simply cataloguing the tactics used by the interested parties. We know in fact that the ecologist movement has relied on a network of associations for a long while. However, the ecologist associations have never been, in contrast to the well-established tradition of the extreme Left, mere top-down conduits for party policy. They have long been the source of the movement's ideas. The political aspect remained of very limited importance, whereas collective action became more and more widespread. At the same time the system of associations did not take on the characteristics of a mass movement. It was a rather élitist movement where quality had precedence over quantity, with a culture where one wins recognition through competence, which has its dignitaries, but which detests leadership. The notion of participative democracy does not really apply to a movement of associations. The latter brings together knowledgeable and energetic people for specific problems, it mobilizes them, but does not demand full-time involvement by the electorate in local and regional politics.

The ecologists' local power base through these associations is thus undeniable. Furthermore, it is on the basis of collective action that the Greens' main leaders have emerged: Didier Anger, Antoine Waechter, Yves Cochet, Andrée Buchmann and Dominique Voynet. The fight against nuclear power, pollution problems and the question of protecting specific sites have all allowed the battle to be fought at local level. But everything has happened as if it was impossible to transform the ecologist wave of enthusiasm into secure electoral seats. It seems, on the contrary, that the ecologist forces wear themselves out with fruitless infighting even though it might be possible for them to gain a strong position in a region. This was the case in Brittany, where between 1986 and 1990 the supporters of Waechter and Cochet fought a merciless battle for control of the Breton Ecologist Federation. In the same period, in 1989, the Greens were to win a remarkable share of the vote:

22 per cent in Vannes, 14.5 per cent at Quimper, 14.6 per cent at St Brieuc (Le Guirriec, 1993). Yet throughout this period the number of registered supporters did not exceed 290. These figures speak volumes about the disparity between the number of signed-up members in the movement and its electoral potential.

This numerical weakness of the Greens seems to be constant historically. In contrast to the Socialist Party, which has drawn widely on the circuit of associations, the ecologists have not been able to find the numbers to strengthen their political influence. When it comes to making a political commitment, the associations have remained more than wary. They have been excellent at drumming up local support favourable to ecologist ideas, but they have never involved themselves in a coherent plan for taking power. For their part, parties like the Greens and Génération Ecologie found themselves condemned to remain small parties without sufficient support to impose a realistic policy. The only region where the Greens have won power is the Nord-Pas-de-Calais. However, it is clear that winning the Nord-Pas-de-Calais is a result of the Socialist attitude. The latter, having become a minority, had no other alternative but to form an alliance with the Greens in order to retain control of the region. The bargaining chip was the Presidency of the Regional Council, which is how Marie-Christine Blandin gained control.

The weakening of the Greens at the national level could have been propitious for a strategy of reinforcement of the local networks. In contrast to the Socialists who, during the 1970s, managed to set up a powerful municipal base, the ecologists have not been able to profit from the positions won at the regional level. The example of the Nord-Pas-de-Calais is symbolic in every way. Here is a region which represents considerable political potential and where the Greens had the opportunity to get established since the other political forces had encountered serious difficulties. Yet we note that after two years in the regional presidency, the ecologists have not really moved local opinion in their direction. What is more, they have not followed a novel policy. Their internal squabbles quickly came to the fore, and for the electors they still seem to be a secondary force. Curiously, just where the ecologists ought to have found fertile ground for their ideas, they seem to be marking time. The Greens had championed local politics; therefore we may legitimately wonder about the small political capital gained from their experience in power.

Part of the explanation probably lies in the idea the ecologists have of their relationships with the grass roots. In their approach to environmental problems the associations have always stressed the inability of the politician to solve fundamental problems. For the ecologists, local politicians are trapped in a system controlled by local élites: elected representatives' sole purpose consists in positioning themselves as mediators between local demands and the representatives of the state: they have agreed once and for all to play a sort of zero sum game in which they try to gain a few concessions from government departments. It is this attitude that the Greens object to; to them, it seems to increase the distance between the citizens and a state which imposes its views regardless of local demands.

One can never emphasize enough the deep mistrust that the ecologist associations have always shown towards local government. Political power is immediately conceived as bad since it can only be the source of dependent relationships. Power is always personalized; it encourages trawling for votes; it forbids all forms of reflection which really take the general good into consideration. Power is thus deeply corrupt and the ecologists consider it to be intrinsically suspect. This vision is consistent with the ethical point of view that they continually advance. For them politicians are motivated by ambition for power and not by the desire to improve conditions for their fellow citizens. Therefore, in their local activity, the Greens have a real predilection for highlighting the particular deficiencies of politicians. With a certain sense of humour, they do not hesitate to award, with full solemnity, the 'little trowel prize' to a councillor who is a builder, or the 'sour puss prize' to a particularly unco-operative sub-prefect.

Participatory democracy

Instead of local élites, whom they oppose, the Greens propose a participative democracy. From the outset the ecologists have set themselves apart from the dominant political forces. They took a long time to become one, and then two parties. The bottom-up model which operates in the Greens clearly illustrates their rejection of traditional political methods. The principal decision-making body of this party remains the General Assembly. Everything is done to guard against centralization. The region plays an essential rôle in this type of organization. The obsession with transparency accords with internal democracy founded on the direct participation of the membership in all strategic debates. Sometimes taken to absurd limits, these methods in effect exacerbate divisions and obscure political choices under the concerted pressure of militant minorities. Another perverse effect of the bottom-up model is the suspicion of power which influences the leaders and hinders their capacity for initiative.

The legitimacy that the Greens claim is not that conferred by their participation in the limited circle of decision-makers; rather it is that which comes from competence and knowledge of the grass roots. For the ecologists, elected representatives are always ready to compromise since they are incapable of scientific analysis regarding an area. At the heart of the ecologist movement a sort of duality can be made out. On one hand there is the lawyer, on the other the engineer, who together form the solid foundations of the structure. The ability to put together complex cases and the art of litigation are the essential ingredients of associative action. In this respect, we may speak of a real 'guerrilla war of litigation' which has allowed the ecologists to win in local disputes. In any case, it is clear that the law is a very effective weapon; the other weapon is knowledge of environmental questions. The leading lights of associative action are uncompromisingly serious in the matter of facts and figures. Reference to expertise and science is at the heart of their arguments. The associations do not hesitate to offer their expertise to the authorities in a positive way. Systematic opposition is out of fashion.

In their approach to environmental problems the ecologists' main demand is often for a better implementation of rules and regulations which, according to them, have been broken to benefit local political interests. It is understood that the ecologists' position may directly oppose that of the local élites. The rigour that the associations demand attacks deeply ingrained habits head-on. Contrary to the local representatives described by P. Grémion (1976) who seek 'to gain concessions from the universality of the law' and 'to resist the pressure from the centre and to respond selectively to bureaucratic action', the ecologist associations behave much more directly. Hence the importance of their legalistic approach which allows them to win the argument.

Similarly, the ecologists have continued to enter the public arena by all available means. Associative work is largely akin to lobbying and it is clear that the ecologists are more at ease with it than traditional organizations, not least of all the unions. In fact, they are seen to be active in very different realms simultaneously, socio-economic, political and even religious. They also know how to make the media report their activities by arguing that it is their competence, and not just strength of numbers, which earns them the right to be present in the public debate.

The mobilization against the Serre-de-la-Fare dam well illustrates the effectiveness of the ecologist movement in local campaigning (Rodier, 1993). This has highlighted the ability of the movement of associations to gain support from a part of the population which until then had been impervious to the ecologist movement. In this battle the ecologists were fighting against the destruction of a site and its surrounding country; it emphasized the need to conserve the countryside as part of the regional heritage. The movement, wholly centred on a regional environmental problem, proved to be very effective as the dam project, instigated by the state with the support of powerful politicians such as the Mayor of Tours, Jean Roger, had to be abandoned. In the Puy commune in the Haute-Loire department, a traditional fief of the Catholic Right, the Greens won three seats in the 1989 elections, and 21.87 per cent of the votes in a municipality traditionally of the Right.

However, if we consider the case of the movement of associations involved with S.O.S. Loire Vivante, we find that its main intellectual organizer, Roberto Epple, is a Swiss senior executive who threw himself into an environmental crusade and who works for an NGO, the World Wide Fund for Nature (WWF). He possesses knowledge and experience which he gained through acting at the European level (he worked on the problems of the Danube). He is not seeking political power. He constantly aims to sharpen up the local movement, and greatly increase its power through a very clever use of marketing and the media. This type of ecological missionary is to be found in other guises in the majority of association circles. We are not dealing with political figures, nor with people who are strongly motivated by their roots in the community, but with knowledgeable people who put themselves forward for particular battles and who rapidly occupy key positions in the associations.

This situation does not, however, benefit political organizations. By definition, the political party can develop only if it focuses resolutely on the conquest of power. In the case of the ecologists, for whom power is by nature suspect, it appears difficult for them to adapt to the logic of creating electoral support. Green elected representatives quickly find themselves sandwiched between the associations which prosper only in an atmosphere of dissent and the political élites who strengthen their influence by perpetual compromise. The Greens' AGMs are where contradiction is most obvious; on the one hand, the desire of its politicians who want to make the movement take root and so make it a real force fit to govern and, on the other hand, the reservations of the party militants who are wary of such a step.

These tensions have resulted in partial paralysis of the ecologists' advance at local level. There is every reason to suppose that henceforth the ecologists have little chance of making their presence felt, except as a supplementary force, when faced with the traditional parties. Even where environmental problems play an important rôle, the Greens will have to reckon with elected representatives who little by little have adopted a significant share of their arguments. The political agenda has considerably shrunk at their expense.

Urban ecology

The most recent attempt at the ideological relaunch of the movement consisted in putting forward the notion of urban ecology. Here again, it is necessary to indicate an ambiguity and to distinguish clearly the conceptual use of this notion from its ideological aspect. Urban ecology stems from a method of study of urban phenomena which developed around the Chicago School.

The principal interest behind the town as a modern society's ecosystem was the introduction of a new methodology which broke with the major sociological investigations of the past. The importance given to qualitative data and the desire for an intensive ethnographic investigation of urban communities characterized this approach. As early as 1925, one of the founders of the Chicago School, R.E. Park, explicitly described his work as being in the anthropological tradition:

> Until now anthropology, the science of man, has devoted itself primarily to the study of primitive peoples. But civilized mankind is just as interesting as a research subject, without mentioning that he is easier to observe and study. Life and urban culture are more varied, subtle and complex but the fundamental impulses are the same in both cases. The patient methods of observation employed by anthropologists like Boas and Lowie for studying the life and behaviour of North American Indians can be employed even more fruitfully in the study of the customs, beliefs, social practices and general ideas about life which prevail in Little Italy or in the seedy areas of Chicago's North Side, or even to relate to the more sophisticated mores of the inhabitants of Greenwich Village or the Washington Square area of New York.
>
> (Grafmeyer and Joseph, 1979: 81)

Thus urban ecology was born, an original approach to contemporary societies which brings the spatial parameter to the fore. It is in its relationships with established disciplines that urban ecology shows its uniqueness. It does not claim to present a global model for social conditions but to offer better tools for studying urban questions. Today the notion of urban ecology has entered the political sphere. That stems for the most part from the fact that in France the town has become a major issue: the urban areas contain a whole gamut of social problems. The disturbances in the suburbs have highlighted the growing tensions on the outskirts of the large towns. The urban question is high on the political agenda. The creation of a Ministry of the Town is a real acknowledgement of this fact by the government. At the same time, this type of initiative has a very specific effect: by bringing the town as such to the foreground, it defines a degree of causality.

For several years the social question has thus been debated in relation to its territorial aspects. Cohabitation in working-class areas and poor quality of life in the suburbs have been denounced as major causes of the malaise. In parallel, the problems linked to unemployment admittedly appeared as the background to this situation but in the manner of a constant factor upon which politics could scarcely have any influence any longer. The President's 'everything has been tried' was echoed by his Prime Minister's caution. Not being able to renounce responsibility right down the line politicians have thus preferred to define a field of activity where the state could play a part, through its social services. The urban policy, once set up, allowed the creation of forms of assistance on the ground in such a way as to prevent new explosions and to demonstrate through the media the existence of help for the most disadvantaged. Progressively the theme of humanitarianism moved from the largely Third-World periphery towards the centre.

It is in this context that we can best understand the reference to urban ecology. Two distinct issues arise from it. The first relates to urban growth and the integration of people in the metropolis. The recourse to urban ecology is found in the extension of an environmental approach to the functioning of the town. We start from the following observation: the developmental problems that modern societies are experiencing no longer spring from rural life; they are becoming primarily urban problems. In these conditions they can be studied as 'scientific ecology' which treats the town as a complete entity encompassing the human and natural domains in a novel construction. Today the heart of the matter is the mastery of, on the one hand, the effects of urban growth within a town planning scenario and, on the other hand, more and more serious dysfunctions linked to the processes of 'deterritorialization' or rootlessness.

The second question that the use of urban ecology aims to tackle is the value systems and images which invade the urban environment. The question of rootlessness is here viewed in another light, that of people progressively marginalized by a global system of production and exchange which relegates part of the population to a sort of no man's land, where everyone loses their identity. From the ethical and political viewpoints these 'non-places'[2] (Augé, 1992) generate a crisis of identity for which traditional ideologies no longer offer any intellectual remedy or any plan of action. This is where urban ecology intervenes as a *deus ex machina*, intended to promote a sort of motivating Utopia based upon a restoration of the values of citizenship and solidarity. This is a thoroughly humanist position and encourages the search for a new perspective when dealing with social issues. But the starting point of the whole enterprise aiming to achieve convergence between scientific ecology and political ecology under the heading of urban ecology is linked to a series of shifts. The first shift, from the social to the territorial, offers politicians the possibility of distancing themselves from the social question: it is removed from centre stage (i.e. from the methods of economic management of our societies and the forms of domination used in them) to the periphery (i.e. to the populace's poor living conditions). A second shift, from the territorial to the urban, is helpful for all those who wish to define the problems of exclusion: to gain a clearer insight perhaps, but also to delimit them within a study of the territorial changes which are affecting our societies. The third shift, which results from the first two, moves from the political to the ethical and indicates that the solution to the problem is to research into the integration of these marginalized populations.

This triple shift has the effect of making obsolete any approach to the social question in terms of the notion of power and power blocks. On the contrary, the highlighting of zones of marginality, the media interest in the signs of isolation and in the disorder which springs up around our largest cities, emphasizes drift and the constant presence of risk: latent anxiety, the backcloth to the social question, is not unrelated to the images conjured up by the 'dangerous classes' in the nineteenth century (Chevallier, 1958). The ecology project as a global outlook for remedying those dysfunctions in a simultaneously scientific and positive way is becoming one resource among many others in a panoply of weapons that people of good will must use to combat social breakdown. It is clear, however, that ecology is no more than one of the possible responses in a situation dominated by humanitarianism and the exigencies it makes.

Conclusion

In total, ecology finds itself trapped between, on the one hand, a continuous process of dissemination which deprives it of its political structures and on the other, a process of alienation, since the theme of urban ecology which appeared in the most recent period of its history is used to support a position built around exclusion. The ecologists find themselves trapped in their attempt to occupy an independent political space.

Like stolid cyclists who have led the field for most of the race but who see victory snatched from them by a hitherto anonymous pack of riders, the Greens today are seeing the parties which they thought they could undermine reappropriate part of their agenda. They themselves seem to have lost their ability to find new forms of expression and opposition. One of the questions which arises in the background is that of militancy which was at the heart of Green action. The novelty of the ecologists on the political scene was due to this militant, participative and grass-roots activity that they exemplified in contrast to the élitism of the established parties. But this desire to subvert tawdry politics had, perhaps, only the appearance of novelty.

In fact, we may wonder whether political ecology is not marking an end rather than a new beginning. Is it not part of the political fall-out from the events of May '68? Its failure would then signify the exhaustion of a style of action which saw itself more and more separated from the public domain. The coincidence of views between the Greens and certain humanitarian ideas taken up by the media could explain the recovery of the ecologists at the end of the 1980s. When the latter tried to develop a form of political action which led them quite naturally to become a party, between the Left and the Right, they were confronted by the insoluble problem of their own transformation into political professionals drawing from a well which would guarantee their distinctiveness. Similarly they undertook a frantic search for legitimacy and they were condemned to run the gauntlet of a succession of local, regional, general and European elections. In order to achieve significant results they had to create a sufficiently solid organization to impose themselves on the electorate.

While the ecologists have managed to get elected to local and regional assemblies, they have not succeeded in becoming indispensable partners since they are not in a position to have significant successes on their own. The classic form of capturing and transmitting power, which is very important at the local level, has represented a

considerable obstacle. The comparison with the ecologist phenomenon in Germany is significant because we are dealing with two
different approaches in very different political environments. The
German Greens have emphasized the notion of an alternative. Defining
themselves as alternative, they marked out a certain political territory in
opposition to the Christian Democrat and Social Democrat giants. In
France the multiplicity of forces on Left and Right is less propitious for
the newcomers in defining their own political sphere. Each may always
overlap slightly onto a neighbour's territory.

In Germany, as the facts have shown, the Greens were able to develop
a specific identity without great risk of being swallowed up by parties
having their own reserves. The other difference is in the German
electorate's receptiveness to alternative ideas. In France the alternative
had taken form with the arrival of the Left: Mitterrand's seven-year
terms had put that idea into perspective. If alternative there was, it
could only be in a realm other than politics. A distinction had to be
marked out and thus followed the success of the move towards an
ethical position. The French Greens took part in the operation without
mastering its political consequences. Today they find themselves as if
deprived of oxygen, witnesses of the realignments which are happening
in other parties, mere extras in a plot they can no longer follow. The
lack of involvement of the ecologists in a situation where the presidential race once again opens the floodgates of a debate on society and
its environment is in itself symptomatic of this political exhaustion.

The question is no longer really whether the ecologists will bounce
back at local and national levels, but rather what will remain of what
some people have called 'the Green tide'. It may be thought that the
reintroduction of the scientific theme into the intellectual climate of
politics, and the parallel revival of a demand for an ethical stance, will
have left some traces. Similarly, as regards content, from the ozone
layer to nuclear power, from the list of hazardous substances to the
search for a better rôle for people within the environment, all have
undoubtedly been original contributions from ecologist thinking. On
the other hand, it is not certain that history will favour the style of
practical politics based on certain types of political activity and grass-
roots democracy advocated by the most committed ecologists. Conversely, procedural conflicts and the rôle of experts will in the long run
be seen as an inheritance from the ecologist movement. Half-way
between alternative political activism and consumer-oriented approaches, ecology will thus have participated, in its way, in the transformation of our political culture.

Notes

1. 'Is ecology marginal? No, it is central ... We must convince ourselves and those around us that the defence of the ecosystem is an essential task which will increasingly challenge all political parties.'
2. For Marc Augé, these 'non-places' are spaces where solitude and similitude replace identity and relationships; places which are only made real through the comments, messages and injunctions which they produce for the benefit of their users.

References

Augé, M. (1992) *Non-lieux. Introduction à une anthropologie de la sur-modernité.* Paris: Seuil.

Chevallier, L. (1958) *Classes laborieuses, classes dangereuses à Paris dans la première moitié du XIXe siècle.* Paris: Plon (republished in 1984 by Hachette).

Fabius, L. (1990) *C'est en allant vers la mer.* Paris: Seuil.

Grafmeyer, Y. and Joseph, I. (1979) *L'Ecole de Chicago. Naissance de l'écologie urbaine.* Paris: Editions du Champ Urbain.

Grémion, P. (1976) *Le Pouvoir périphérique.* Paris: Seuil.

Le Guirriec, P. (1993) 'Dix ans d'écologie politique en Bretagne' in M. Abélès (ed.) *Le Défi écologiste.* Paris: L'Harmattan.

Rodier, F. (1993) 'Face au barrage: les écologistes du Puy-en-Velay' in M. Abélès (ed.) *Le Défi écologiste.* Paris: L'Harmattan.

Index